T0146929

CHRISTIANITY VS. NATURALISM

Weighing the Evidence

MICHAEL HALL

WESTBOW
PRESS®
A DIVISION OF THOMAS NELSON
& ZONDERVAN

WestBow Press books may be ordered through booksellers or by contacting:

WestBow Press
A Division of Thomas Nelson & Zondervan
1663 Liberty Drive
Bloomington, IN 47403
www.westbowpress.com
844-714-3454

ISBN: 979-8-3850-0714-1 (sc)
ISBN: 979-8-3850-0715-8 (hc)
ISBN: 979-8-3850-0716-5 (e)

Library of Congress Control Number: 2023917289

Print information available on the last page.

WestBow Press rev. date: 12/05/2023

ACKNOWLEDGEMENTS

I would like to recognize my wife for her hours of listening to me discuss the information in this book *ad infinitum*, and her willingness to read and edit my many versions before the book was ready to be published.

I would also like to acknowledge the many people who have been both my proponents and opponents in the many debates that I have encountered over the years. My proponents encouraged me to get past my own closed-mindedness, while the opponents challenged me to dig deeper into finding the facts that supported my faith.

I would also like to thank my mother in her efforts to raise me as a Christian.

Last, I'd like to thank the churches who have let me teach Sunday School on these topics, and many others, as they helped me to overcome my aversion to speaking in public, coalesce the information into discrete and succinct topics, and forced me to create many of the graphic images that enables others to readily understand some the topics.

CONTENTS

TABLE OF FIGURES

INTRODUCTION

Many Christians today lack a basic understanding of the evidence that supports a Christian *worldview*. The purpose of this book is to provide the evidence for the main religions of America, both the supporting evidence and the undermining evidence. The intended audience of this book is any openminded person with a high school education or more—it is not just for Christians struggling in their faith, but for anyone open to considering some of the major evidence available today. In a nutshell, it is for the average person.

Most books on this topic are intended for one with an interest in theology or philosophy—focusing on the defense of Christianity rather than its differentiation between other religions. These types of books tend to fall short for those convinced that Christianity is not logical and are thus not interested in a philosophical argument advocating the Christian narrative. To interest those that are uninterested, one must be skeptical and put the viewpoint to the test. As the French philosopher Denis Diderot (AD 1713–1784) wrote, "What has not been examined impartially has not been well examined. Skepticism is therefore the first step toward truth."[1] The focus of this book will be upon the undisputed evidence accepted by all.

A worldview is defined by the *Merriam-Webster* "as a comprehensive conception or apprehension of the world especially from a specific standpoint."[2] There are two predominant worldviews in America today, Christianity and Naturalism. Predominantly, this book will be comparing the evidence for each of these worldviews from a skeptical viewpoint.

Christianity has many different forms, branches, and differing interpretations. For this book, Christianity will be defined as what is found in the Old and New Testaments of the Bible and will adhere to a literal interpretation of the quoted verses. Other categories, like the deuterocanonical and the apocrypha books will be discussed later in the book. However, except for those sections dealing with those topics, when the terms Christianity or the Bible is used, it is referring to just the Old and New Testaments as it is those group of books that are the most widely accepted definition of Christianity across all the branches of Christianity.

Naturalism is another worldview. It presumes that our world came about through natural causes, not a supernatural cause. It has five main tenets, called scientific theories, and they are taught in our schools as if they are established facts.

However, with a skeptical view of both while analyzing the evidence for each, one would find that Christianity is on the one-yard line before the touchdown, while Naturalism has ninety-nine yards to reach the touchdown zone.

This book will be using the process given by Dr. L. Russ Bush in his book *A Handbook for Christian Philosophy* to sort through the evidence to reach a conclusion. While his book is from a Christian perspective, it is applicable to all walks of life, including faith, science, and even everyday life. Philosophy is defined by *Merriam-Webster* as the "pursuit of wisdom."[3]

He gave four guiding principles of the proper search for wisdom. 1) Test of Logical or Rational Consistency. True wisdom will be rationally consistent with other knowledge. 2) Test of Empirical Adequacy. True wisdom must consider all evidence, without creating false evidence. As a result of this, it cannot willingly ignore known facts. 3) Test of Explanatory Power. True wisdom must explain all the issues. If known issues are neglected, then it is not wisdom guiding the conclusion, but a biased opinion. And 4) Test of Practical Relevance. Any conclusion(s) reached must be relevant to the person hearing the conclusion. For example, how many people would care about the number of hairs on another person's head? Very few people would consider this factoid to be relevant. They may consider the number of hairs on their own head to be relevant, but not another person's head.[4]

CHAPTER I

MY JOURNEY FROM NATURALISM
TO BIBLE-BASED CHRISTIANITY

B efore I get into the meat of this subject, I need to tell you about myself—my personality, my experience, methodology, and such. If I were to compare myself to one of Jesus's disciples, I would most closely match with Doubting Thomas because I feel the need to touch the wounds (*i.e.*, see the facts) before I believe.

My Myers-Briggs personality is ISTJ (Introvert, Sensing, Thinking, and Judging). I excel at objectivity. During a marriage counseling session, I took a test so the counselor could better relate to my wife and me. One measurement stood out to me—the "objectivity vs. subjectivity" measurement. This is the measurement of how objective a person is in life, with the normal healthy range being between 50 to 95 percent. My score was an unhealthy 97 percent. All this means that I am not easily swayed by emotions or how a topic may impact me personally. I tend to approach new subjects with a strong sense of skepticism. My career experience as a programmer, analyst, and modeler, has also taught me the value of looking at data objectively.

Like most Americans in public schools today, I was *indoctrinated* into the Naturalist religion—being taught that our universe was created by a big bang and then evolution caused the various species that exist today. Indoctrination is defined in the *Cambridge Dictionary* as "the process of repeating an idea or belief to someone until they accept it without criticism or question."[1] At the same time, I was raised in a weak Christian household, rarely attending any church while in my preteen and teenage years.

By the time I was in my teens I had a hybrid belief in Christianity and Naturalism, and I was questioning my parents' belief in Christianity. By my late teens, I had concluded (without any research) that Jesus did live on earth, but while He was a good teacher, He was not the Son of God because there was no god.

Shortly after I reached this conclusion, I had a personal encounter with God, which I will describe at the end of this book. As a result of this encounter, I moved to a hybrid belief of Christianity and Naturalism, as many Christians have today. But I was not really grounded in my faith in Christianity. Having said that, due to my indoctrination into Naturalism in our public schools, I was fairly grounded in the Naturalists' theories of the big bang and the millions of years of evolution. Seventeen years after I had switched back to my hybrid belief system, I became engaged in debates between Christians and Naturalists.

While I defended the Christian worldview in the debates, I strongly desired that, regardless of what evidence I uncovered, I would follow the evidence to whatever was best supported by the available evidence. Even after uncovering most of the evidence presented in this book and after attending a course in seminary in philosophy, I still held on to a hybrid Christian and Naturalism belief system. I believed that God created the world through a big bang and evolution over millions of years. A few years after seminary, I finally shook off any belief in Naturalism because I had realized that Naturalism lacks *any* empirical support to justify a belief in it.

Hence, I know a reader of this book will not change their viewpoint anytime soon. It will take a reader a lot of thinking and consideration of the evidence before they change their beliefs. As such, my purpose of this book is not to change a person's beliefs, but to help remove major obstacles to deepening one's faith with the biblical God.

To be objective, one must understand the worldview from the believer's perspective, not just the opponent's viewpoint. Appropriately, I sought out information published by respected Naturalists and Christians to understand their beliefs, their reasoning, and their evidence. However, what I was looking for in my research was evidence that would weaken or strengthen each religion, while being written by a writer supporting that belief system. Furthermore, I did not limit my research to just a few books but reading more than two hundred books on the two religions. Nor did I limit my reading to just books, seeking out information on the internet, and any other source that could be used to disprove or verify either religion. While a lot of my information found in books was used to form my convictions, I decided to lean on internet sites for this book when they were an option so that the reader can verify the information for themselves.

These sources were split with about 60 percent of them supporting Naturalism and 40 percent supporting Christianity because I really wanted to find the empirical evidence that supports the Naturalist viewpoints, and it was difficult to find. I also briefly considered other religions as well, but my focus was on these two religions since they dominate the American landscape. What I found in my research was astounding. School children are convinced that Naturalism is the only religion supported by evidence. My research found the opposite to be true.

CHAPTER 2

DEFINITIONS AND CONCEPTS

While many readers will be familiar with most of the terms below, numerous definitions are given to ensure that any reader of this book understands the terminology and concepts that must be used while discussing the topics within this book.

❖ Religion

Many people will protest the idea that a belief in science, as taught in our public schools, is a religion. However, religion is defined by the *Merriam-Webster* as a "a cause, principle, or system of beliefs held to with ardor and faith."[1] Anything that ends with the suffix "-ism"[2] is a system of beliefs. And anything that ends with suffix "-ist"[3] is a person who holds to the set of beliefs of that "-ism" religion. The *American Heritage Dictionary* defines *doctrine* as a "principle or body of principles presented for acceptance or belief, as by a religious, political, scientific, or philosophic group."[4] Note that this definition could include all of today's sciences.

Consequently, a scientist is one that adheres to or advocates the scientific doctrine—which could be alternatively stated as the religion of science. A scientist is a person who strongly believes that following the scientific method will lead to true knowledge. Yet even a scientist can interpret the evidence to suit his or her preconceived beliefs. This is why the scientific method holds that a belief must be tested and supported by evidence and must be able to be tested by opposing scientists who will reach the same conclusion.

Most of what is called science today fails that second criterion. It is published in the popular media with little to no peer-review process. Thus, most of what is considered proven science is really a religion. Yet, all scientific theories must be verified. Once a scientific theory is sufficiently verified and widely accepted, it is referred to as a scientific law. It usually takes more than one hundred years from when the scientific theory is first published to its universal acceptance as a scientific law. Some take much longer. Both the big bang theory and the theory of evolution still fall into the scientific-theory status because they have not been verified through scientific studies and there is evidence against them—more than most people realize.

❖ Empirical Evidence and Faith

Empirical evidence can be measured by one of the five senses of the human body—see, touch, smell, taste or hear. Empirical evidence is the core concept of the scientific method. It is also the core concept used in this book. You will be able to see the evidence with *your* own eyes, and *you* will determine if it meets the acceptance criteria set by *you*.

Few of us recognize the outsized impact that faith has on our daily lives. Most of us do not realize our dependence on faith—and even fewer of us would call it faith. We are taught that faith requires a supernatural being. But this is only a falsehood that is used to distract us from the truth that faith is practiced everyday of our lives.

Let us take a well-known historical example to demonstrate this concept—Captain "Sully" on flight Cactus 1549 and is also known as the "Miracle on the Hudson." This flight was known as US Airways Flight 1549 and was scheduled to be flown on January 15, 2009, from LaGuardia, NY to Charlotte, NC. Everyone on the airplane that day expected (*i.e.*, had faith) that in a few hours they would safely land in Charlotte. No one that boarded, including Sully himself, believed that they would have a water landing in the Hudson River less than five minutes after takeoff from LaGuardia. All 155 people on board survived the landing on the river, but this book is not about recounting what happened during and after this event. Rather, it is about how faith influenced everyone's actions—on that day and all the days of our lives.

On a more personal level, every day you wake up to go to work or school, you have faith that nothing other than the usual will occur on that day. Everybody on earth lives their daily lives heavily invested in the faith that nothing unusual exists. Most of that faith is based upon the empirical evidence that has occurred in our lives prior to that point in our lives. Almost every day we experience the events that we expect to occur during the day. Our faith is grounded in the empirical evidence that unusual episodes rarely occur in our lives. But it is important to recognize that we are still living our daily lives based upon faith every day and that living by faith is not a bad thing—if that faith is well-grounded with empirical evidence.

❖ Fact, Belief, and Truth

Last, three related terms—which are often used interchangeably erroneously—must be defined. These terms are facts, beliefs, and truth. When used in this book, the term *fact* will mean empirical evidence that is accepted as true by 99 percent or more of the experts on *both* sides of the issue. Some people, including some experts, will refuse to accept anything that does not agree with their preconceived beliefs, but that is another issue. This is the only reason the bar is set to 99 percent of experts instead of all experts. Universally, when the term fact is used, it means all experts on *both* sides can see this and accept it as true. Sometimes acceptance will be the simple acknowledgment that "yes, expert-I wrote that statement." Other times acceptance means that it will be observable, like the issue of "the sun is still burning." And even you, yourself, once acquainted with the evidence, will accept the issue as a fact.

The next term to address is *truth*. In this book, the term truth will be used to designate the conclusion reached when all the facts are known, and there are *absolutely no beliefs* left in the equation. This worldview truth can never be determined while we are here on earth, and while we are constantly gaining knowledge. Using the Captain Sully event, the truth was only learned after about five minutes into the flight, too late to change anyone's decision.

The last term is *belief*, which refers to the distance between the facts and the truth. It is that final leap of faith to get us to what we regard as truth. This book seeks to help you narrow your "leap of faith" in your quest for the truth, before you reach the "final destination."

Fact, Belief, and Truth—a Demonstration

Using a rifle bullet and a target demonstrates these definitions. The bullseye is the truth. The length of the rifle barrel is equivalent to the empirical facts—it only carries the bullet so far. The distance between the end of the rifle barrel and the target is where one's beliefs exist.

When a sniper fires a rifle bullet at a target, gravity pulls the bullet down, while the wind blows the bullet sideways. To compensate for these environmental disturbances, the sniper adjusts the scope to cause the barrel point away from the bullseye but to where the sniper believes it will cause the bullet to reach the bullseye after compensating for all the environmental disturbances. This is the effect that beliefs have on our conclusions. If the sniper's rifle barrel is next to the target, then no adjustment is needed. If the sniper is a mile from the target, then careful adjustments will be needed to score a bullseye.

The main problem here is that no one really knows where the truth lies. So, the more empirical facts that are available, the less likely a miss of the bullseye will occur. When few, or no, empirical facts are to be had, then the shooter is firing blindly—and will miss the target almost every time.

❖ Persons Holding a Worldview

Merriam-Webster defines an *atheist* as "a person who does not believe in the existence of a god or any gods."[5] This person ardently adheres to the Naturalist religious viewpoint. Atheists are firmly convinced that the universe originated from a singularity, which exploded via the big bang theory, life began through one or more random events, and then evolution changed the original species into the various species we see today.

Merriam-Webster defines an *agnostic* person as "one who is not committed to believing in either the existence or the nonexistence of God or a god."[6] In practice, most agnostics are really atheists because if the person desired to find any evidence for a god, it is readily available today. It just takes time, lots of time usually, to find that evidence. But the agnostic chooses to either not search for the knowledge or to ignore the knowledge currently known.

Merriam-Webster defines a *theist* as "a person who believes in the existence of a god or gods."[7] A *monotheist*[8] is a person who believes there is only one god. Christians are considered monotheists, as they consider the biblical God to be the creator of life on earth—the One True God. *Polytheists*[9] believe in more than one god. This belief system is not as prevalent today as it was in the past, so it will not be addressed in the book.

Last, the term *anti-Christian* will be used to designate any person who seeks to constantly attack any Christian viewpoint, especially when the anti-Christian senses the Christian is weak in their knowledge of Christianity. They generally fall into the atheist religion, but they frequently appear in discussion forums to primarily attack and ridicule Christians on the forums. They are usually armed with falsified conclusions, and those conclusions may appear valid until examined closely. They will rarely address any rebuttal provided by a Christian to these false conclusions, instead resorting to mockery and defamation. Some of this book will address the most common of these false conclusions presented by anti-Christians by providing empirical evidence to show why it is false. If you are already a Christian believer, this will help equip you to defend your reason for believing in Jesus.

❖ Hypothesis, Theory, Premise, Tenet, and Law

Merriam-Webster defines a *hypothesis* as "a tentative assumption made in order to draw out and test its logical or empirical consequences."[10] Every hypothesis starts with one or more *postulates* or *premises*. *Merriam-Webster* defines a postulate as "to assume or claim as true, existent, or necessary."[11] *Merriam-Webster* defines a premise as "something assumed or taken for granted."[12] So, they are different words that essentially mean the same thing. A scientific theory starts as a hypothesis, but its proponent provides some preliminary evidence to lend it creditability.

When a scientific theory reaches a certain level of acceptance, it becomes a scientific *tenet*. *Merriam-Webster* defines tenet as "a principle, belief, or doctrine generally held to be true."[13] In short, it still falls short of being proven true, and it could be falsified at any time with new empirical evidence.

When a scientific theory has been thoroughly tested by many scientists without finding *any* evidence against the original conclusions reached by the hypothesis, then a consensus within the scientific community raises it to the highest level of *scientific law*, and it is universally accepted as a fact by all. One example of this progression is that Newton's theory of gravity is now known as Newton's Law of Gravity.[14] This testing process takes a long time, usually a hundred years or more.

When testing a scientific theory, if all the premises are valid, then the hypothesis's conclusion is presumed to be valid as well. Opponents of a theory's conclusion will test each premise, comparing it to the empirical evidence either supporting it or undermining it, some of which the original scientist(s) may not have considered. Either they *falsify* (*i.e.*, prove it false) one or more of the premises or they validate the original conclusion by providing evidence that the premises have some evidence to validate the hypothesis. Alternatively, they could validate the underlying premises, but reach a different conclusion—but this area out of scope for this book.

If the theory is falsified, then its proponents often adjust the original hypothesis to accommodate any new evidence. This cycle continues until a scientific theory passes all tests, and it becomes a scientific law. Alternatively, it is restated *ad infinitum* until a new and better theory explains the original conundrum, and the old theory is replaced with the new theory. *Merriam-Webster* defines ad infinitum as "without end or limit."[15]

CHAPTER 3

SETTING THE STAGE

The two worldviews that are explored in this book are: 1) Our world came about through natural means starting with the big bang, creation of life, millions of years of evolution (slow changes over time creating a new and better species through mutation), that give us the world as we observe it today; and 2) Our world was created by the biblical God. Unless we can articulate a scientific theory for the biblical God, we cannot test it against the empirical evidence. There are two claims that most Christians acknowledge: a) The Bible is the Word of God, and b) This God is omnipotent (all-powerful) and omniscient (all-knowing).

The Bible has many other attributes for the biblical God, but they can only be evaluated through the lens (*i.e.,* the acceptance) of the Bible's validity. Thus, all other attributes of the biblical God are outside of the scope of this book. A few other religions will also be explored, along with their ability to guide one's life and actions. But there are too many religions in this world to attempt to cover them in any one book, so only four alternative religions will be discussed, and the discussions will be brief.

NATURALISM

CHAPTER 4

INTRODUCTION TO NATURALISM

Naturalism is a worldview that holds that the world we observe today came into being through natural means, rather than a supernatural being. It is based upon five major tenets: the natural origins for the universe, the natural origins for life, the evolution of that early life into today's diversity of life, this evolutionary process took millions of years to occur, and there were many transitional steps between the first life and today's diversity of life. The undergirding of this worldview is that these concepts can be postulated as scientific theories and can be subsequently proven true or false. Its proponents acknowledge that some of these theories will be proven false and subsequently replaced by new, testable theories to guide them to the final answer.

Most people believe that scientific theories are postulated, tested, verified, peer reviewed, and then the findings are published in the media when the results would be of interest to the public. Nothing could be further from the truth. Hundreds of years ago, before the information age, that may have been true. But in today's information age, as soon as a scientist reaches a conclusion supporting the scientist's viewpoint, the findings are published in a publication with little to no peer-review process conducted, and they are often announced in the major news media for their readers' consumption.

The reason the process works this way is all about money. The scientist gets funding from some source, and if the scientist does not produce satisfactory results within a reasonable amount of time, they lose their funding and have no job. This encourages publishing early, non-peer reviewed conclusions. Often, many of these conclusions are subsequently proven false (falsified) by other scientists. But since the public media is less interested in the latter conclusions, they are not usually published in places where the public has access to them. The public is left with the belief that science is finding new things out all the time, and the scientific method is at work keeping the falsehoods out of the public's eye. But let us look at how the scientific method is supposed to work, how it does work, and a real-life example of how it actually works in today's information age.

❖ The Scientific Method

The scientific method is a process to find true knowledge. In its pure form, it does not care which direction the researcher desires to go. All that matters is that the research is: 1) Testable, 2) Supported with empirical evidence, 3) Can be reviewed and tested by other researchers, and 4) That it can be falsified if research finds empirical evidence that contradicts the original theory. Many people don't understand the difference between a scientific theory and a scientific research program—but there is a major difference between the two terms.

❖ Research Programs

A research program is a group of scientific theories, with each theory able to be falsified while the program itself is almost impossible to be falsified through any empirical evidence. *Merriam-Webster* defines *programme* (the British spelling of program) as "to predetermine the thinking, behavior, or operations of as if by computer programming."[1]

According to Imre Lakatos (1922–1974), a Hungarian philosopher of mathematics and science, there are two types of scientific research programs, progressive and degenerative. In a progressive research program, the theory leads to new facts. In a degenerative research program, it either fails to predict new facts or has those predictions systematically falsified. However, Naturalists would rather have a degenerate research program "than to sit down in undeluded ignorance."[2] Thus, even a failing research program is better than no program advocating for a natural origin for the world that we see today. According to *Stanford Encyclopedia of Philosophy*, Lakatos's philosophy of science was "Does this mean that no research programme should be given up in the absence of a progressive alternative, no matter how degenerate it may be? If so, this amounts to the radically anti-sceptical thesis that it is better to subscribe to a theory that bears all the hallmarks of falsehood . . . *than to sit down in undeluded ignorance.*"[3] [Emphasis added]

Consequently, even if every one of Naturalism's tenets fall into a degenerate research program category, they are content to continue down that path rather than falsify any of the necessary tenets needed for a belief in Naturalism. Why is this true? It is because most scientists today subscribe to Lakatos's philosophy of science.

[F]alsifiability continues to play a part in Lakatos's conception of science but its importance is somewhat diminished. Instead of an individual falsifiable theory which ought to be rejected as soon as it is refuted, we have a sequence of falsifiable theories characterized by shared a *hard core of central theses that are deemed irrefutable*—or, at least, refutation-resistant—*by methodological fiat.* This sequence of theories constitutes a research programme. The shared hard core of this sequence of theories is often unfalsifiable in two senses of the term. Firstly scientists working within the programme are typically (and rightly) reluctant to give up on the claims that constitute the hard core. Secondly the *hard core theses by themselves are often devoid of empirical consequences.*[4] [Emphasis added]

So, what most people read about in the public media are considered scientific theories and are subject to falsification. But the hard-core research programs (*i.e.*, Naturalists' tenets) are not subject to this falsification process. Instead, what happens is that when a Naturalist tenet is falsified, scientists "put it on ice" until they can develop an alternative theory to replace the tenet before announcing the earlier theory as falsified. And this is an endless cycle. Once theory number one is falsified, work commences on theory number two until enough support is found to transition to theory number two. Later, as additional research into theory number two finds empirical evidence contrary to the theory, it too is put-on-ice until a replacement theory can be announced. This creates the illusion that science is always advancing, rather than the truth that the hard-core program has been falsified multiple times with multiple alternatives theories. This is why there are so many articles published that appear to propose an alternative theory that fits the empirical evidence that the researchers set out to address.

❖ Example of the Scientific Process

To demonstrate this issue, let us look at a renowned theory that is widely accepted today but still falls short of the standard to become known as a scientific law—the theory of general relativity. This theory was developed by Albert Einstein between 1907 and 1915. It is well known that many subsequent studies have confirmed this theory—almost to the point that it is considered a scientific law. What is less known is that this theory has also been falsified, albeit in a very limited situation.

About the same time that Einstein was working on his theory of relativity, German physicist Max Planck was working on another theory—the quantum theory.[5] The quantum theory explains behaviors on the atomic level—about three molecules or less. And the quantum theory has likewise been verified and is universally accepted by the scientific community. Yet, it too has been falsified by scientific studies. Why?

General relativity works exactly as expected above the quantum level but fails to explain the results below that point. Likewise, quantum theory explains our universe at the atomic level but fails to explain our observations above that point. So, they are both verified within a limited range of study and falsified outside of that range. Scientists understand this discrepancy and are working on what Stephen Hawking called a "unified theory"[6] in his book *A Brief History of Time*. In practical terms, there is no impact on the scientific understanding of our universe.

But it does call out the amount of time that it takes for a theory to undergo rigorous testing to reach the esteemed level of a scientific law. And until it reaches the status of a scientific law, every Naturalists' tenet is subject to be dismissed as truth. All scientific theories start off as progressive research programs, but some degenerate into pseudoscience or pathological science. But in today's information age, the scientific method takes a detour. It is caused by the underlying problem of money—how does a researcher get their funding?

❖ Announcing Scientific Discoveries

The root cause of the problem is how today's scientists are enabled to conduct their research. According to the *Smithsonian Magazine*, in the early days of science, the scientist funded his or her own research with, maybe, a little help from friends and family.[7] Nowadays, according to the *National Science Foundation*, scientists are funded by governments and institutions.[8] These entities set expectations, specifically the support for believing in Naturalism—which presumes that our world came about through natural causes, not a supernatural cause.

The overall research and development sector for science and engineering totaled $548 billion in 2017 in the U.S. alone. This includes many areas outside of the Naturalists' religion but can be used to get a general understanding of how funding plays a role in scientific research. The business sector provided the largest funding, with 73 percent, followed by universities and colleges with 13 percent, and the third largest funding institution is the federal government at 10 percent of the money.[9]

If a scientist desires to research a topic that goes outside of these general guidelines, scientists often do not get the funding to conduct the research. So, there is an unnatural constraint on which topics can be researched. Additionally, to get further funding, the researcher is encouraged by the process to publish their findings before any peer-review can be conducted. This perpetuates the disfunction in the scientific community. Subsequent findings, both supporting and contradicting the original conclusions receive less attention, especially when the additional research conclusions are contradictory.

According to a recent article in *The Guardian*, recent research found that the number of scientific studies that have been retracted because of failing to meet scientific standards has risen in recent years.[10] For example, in 2000 the number of retractions was about forty retractions, while in 2020 alone, it rose to nearly 5,500 retractions. While this is only a small percentage of the number of scientific research publications, only about one per 1,000 studies, it reflects the push of publish-or-perish mentality that pervades today's scientific culture. These retractions are a result of two main reasons, more volunteer sleuthing and "major publishers' (belated) recognition that their business models have made them susceptible to paper mills."[11] Another problem is that any criticism of published scientific work is often restricted, with the authors having overall approval of the publication of any criticism. And, when the corrections or retractions are acknowledged, it can take years for them to be printed—and may never be printed at all.[12]

How bad is this issue? It is very bad. An infamous example of this dysfunction will demonstrate its impact upon the public, along with the subsequent coverup by the scientific community. This coverup and reintroduction with a new hypothesis is known as a *pathological science* and is a very common issue in the scientific community today. *Wikipedia* defines a pathological science as "an area of research where 'people are tricked into false results ... by subjective effects, wishful thinking or threshold interactions.'"[13] The term was introduced by Irving Langmuir, a Nobel Prize-winning chemist, during a speech in 1953. The quintessential example of pathological science is the discovery of *polywater*.

❖ Polywater

In the mid-1960s, Russian scientists Nikolai Fedyakin and Boris Deryagin "discovered" polywater,[14] a polymerized form of water that, if it escaped out of the laboratory, could prove to be extremely dangerous to all life on earth. Fedyakin published his findings and conclusions, including its threat to humankind, with Deryagin subsequently testing and concurring with his conclusions. By the late-1960s, the media got caught up in the brouhaha. Panic started to set into the general public's mindset. With the increase in the public's interest, more funding was provided to the scientific community to quantify the potential dangers and possible solutions.

Some of these scientific experiments verified polywater and its dangers, while others falsified it. By 1973, a scientific consensus was reached—polywater was just ordinary water with some contamination in the water. It posed no more danger than regular water mixed with any number of common compounds.[15] However, the issue dropped out of the popular press well before the consensus was reached, so those who were not following the scientific research never heard about the resolution.

❖ Introduction to Naturalism Conclusion

Historically, a scientific theory usually takes more than one hundred years before sufficient research has been conducted to verify it without any contrary empirical evidence. After scientists have researched all the plausible means of falsifying the theory and have failed to do so, only then can it become universally accepted as truth and the name of the original scientific theory is changed to the name of a scientific law, like the theory of gravity became known as Law of Gravity.

This book will show that each of the major tenets of Naturalism has been falsified. But because they are hard-core research programs, they are deemed immune to falsification by methodological fiat. Only Stephen Hawking has been open to admitting to the falsification of a major tenet of the Naturalists' religion. As might be expected, by the time he had admitted to the falsification, he was at the height of his career, and he was advancing his own theory of a natural origin of the universe —what he hoped to replace the big bang theory. No one else has been brave enough to tell the truth that a Naturalist hard-core research program has been falsified until they have an alternative theory ready to take the place of the current favorite research program, and that theory has gained sufficient traction in the scientific community. Thus, every major tenet of the Naturalist religion falls under the category of pathological sciences, also known as a degenerative research program.

CHAPTER 5

ORIGINS OF THE UNIVERSE
(COSMOLOGY)

For the Naturalists' worldview to be valid, there must be a scientific theory on the natural origins of the universe that is tested, and with empirical evidence to support that theory. Naturalists have produced many postulates to advance the idea of a natural origin for our universe. The theories that have received the most attention historically are addressed in this chapter. The major cosmological hypotheses are the static state model, the steady state model, and the big bang theory—which was subsequently modified into the inflationary model.

❖ Static State Model

Per *Wikipedia*, scientists studying cosmology in the early 1900s assumed that the universe was in a static state.[1] However Isaac Newton's work on physics, in the late 1600s, compelled scientists to reevaluate this cosmological model. Newton's Law of Gravity[2] describes the force of attraction between two objects. This gravitational force is proportional to the product of the masses, and inversely proportional to the square of the distance between them.

Scientists realized that a static model could be falsified because gravity would attract the various celestial objects together into a single mass, with the only premises being that: a) the Law of Gravity is correct, and b) given sufficient time for this to occur. Since the Law of Gravity had been tested and verified for hundreds of years by the early 1900s, then the only real obstacle was the sufficient time requirement.

The only way to bypass this requirement would be the creation of the universe by a supernatural force—which is an *anathema* (intense dislike) to Naturalists. There were other objections to the static model, but they will not be addressed here since the core issue is that scientists universally consider the static model of the universe to be falsified.

❖ Steady State Model

The next cosmological model advanced was known as the steady state universe[3], which presumed that the universe is always expanding while maintaining a constant average density. As demonstrated, it was just a slight improvement over the static state model—addressing the flaw that the universe would collapse if the universe were static. The hypothesis was that the inertia force of the expanding celestial bodies would prevent the collapse due to the gravitational forces.

However, in 1965, two scientists (Penzias and Wilson) discovered cosmic background radiation (CBR).[4] CBR is an electromagnetic radiation that fills all the space in our universe. According to astrophysicists, this energy should not be found in a steady state universe. Once again, another cosmological model was universally rejected by scientists.

❖ Big Bang Theory / Inflationary Model

While scientists were considering the various cosmological models, in the 1920s, a Belgian astronomer named Georges Lemaitre proposed a cosmological model that the universe began in a cataclysmic explosion. The media mocked it by calling it the "big bang," and the name stuck. In the late 1960s to early 1970s, several scientists conducted separate studies on the possibility of the Big Bang theory and found that mathematical models proved that an expanding universe required a *singularity*. A singularity is an infinitely small point in space where all matter, energy, and time are collapsed into that single point. A singularity implied an explosion—as proposed by Lemaitre. The explosion would explain the evidence of the cosmic background radiation found in 1965. In 1965–66, Roger Penrose and Stephen Hawking proved that a singularity existed for all solutions to Einstein's theory of general relativity. In 1970, Hawking and Penrose published their research justifying the singularity, and a consensus was reached in the Naturalist community that allowed the Big Bang theory to become a recognized scientific theory. Nevertheless, there was also evidence that falsified the Big Bang theory.

One of those problems was that the universe appears homogeneous in all directions. To solve this problem, several theoretical physicists proposed a modification to the Big Bang theory in the 1970s and early 1980s. They proposed that the early universe expanded exponentially fast for a fraction of a second after the big bang. This new model became known as the Inflationary Model, and it has now become the de facto replacement for the Big Bang theory for scientists. It is the predominant cosmological scientific theory today, and both terms—Big Bang theory and Inflationary Model— are used almost interchangeably today.

In 1988, Stephen Hawking wrote *A Brief History of Time* on the problems with the inflationary theory and proposed a new theory. Excerpts from his book calling out the problems with both the Big Bang and its replacement theory, the Inflationary Model, are given below.

1. Why was the early universe so hot? ...
2. Why is the universe so uniform on a large scale? ...
3. Why did the universe start out with so nearly the critical rate of expansion that separates models that recollapse from those that go on expanding forever? ...
4. Despite the fact that the universe is so uniform and homogeneous on a large scale, it contains local irregularities, such as stars and galaxies. ... What was the origin of these density fluctuations? ... [5]

His conclusion is also worth quoting. "In my personal opinion, *the new inflationary model is now dead as a scientific theory*, although a lot of people do not seem to have heard of its demise and are still writing papers as if it were viable"[6] [Emphasis added]. He also opined that "if we do discover a complete theory, it should in time be understandable in broad principle by everyone, not just a few scientists."[7] To replace it, Hawking proposed what he called the string theory. Many variations on the string theory have since emerged, but no consensus has been reached by the Naturalist scientists.

Center of the Universe

Another factoid against the hypothesis of the universe coming from a singularity via a big bang is the lack of a center for the origin of the singularity. In the last fifty years, scientists have been observing celestial objects that they have calculated to be from the early universe. They believe that these objects are some of the first objects created after the Big Bang. Scientists, namely theoretical astrophysics, use instruments like the Hubble Space Telescope, the James Webb Space Telescope, and the Chandra X-ray Observatory to search space for unusual objects to support or detract from the hypothesis they are researching. This results in finding unusual objects in space, which are referenced by two terms: right ascension (abbreviated RA) and declination (abbreviated Dec). Right ascension is the angular distance to the identified object measured eastward along the celestial equator from the sun at the March equinox to the point in question above the earth. Declination is the angular distance of a point north or south of the celestial equator. Essentially, these astronomical coordinates specify the location of a point on the celestial sphere in the equatorial coordinate system, whereby other astronomers can use to point their telescopes to observe the object.

There are many unusual objects in space, but the ones that are of special interest are the ones identified by scientists as being created shortly after the big bang occurred. A list of a few of these unusual early objects is given below. The metrics for these objects were obtained from *Wikipedia* from their respective web pages, and are provided as a numbered list below for the reader to allow verification of the subsequent paragraphs that calculate the distance between two of the objects.

1. HDI (galaxy), 13.5 billion years old, RA 10h 01m 51.31s; Dec 02° 32' 50.0"; Distance: 33.4 billion light years.[8]
2. JADES-GS-z13-0 (galaxy), 13.6 billion years old, RA 03h 32m 35.97s;Dec -27° 46' 35.4"; Distance: 33.6 billion light years.[9]
3. GLASS-z12 (galaxy), 13.6 billion years ago, RA 00h 13m 59.76s; Dec -30° 19' 29.1"; Distance: 33.2 billion light years.[10]
4. GN-z11 (galaxy), 13.4 billion years ago, RA 12h 36m 25.46s; Dec +62° 14' 31.4"; Distance: 32 billion light years.[11]

Some of the above galaxies are in the northern hemisphere, while others are in the southern hemisphere. Those celestial objects in the northern hemisphere have a positive declination, while those in the southern hemisphere have a negative declination. The maximum declination in either direction is ±90 degrees. In the list above, we see one near the equator (HDI: +02 degrees), one two-thirds of the angle to the north pole (GN-z11: +62 degrees), and two that are one-third of the angle to the south pole (GLASS-z12: -30 degrees, and JADES-GS-z13-0: -27 degrees).

This means that GLASS-z12 (#3) and GN-z11 (#4) are ninety-two degrees (30 south and 62 degrees north) apart with an average distance of 32.6 billion years from the earth. Using the declination coordinates, their respective distances from the earth, and combined with the trigonometric law of cosines, it reveals that these galaxies (GLASS-z12 and GN-z11) are 47.1 *billion* years apart. Even now, Naturalists claim that the age of these galaxies were only 400 *million* years old—since the occurrence of the big bang. This is contrary to logic. The problem is that the universe is 13.8 billion years old. So, how did two objects get 47 billion years apart in a universe that has only existed for 14 billion years? And how did they do it within the first 400 million years of their creation?

As per *Live Science*, Naturalists have calculated that the Big Bang occurred approximately 14 to 13.6 billion years ago.[12] They base this claim upon the earliest objects they can find in the sky. Thus, the empirical evidence shows one of two conclusions: there were multiple singularities and big bangs, or the Big Bang theory is falsified.

Cosmological Conclusion

Each postulated scientific theory for a natural origin for our universe has been falsified over time, often taking decades or centuries to do so. The newest cosmological category was started in the 1980s with Hawking's string theory—which postulates that the universe is forever in existence but switching between different universes often through the black holes known to be in our universe. But it will take decades or longer to be able to find empirical evidence that supports or contradicts this category of postulates.

As mentioned earlier, Naturalists are disinclined to falsify a required tenet that supports their belief of a natural explanation for our world until its replacement can be accepted by the community. Consequently, the average person is still being indoctrinated in public schools to believe that the Big Bang theory is a fact accepted by scientists. Nonetheless, this major tenet of the Naturalists' worldview is lacking empirical support to accept it as probable, much less empirically verified.

CHAPTER 6

ORIGINS OF LIFE
(ABIOGENESIS)

I f a supernatural explanation is to be ruled out, then Naturalists must also have a scientific theory for the origins of life on earth. This area of study is known as *abiogenesis*. This term comes from the Greek root word "a-" meaning "not", combined with the Greek root word "bio" meaning life, and "genesis" meaning "beginnings or origins." Put them altogether, this term equates to "from non-life to beginning of life."

The Naturalist hypothesis is that life has arisen from non-life by the natural, random combination of elements into simple organic compounds—called amino acids. According to *Amino Acids Guide*, there are over 700 types of amino acids that have been discovered in nature.[1] These amino acids would subsequently form peptides and proteins, the building blocks for all living things on earth. Starting in the mid-1900s, scientists hypothesized that these organic compounds could have been created naturally in the early history of the earth. The Miller-Urey experiment, which started in 1952, and was published in 1953, first tested this theory.

❖ Miller-Urey Experiment

The Miller-Urey experiment[2] was a chemistry experiment that was thought to simulate the conditions of the early earth atmosphere in an enclosed laboratory experiment. The early elements were thought to be hydrogen, methane, ammonia, and water vapor. So, the scientists used these elements in their experiments. The experiment would heat the mixture into a gas, which would then rise and pass through a section that would simulate lightning—a reoccurring spark like the sparkplug in a gas-powered engine. Then, this vapor would condense, cool, and then return to the heating chamber to start the process all over again. The goal of the experiment was to produce amino acids. The experiment was considered a partial success by the Naturalists, since three of the twenty-two amino acids needed for life were created (proteinogenic).[3] The experiments did create a total of five amino acids, but only three of them were needed for life. The others were among the other seven hundred amino acids found on earth. But science requires a peer-review after the publication to confirm or deny the conclusions reached.

Problems with the Miller-Urey Experiment

Counter researchers found problems with the Miller-Urey experiment. Since it was an enclosed system, unlike the earth's open system, it allowed the buildup of an excess of hydrogen. In an open system, the excess hydrogen would escape the earth's gravitation force and dissipate into space. Without this excess hydrogen, the amino acids could not be created. Another problem was that the scientists knowingly excluded free oxygen from the experiment because they understood that hydrogen and oxygen will produce an explosion when combined with a spark. Additionally, oxygen is known as an oxidizing element—meaning that it breaks down organic compounds to provide the energy for life on earth. On that account, the inclusion of oxygen in the experiment would have broken down the amino acids as fast as they were produced if it were included in the experiment. The earth's present atmosphere comprises almost 21 percent oxygen today. But how much oxygen was in the early earth's atmosphere?

Miller-Urey postulated a low-oxygen (*i.e., reducing atmosphere*) for the early earth atmosphere, since an oxygen-rich environment would destroy the amino acids before life could begin. Thus, their hypothesis was that the early earth atmosphere was a low-oxygen environment conducive to the creation of the necessary amino acids. Then, these amino acids formed the first species, which in turn caused the rise in oxygen levels to today's known levels. But the evidence provided by other Naturalist studies contradicts this premise.

In 1976, Canadian scientists Dimroth and Kimberly wrote "In general, we find no evidence in the sedimentary distributions of carbon, sulfur, uranium, or iron, that an oxygen-free atmosphere has existed at any time during the span of geological history recorded in well preserved sedimentary rocks."[4] Research by Naturalists published in *Geology*,[5] in 1982, and *ScienceDaily*,[6] in 2009, also found empirical evidence from the earliest strata layers (*i.e.*, the oldest rock layers on earth) showing a red tone in the layer. These strata layers are referred to as *red beds*. Red beds are formed when metal—usually iron—combines with oxygen and forms rust. This rust stains the rock layer with a red tint. The researchers found that these rock layers have been dated to be about 3.7 billion years old—namely around the time they believe that life first developed.[7] This indicated that the earth's early atmosphere was an oxygen-rich environment. All this scientific research proves that the Miller-Urey experiment did not reflect the conditions of the earth's early atmosphere.

Subsequent scientific experiments, with slight variations of the Miller-Urey elements, on abiogenesis have also failed to produce the organic compounds necessary for life. Some of these experiments were able to produce many more amino acids (as many as nine of the twenty-two needed), but still less than the total of the amino acids needed for life on earth. So, currently, there is no Naturalist scientific consensus on a theory for the origins of life. This is usually ignored by the acolytes of Naturalism, as they believe that science will eventually answer this dilemma.

❖ Abiogenesis Conclusion

While there have been many attempts to create all the amino acids necessary for life, there have been no experiments to create life, via peptides and proteins, from these amino acids. Even the experiments to create the necessary amino acids have failed to create all the necessary amino acids for life on earth. So, this major tenet of the Naturalists' worldview is lacking any empirical support to accept it as possible, much less probable.

CHAPTER 7

THEORY OF EVOLUTION

E volution is generally recognized as the upward progression from simple life forms to today's complex life forms. Although Naturalists will readily admit that some species may *devolve* (evolve into a less complex species), this definition of evolution will be ignored since the nexus of the matter is reaching today's diversification of species.

Most people today believe that Charles Darwin was the first person to propose the theory of evolution in his *On the Origins of Species* book. This is incorrect. In fact, two scientists, one of them was Darwin, were working simultaneously on dusting off a previously falsified theory of evolution from ancient Greece and publish their conclusions. Darwin won the race by publishing his book in 1859. In consequence, all Darwin did was to research an ancient theory, microsize it to the point of it being unfalsifiable in his time, and publish his work.

❖ History of the Theory of Evolution

The ancient Greeks were the first to propose the theory of evolution. Anaximander of Miletus (610–546 BC) was the first to propose that the first animals lived in water, and that land animals evolved from them, partly dwelling in water and partly on land, before finally evolving further to live fully on the land alone.

Empedocles (*fl* 445 B. C., in Sicily) developed to a further stage the idea of evolution. Organs arise not by design but by selection. Nature makes many trials and experiments with organisms, combining organs variously; where the combination meets environmental needs the organism survives and perpetuates its like; where the combination fails, the organism is weeded out; as time goes on, organisms are more and more intricately and successfully adapted to their surroundings.[1]

Like modern scientists, the ancient Greeks considered the hypothesis, observed the evidence, and reached a conclusion. They observed that wounded soldiers did not pass on their mutations to their offspring. For example, an individual whose arm was cut off in battle did not beget one-armed children after the soldier's arm was lost in combat. Thus, they dismissed the theory of evolution, and it laid in the dustbin until the 1800s when Darwin resurrected it.

After Darwin republished the ancient Greek theory of evolution, other Naturalists began to work on verifying or falsifying his hypothesis. Naturalists had a dilemma in the theory of evolution. If evolution were to occur, it would either be frequent enough to measure or it would be too rare to observe—like millions of years before a speciation event would occur.

❖ Speciation Event—The Spawning of a New Specie

According to the University of California Museum of Paleontology, a speciation event is when a mutation occurs in a species that births a new specie[2]—one that is unable to mate successfully with the parent specie. Since there had been no speciation events in known history, evolutionists were left with the only possible solution—that evolution happened with hundreds of thousands of years or even millions of years between each speciation event. This left the Naturalists in a quandary, as science is based upon empirical evidence that can be tested and repeated by other scientists. Nor could they wait the required number of years to test their hypothesis. As such, they looked for alternative means of testing the hypothesis.

❖ Evolution Experiments

Scientists studying biology in the late 1800s discovered that the fruit fly (*i.e.,* *Drosophila Melanogaster*) was a good genetic research subject because it could be bred cheaply and reproduced quickly. The fruit fly is a small, red-eyed fly that is covered in small hairs, has two large wings, and two small wings (called halteres), the latter of which are used for balance and control during flight. And it was attracted to, and fed on, fruit, hence the common name of fruit fly.

In 1910, before biologists had specialized into studying genetics, Thomas Morgan (1866–1945) observed that a male fruit fly had white eyes, rather than the usual red eyes. Morgan and others thus confirmed the theory of chromosomal inheritance, which hypothesized that traits could be passed from one generation to the next through chromosomes.[3] In 1927, Hermann Muller (1890–1967) discovered that x-rays could induce mutations in chromosomes (*Artificial Transmutation of the Gene*).[4] Muller's experiments would expose the fruit fly eggs to x-rays, altering their chromosomes. Then, raise that egg to adulthood to find out if the change in the chromosomes carried on to the next generation of the fruit fly. When combined, these began the research field of genetics.

The next logical step was to test the process of repeated mutation, raising the next generation from these mutations, and then causing further mutation upon the next generation—hopefully leading to a speciation event. The most obvious candidate species was the fruit fly, as it was cheap to raise, and reproduced quickly—as in two weeks from the laying of the egg to the newly developed adult fruit fly being able to reproduce. And the geneticists had identified the tool to use to create mutations—the x-ray. Given the rapid cycling of generations of fruit flies, they could recreate the equivalent of millions of years of natural evolution in a laboratory setting in less than two years of scientific research. What they found is that the species could be changed, but only within a limited range of mutation.

They were able to cause more or fewer hairs to grow on the resultant fruit fly. Richard Mann and Ryan Loker found that they could cause the halteres to grow large enough to resemble the normal pair of wings, giving the appearance of a four-winged fruit fly which could not fly.[5] And, as

Morgan discovered, they could also change the color of the eye. There were other changes, too. For some mutations, the mutated egg could not develop into a larva, so that line of mutation research ended.

❖ Evolution Conclusion

Since the early days of fruit fly experiments, many other researchers have conducted similar experiments, all with similar results. Every time the research was conducted, it was found that the range of survivable change was limited, and that for every change induced, the resulting adult fruit fly was similar or worse off than its parent-generation fruit fly. Though many Naturalists have set out to prove the theory of evolution, they all have resulted in falsifying the theory of evolution. Yet, Naturalists are unwilling to admit this fact, choosing instead to believe that someday a geneticist will prove the theory. Yet again, this major tenet of the Naturalists' worldview is lacking any empirical support to accept it as possible.

CHAPTER 8

TRANSITIONAL SPECIES

Transitional species is a concept that refers to the idea that one species will give birth to (beget) a new species, which in turn will beget yet another species. The middle species is referred to as a transitional species. Technically, all three species would be considered transitional species if a connection could be established between all three species since the first species must be transitional from the first life, and the last species would eventually evolve into another species. Following the theory of evolution, a single-cell species will beget an entire string of transitional species until one arrives at today's known species that inhabit planet earth. Evolutionists are reluctant to put a number on the required number of transitional species to reach today's diversity of life, so one must dig into the matter, and extrapolate the required information.

To begin, a few basic concepts of evolution are needed. The first concept is that evolution is random, not directed. Second, every branch of evolution is equally likely to beget a new species. Third, is that given enough time, every branch of evolution will beget a new species. The key concept is "given enough time." A given evolutionary branch may not beget a new species at the same time as another branch, but over the millions of years available, every branch should beget the same approximate number of speciation events. In a nutshell, one branch may have a few more, or fewer, speciation events than another—but this does not matter in the overall conclusions we can reach if we follow this to its mathematical conclusion. For this analysis, we will keep it simple and assume that every branch has an equal number of speciation events, while acknowledging that the margin of error could be as high as 10 percent. And, even with a much higher margin of error, the overall conclusion would be the same.

❖ Number of Speciation Events

To be objective, we must begin with a number of speciation events provided by a respected Naturalist. Unfortunately, a quote on the number of speciation events from first life to modern life is impossible. The best available is a quote from Richard Dawkins in his book *The Blind Watchmaker* concerning the "evolution of the eye, from no-eye to modern-eye." It is not ideal, but the total number of transitional species *must* be higher since many more evolutionary steps would be needed to evolve from early life to a life with no-eye. And the number of transitional species needed even with this *very small* number of steps from "no-eye to modern-eye" boggles the mind of a skeptic. In his book, Dawkins postulated the following premises for the evolution of the human eye.

1. Could the human eye have arisen directly from no eye at all, in a single step? ...
2. Could the human eye have arisen directly from something slightly different from itself, something that we may call X? ...
3. Is there a continuous series of Xs connecting the modern human eye to a state with no eye at all? ...
4. Considering each member of the series of hypothetical Xs connecting the human eye to no eye at all, is it plausible that every one of them was available by random mutation of its predecessor? ...

It seems to me clear that the answer has to be yes, provided only that we allow ourselves a sufficiently large series of Xs. You might feel that 1,000 Xs is ample, but if you need more steps to make the total transition plausible in your mind, simply allow yourself to assume 10,000 Xs. And if 10,000 is not enough, allow yourself 100,000, and so on.[1]

These numbers do not appear that large, and they seem reasonable. But the mathematical application of these stipulated Xs will prove them to be unreasonable. For mathematical reasons explained later, a number near the lowest provided Xs will be used for the calculations, specifically 1,007 Xs.

Evolutionists do not care about mutations within a species, which are called traits, that could be passed from one generation to the next through chromosomes (like blond hair, blue eyes, etc.). What matters to them is when a mutation will spawn a new species. Dawkins labeled this event as "Xs". This spawning of a new species is known by evolutionists as a *speciation event*. The University of California Museum of Paleontology defines "Speciation [as] a lineage-splitting event that produces two or more separate species."[2] This translates to a doubling of species every time a speciation event occurs, since both the parent and the child species will exist after the speciation event. But, how long has evolution been occurring on earth?

"Scientists think that by 4.3 billion years ago, Earth may have developed conditions suitable to support life. The oldest known fossils, however, are only 3.7 billion years old."[3] This translates to a speciation event approximately every 3.7 million years, on average—if one were to use the lowest number of speciation events postulated by Dawkins (3.7 billion divided by 1,000). A single speciation event could occur, and then 7.4 million years later, two speciation events could occur back-to-back—resulting in an average of a single speciation event every 3.7 million years. Likewise, some branches could die off, resulting in a dead-end. To keep things simple, we will just assume that speciation events occurred every 3.7 million years. The conclusion reached is the same—regardless of *any and all* contortions applied to the calculation.

❖ Centillion Species

Beginning with a single species, after the first speciation event the earth would have two species. After the next speciation event, there would be four species, then eight, then sixteen, then thirty-two species after just five speciation events. Jumping forward, the earth's number of species would rise to 1,024 after ten speciation events, over one million species after twenty speciation events, and over two million species after twenty-one speciation events—more than all currently identified species on earth today. Plotting this formula in a spreadsheet, *i.e.*, doubling after every speciation event, would result in more than one *centillion* species (1.3715E+303) that have lived on earth since life first evolved after just 1,007 speciation events. And this number of species is just for the evolutionary transitional step of "no-eye to modern-eye."

Merriam-Webster defines a centillion as "a number equal to 1 followed by *303 zeros*,"[4] following the US definition. It is the largest mathematical number that has been named and can be used in calculations, which is also why the number of speciation events used in the calculation was limited to 1,007 speciation events. Not to mention, Microsoft Excel's calculations will crash after 1,023 speciation events, so further calculations are impossible. It (1,007 speciation events) is also at the low end of Dawkins's estimate—so the lower the number of speciation events, the more likely we can prove evolution's concept of transitional species as correct.

Biologists have currently identified less than two million species, with speculations reaching as high as eight million possible species. Using the spreadsheet, the number of speciation events needed for two million species is just twenty-one speciation events, and an upper limit of twenty-three speciation events as an upper limit for eight million species. So, why haven't Naturalists been able to identify these twenty-one (or twenty-three) speciation events?

The actual percentage of known species that have left fossil evidence behind is not known, but if just one percent (a *very* conservative number considering the number of fossils found today) of all transitional species left fossil evidence behind, then evolutionists should be able to find 1.3715E+301 (one followed by 301 zeros)—in other words, almost one centillion species. This number is not materially different from the lowest number of Dawkins's proposed transitional species for the evolutionary step of "no-eye to modern-eye"—i.e., about one centillion species.

❖ Transitional Species Conclusion

This number of transitional species needed for the theory of evolution to be correct, from first life to today's diversification of life, is far beyond human comprehension. We should be stumbling over hundreds of new transitional species every single day, and we still would not be able to identify them all. The fact that we are not finding a new transitional species every single day falsifies the theory of evolution tenet of transitional species. Naturalists will attempt to name a species as a transitional species but cannot prove the grandparent-parent-child relationship required for it to be considered as a true transitional species. As a result, this major tenet of the Naturalists' worldview is lacking sufficient empirical support to accept it as possible.

CHAPTER 9

MILLIONS OF YEARS SINCE
THE DINOSAURS

The evolution tenet that postulates that "millions of years of evolution has occurred" began to unravel the year that the movie *Jurassic Park* came out in 1993. The obvious question on everyone's mind when the movie hit the theaters was "Could dinosaur DNA survive long enough to bring them back to life?"

❖ Scientific Research into Survival of Dinosaur DNA

Meanwhile, Tomas Lindahl was a Swedish-British scientist who focused on cancer research and specialized in DNA research. While he wasn't working on the *Jurassic Park* issue, it did result in answering the question on everyone's mind. In 1993, Lindahl published an article that countered the idea postulated by *Jurassic Park*—that dinosaur DNA could survive millions of years, and that dinosaurs could be brought back to life. His conclusion was: "Hydrolysis, oxidation and nonenzymatic methylation of DNA occur at significant rates in vivo, and are counteracted by specific DNA repair processes. The spontaneous decay of DNA is likely to be a major factor in mutagenesis, carcinogenesis and ageing, and also sets limits for the recovery of DNA fragments from fossils."[1] *Merriam-Webster* defines *in vivo* as "in the living body of a plant or animal."[2]

In essence, Lindahl found that DNA (as well as soft tissue and blood cells) would completely degrade in a temperate environment (a climate zone) in less than 10,000 years after an animal's death because the natural repair processes that keep DNA intact would stop the moment the animal died. Almost all dinosaur fossils are found in temperate environments.

Wikipedia defines the four climate zones as the Artic, the Temperate, the Subtropic, and the Tropic.[3] Most of the 48-contiguous states in America fall into the Temperate Zone, along with most of southern Canada. Some of the southernmost 48-contiguous states fall into the Subtropic Zone. In consequence, pretty much anywhere researchers can easily explore falls into a temperate or warmer environment and the degradation of dinosaur soft tissue would be in 10,000 years or less. So, Lindahl's research put an end to the hope of resurrecting dinosaurs—or so the world thought. The next big discovery was the discovery of mammoth soft tissue / DNA.

Mammoths were thought to have died out about 10,000 years ago (with some speculating as little as 4,000 years ago), so the discovery of mammoth soft tissue started the wheels of pathological science into churning out "reasonable" explanations. They hypothesized that soft tissue and DNA in Artic conditions would survive for as much as 100,000 years. Things settled down, and Naturalists breathed a sigh of relief—only to get the next shock.

Molecular paleontologist Dr. Mary Schweitzer found the first evidence of dinosaur soft tissue from 68 million years ago.[4] This dinosaur, a T-Rex known as MOR 1125, was found in Montana—a temperate environment. Dinosaurs were thought to have died out 65 million years ago, so this put dino soft tissue survival well outside the 10,000 years proven by Lindahl in his scientific research study, and even beyond the hypothesized 100,000 years for Artic conditions.

During an extraction of a Tyrannosaurus skeleton (MOR 1125) in the Hell Creek Formation in Montana, the T-Rex's femur (thigh bone) was too large to lift out by a helicopter. This forced the extraction team to break the dinosaur's femur into two so it could be lifted out by a helicopter. Prior to this event, no scientist had ever deliberately broken a dino fossil into two or more pieces, so this was new ground, scientifically speaking.

This breakage gave Schweitzer the opportunity to examine the interior of a fossilized dinosaur bone.

❖ Discovery of Dinosaur Soft Tissue, Blood Cells, and DNA

The pieces of the T-Rex's fossils were subsequently turned over to Schweitzer to analyze. She discovered the existence of dinosaur soft tissue, including red blood cells and blood vessels within the broken pieces of the T-Rex femur. In May 2006, Helen Fields reported in the *Smithsonian Magazine* the following.

> What she found instead was evidence of heme in the bones—additional support for the idea that they were red blood cells. Heme is a part of hemoglobin, the protein that carries oxygen in the blood and gives red blood cells their color. "It got me real curious as to exceptional preservation," she says. If particles of that one dinosaur were able to hang around for 65 million years, maybe the textbooks were wrong about fossilization. ... Of course, what everyone wants to know is whether DNA might be lurking in that tissue. Wittmeyer, from much experience with the press since the discovery, calls this "the awful question"—whether Schweitzer's work is paving the road to a real-life version of science fiction's Jurassic Park, where dinosaurs were regenerated from DNA preserved in amber.[5]

Numerous news stories about Schweitzer were published. One of the earliest articles was in March 2005, from *NBC News* showing images of the stretched ligaments (i.e., collagen) from the T-Rex.[6] Later, other articles showed more information, like the May 2006 report in *Smithsonian Magazine* showed images of blood cells inside of blood vessels.[7] In November 2013, a report by *Live Science* quoted Schweitzer as saying that "What we found was unusual, because it was still soft and still transparent and still flexible. ... They've even found chemicals *consistent with being DNA*."[8] [Emphasis added]. Naturalists were seeking to find an explanation on why dinosaur soft tissue could be found after 65-million years. The *Live Science* report went on to explain Schweitzer's research into why the improbable could exist, stating that ""The free radicals cause proteins and cell membranes to tie in knots," Schweitzer said. "They basically act like formaldehyde." Formaldehyde, of course, preserves tissue. It works by linking up, or cross-linking, the amino acids that make up proteins, which makes those proteins more resistant to decay."[9] There is a major problem with this explanation. Formaldehyde only *slows* the decay rate down—It does not stop it. Writing for *Funeral Circle*, Alex Marcombe wrote the following article on the effects of formaldehyde on the body.

> Embalming is the process of injecting a mixture of chemicals, including formaldehyde and other preservatives, into the bloodstream of a deceased person to delay decomposition. ... Natural decomposition of an embalmed body will begin within *a few days to several weeks* of the procedure. The longevity of embalming depends on a variety of factors, including the techniques used, the condition of the body at the time of embalming, and the environment in which the body is stored. It's important to note that embalming does not permanently preserve a body and it will eventually begin to decompose.[10] [emphasis added]

So, Schweitzer's conclusion that formaldehyde preserves tissue is both true, but highly misleading. It only slows the decay process for a matter of weeks, not the 65 million years since the dinosaurs roamed the earth.

Collagen and DNA are similar yet serve different functions within the body. DNA is a double helix structure of proteins (amino acids or organic compounds) that carries the chromosomal genes to replicate the body. Whereas collagen is a triple helix structure of proteins that provides elasticity to the body. Since they are both chains (helix structures) of proteins, they should degrade in a similar manner—because the repair processes that would otherwise maintain them would end with the death of the animal. The collagen begins to degrade after the animal hits its prime years. Collagen makes skin elastic, tendons, and ligaments for the bones. This loss of elasticity, due to degrading collagen, is why we see older people with sagging skin on their bodies. Since both collagen and DNA are protein structures, this means that the scientific findings on DNA should apply to collagen, too.

The finding of dinosaur soft tissue has caused an uproar in the Naturalist community. However, as time passed, more and more researchers were finding the same results—too many to quote here. One key finding is that even in the most poorly preserved fossils, dinosaur soft tissue could be found, as reported in *Science News's* 2015 report. "Researchers from London have found hints of blood and collagen in a hodgepodge of 75-million-year-old dinosaur bones. The fossils were poorly preserved, suggesting that dinosaur bones containing traces of soft tissue *may be more common than previously thought*, the scientists argue June 9 in *Nature Communications*."[11] [Emphasis added].

❖ Millions of Years Conclusion

The discovery of abundant dinosaur soft tissue has destroyed the Naturalists' hopes of the millions of evolutionary years needed for a natural origin's explanation for the diversity of life found in today's world. While Naturalists have tried to explain the issue, it only goes to show how far they will go to preserve their tenet of millions-of-evolutionary-years, giving the appearance of a pathological science. The only alternative explanation would be a short cycle in evolution, but there is no evidence to suggest this explanation since it would mean that evolution should be observable in modern times. Thus, this major tenet of the Naturalists' worldview is lacking any empirical support to accept it as possible.

CHAPTER 10

THERMODYNAMICS AND EVOLUTION

Merriam-Webster defines *thermodynamics* as the "physics that deals with the mechanical action or relations of heat."[1] The scientific laws of thermodynamics are universally accepted as an empirical fact by scientists. These laws define the interaction of mass, energy (*i.e.*, temperature), and *entropy*. *Merriam-Webster* defines entropy as "a measure of the unavailable energy in a closed thermodynamic system that is also usually considered to be a measure of the system's disorder."[2] In simple terms, entropy is the unusable energy of a thermodynamic system.

Traditionally, there are three recognized laws in the field of thermodynamics, although a fourth law has been advanced. The first two laws were formally stated in the 1850s by Rudolf Clausius and William Thomson (Lord Kelvin). The focus in this chapter will be on the first two laws since they play a significant role in the falsification of the theory of evolution. Gordon W.F. Drake, in *Encyclopaedia Britannica*, states these two laws as:

1. [E]nergy can not be created or destroyed but merely converted from one form to another.[3] (aka: law of the conservation of energy).
2. [T]he entropy of a closed system, or heat energy per unit temperature, increases over time toward some maximum value. Thus, all closed

systems tend toward an equilibrium state in which entropy is at a maximum and no energy is available to do useful work.[4] (i.e., entropy always increases when work is done).

In short, energy/matter cannot be created or destroyed and entropy (*i.e.*, disorder or unusable energy in the system) always increases when work is being done. Note that in a thermodynamic system, matter and energy are considered interchangeable (for example, gasoline ignites releasing its heat to drive the car's engine).

❖ Application of Thermodynamics to Evolution

Many Evolutionists will protest the application of the thermodynamic laws to evolution, claiming that the Second Law only applies to closed systems. The reason for this protest is that thermodynamics could become a means to falsify the theory. Thermodynamic expert, Donald T. Haynie, wrote in his book *Biological Thermodynamics* that "Sir Arthur S. Eddington (1882–1944), the eminent British astronomer and physicist, has said, "If your theory is found to be against the Second Law of Thermodynamics I can give you no hope; there is nothing for it but to collapse in deepest humiliation"."[5] If thermodynamics applies to evolution, then it is possible to falsify evolution using the Second Law. So, evolutionists will claim that the Second Law only applies to closed systems. But the thermodynamic experts say otherwise. In *Biological Thermodynamics* Haynie clarified this by stating that "The Second Law of Thermodynamics. No Process will occur spontaneously unless it is accompanied by an increase in the entropy of the universe. *This applies to an isolated system, a closed system, and an open system.*"[6] [Emphasis added].

As demonstrated, the experts say it applies to all systems. For this reason, it would include evolution, regardless of the Naturalists' objections. Technically, the Second Law only applies to closed systems. Scientists solve this problem by creating a temporarily closed system. But what are the various thermodynamic systems and how are they related to the thermodynamic laws?

Anti-Christians will often argue that thermodynamics does not apply to evolution because the rise in order would be matched by a rise in entropy within the universe. This objection is partially true, but still misleading. There are six categories of thermodynamics and it application to a problem. These are the 1) Classical thermodynamics, 2) Statistical thermodynamics, 3) Chemical thermodynamics, 4) Equilibrium thermodynamics, 5) Non-equilibrium thermodynamics, and 6) Axiomatic thermodynamics. Classical thermodynamics accounts for this rise in entropy, so it negates this argument. This chapter focuses on the use of classical thermodynamics. By properly defining the system, classical thermodynamics addresses the rise of entropy.

❖ Thermodynamic Systems

According to *Bright Hub Engineering*, there are three types of thermodynamic systems; 1) an open system, where mass and energy are free to enter and exit the system, 2) a closed system, where energy is free to exit the system, but mass is restricted, and 3) an isolated system, where neither energy nor mass is free to enter or exit the system.[7] Only the universe is a truly isolated system when all time constraints are removed. So, scientists, engineers, and physicists will place artificial constraints on an open system to create a temporarily closed system. Within these time constraints, the laws of thermodynamics can thus be applied.

Scientists often do not care to measure the amount of entropy in a system, so they will ignore the measurement of the unusable energy in the system or at the least put less focus on the rise in entropy—an exception to this idea is when they are trying to increase the system's efficiency. Their focus is on the work accomplished in the system, limited by the available energy to the system, not the gain of entropy (*i.e.*, increase in disordered/unusable energy). As a result, scientists will accept the First Law of Thermodynamics as a fact and concentrate on the Second Law of Thermodynamics. Next is a demonstration on how an engineer could apply the Second Law for a gas-powered automobile.

❖ Thermodynamics—a Demonstration

We all know that we put gasoline into our cars and the gasoline is converted to work and heat, *i.e.*, the explosion of the gas is converted to a mechanical force that moves the car forward, while the engine heats up as the gas tank empties. This is the basis for understanding the Second Law of Thermodynamics. Thermodynamics is the calculation of the conversion of the energy in gasoline into the work of the pistons going up and down in the engine to turn the crankshaft, drive train, and wheels. This resulting work moves the car forward. It is a concept many people utilize and understand every day, even if they do not understand the mathematics behind the concept. Since our focus is on our understanding of the process (and not the math), a minimal focus will be on the mathematics in this book.

Thermodynamically speaking, a car's engine is an open system because we can add gasoline to the tank any time we need. Furthermore, the engine's excess heat is dispersed via the radiator, additional heat is dispersed when we step on the brakes, and the loss of mass via exhaust fumes. This is the entropy of the system. In this manner, we have mass going in, converting to energy, with work being done in the process. In our demonstration, the filling of the gas tank will mark the beginning of the closed system. For our virtual system, we will assume that the exhaust fumes are captured in an undefined container to satisfy the requirements of a closed system.

For our demonstration, we will assume that one tankful of gas will take the car four hundred miles. That is the measure of the work that is accomplished during the experiment. In our example, we turn an open system into a temporarily closed system by 1) Limiting the input of mass (*i.e.*, gasoline), 2) We will ignore the increase in disordered energy—the gain in entropy—lost in the process, and 3) We trap the exhaust fumes to keep the system closed (just to satisfy the closed system requirement). Our only concern is measuring how far our car will travel (*i.e.*, its work) with the gas available in the gas tank. This is a simplified explanation of turning an open system into a closed system to allow for the application of thermodynamic laws to the system. The next challenge is to design a closed system for testing evolution, even though the earth is an open system.

❖ Testing Evolution with Thermodynamics

Almost all life on earth is powered by the sun. Incidentally, this energy from the sun is entropy to the sun's thermodynamic system, but still usable energy in the earth's system. Accordingly, entropy of a system is not always a bad outcome, as it can be used by other thermodynamic systems downstream of the energy chain. One example is the sun's entropy. The sun's entropy is usable energy for earth. It is converted into mass via photosynthesis in plants. Plant-eating animals, herbivores, consume this mass to power their bodies. In turn, carnivores, meat-eating animals, consume their prey's bodies to obtain the energy they need for their biological processes. Consequently, most of life on earth is powered through this process, although there are some known exceptions to this process.

Evolutionists believe that life formed 3.7 billion years ago, and that evolution occurred over those 3.7 billion years. Given sufficient time, thermodynamics proves that all systems will reach a state of equilibrium if the available energy is constant. According to *Wikipedia*, all sides agree that the sun's output remains relatively constant (at 1.3608 ± 0.0005 kW/m²).[8] For life on earth, this would mean that life would expand until all available energy was being used, even before the first evolutionary step could be completed (based upon Dawkins's postulated 3.7 million years between speciation events), creating a balanced thermodynamic system where all the available energy is used to power the work being done within the system. So, our thermodynamic model will utilize this factoid as a constraint to the model.

Light travels from the sun to the earth in about eight minutes. This is not long enough to design a thermodynamic system to test the viability of evolution. In consequence, a virtual closed system will need to be created, one which will have sufficient energy from the sun to run through the complete cycle of a test subject. In this example, the test subject is a single-cell plant life called algae, since the first step in the evolutionary process is the necessity to create a multi-celled species from a single-cell species before any further evolutionary processes can continue.

To keep the demonstration simple, it will be assumed that a single alga uses one watt of the sun's energy per time cycle. This level of stated energy is *very* excessive for a single-celled species, but watts are readily understood by most people. Accordingly, watts will be used to represent the measurement of energy available to the system. The actual number would be much lower, but specifying the actual energy used could distract readers from a basic understanding of the thermodynamic processes that would occur in our virtual system. Furthermore, it will be assumed that there are three algae in our virtual closed system, and that the system only provides three watts of energy per time unit—to represent the balanced thermodynamic system on earth after the 3.7 million years from when life first arose. Thus, only the three algae can be sustained with the available energy. Until one of the algae dies, evolution is impossible because it takes energy to build a new life form, and all the available energy is being utilized within the thermodynamic system.

For our example, it will be assumed that four units of time will occur, not including the initial unit when all cells are still living. These units of time will be called a lifecycle. The attempt at evolution begins the moment a single alga within the system dies. At that moment, both remaining two algae will begin their process, each algae utilizing 1.5 watts of energy per lifecycle. This assumption is scientifically sound, as both algae have the same surface area as the other and thus could not absorb any more energy than the other. One will be called alga "A" and will attempt to create a new single-celled alga ("C") through the normal replication of the species (*mitosis*) process. Mitosis is defined by *Merriam-Webster* as "a process that takes place in the nucleus of a dividing cell ... result[ing] in the formation of two new nuclei."[9] The other, which will be called alga "B", will attempt to create a new two-celled algae ("2D") through evolution. The reason for the two-cell attempt is that one of the first required steps in evolution would be the evolution of a single-cell species into a multi-celled species. This example is taking the solution with the least amount of required energy needed to demonstrate the thermodynamic process—a two-celled species rather than a multi-celled species.

In the first lifecycle, alga A successfully builds one-third of a new alga (C) via mitosis, while alga B successfully builds one-sixth of a two-celled new species (2D) via evolution. It is one-sixth, because the alga can only build the equivalent of one-third of a single cell within the time and energy constraints, and there are two cells of the new evolution-species (2D) to be built. In the second lifecycle, alga A successfully completes two-thirds of a new alga (C), while alga B successfully builds two-sixths (*i.e.*, one-third of the new evolved species) of a two-celled new species (2D). In the third life cycle, alga A finalizes the mitosis process and completes a new alga, and alga C is born—or split off. Meanwhile, alga B successfully builds three-sixths (*i.e.*, one-half of the new evolved species) of a two-celled new species (2D). In the fourth lifecycle, algae A, B, and C consume all the available energy, with each consuming one watt of the sun's energy. Meanwhile, B's new evolutionary 2D species dies off due to lack of energy.

Here are the results in a time-lapsed graphical format to demonstrate this process.

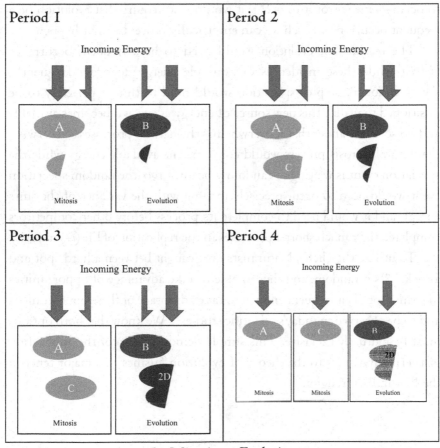

I - Mitosis vs. Evolution

Thus, the theory of Evolution is contrary to the Second Law of Thermodynamics, and "there is nothing for it but to collapse in deepest humiliation," as stated by Sir Eddington.

❖ Evolution and Thermodynamics Conclusion

This major tenet (evolution) of the Naturalists' worldview has empirical evidence that proves it to be impossible, if the premises given in the example hold up. The energy from the sun is pretty much constant, with some variance occurring due to the tilt of the earth's axis which gives our seasons, and the sun's eleven-year cycles. We also know that mass die-offs occur periodically. These exceptions do provide an opportunity for evolution to occur—*however* for it to occur, it would also require that evolution be a frequent occurrence, which we can empirically prove does not happen.

The reason that evolution would need to be a frequent occurrence is that while these incidences of available energy do occur frequently, the evolutionary step of speciation would need to time it perfectly to be positioned to utilize this new source of energy *as soon as* it becomes available and do so in a manner that it overwhelms the natural processes. Otherwise, the natural mitosis process would consume the available energy while the speciation event is waiting to randomly occur. Ergo, the random speciation event would need to occur precisely in time with the variance of the sun's energy, and it would need to complete its process before other competitors completed their much shorter processes in the replication of life (*i.e.*, mitosis).

To utilize the cliché, Naturalists are "caught between a hard spot and a rock." "Is it random, and thus unable to take advantage of opportunities like this?" or "Is it frequent enough to take advantage of these opportunities and to be observed in today's scientific studies?" We know that both options must be mutually exclusive. This simple demonstration of the application of thermodynamics to the theory of evolution falsifies this major tenet in the Naturalists' religion.

CHAPTER 11

RADIOMETRIC DATING

Since one of the primary assumptions of Naturalism is that life evolved millions of years ago it is necessary to understand how dating of fossils and rock strata is accomplished—one of these methods is known as radiometric dating. *Wikipedia* defines radiometric dating as the "technique which is used to date materials such as rocks or carbon, in which trace radioactive impurities were selectively incorporated when they were formed. The method compares the abundance of a naturally occurring radioactive isotope within the material to the abundance of its decay products, which form at a known constant rate of decay."[1]

To understand how radiometric dating works, a basic understanding of the atomic elements is needed, namely the radioactive isotopes that are used in the radiometric dating process. All matter (mass) in the universe is composed of atomic elements, which we categorize in the Periodic Table of Elements. Elements are composed of two or more atoms of the same type and have several subatomic particles called protons, electrons, and neutrons. When discussing these subatomic particles, the number of particles is in reference to the atom, itself, and not the element. They are classified by the number of protons within the atom and will always have the same number of protons, regardless of the number of electrons or neutrons. Elements are composed of a specific number of protons, usually the same number of electrons, and often—but not always—with an equal number of neutrons. For example, hydrogen, the smallest atom, has one proton, one electron, but no neutrons. However, carbon usually has six protons, six electrons, and six neutrons. This type of carbon is stable and is called carbon-12, because the number of protons and neutrons added together equals twelve.

❖ Radiometric Carbon Dating

To determine the age of a fossil, scientists usually take random samples of a long-dead organism to determine the age since that species, an animal or plant, was last alive. They use multiple samples from that species to create a range for the "age" (the years since it was last alive) to come to a statistically relevant date for the fossil's age. Using these samples, the researchers compare the *isotopes* (parent element) to its *stable element* (child or daughter element). The *LibreTexts Libraries* states "[a]lthough most of the known elements have at least one isotope whose atomic nucleus is stable indefinitely, all elements have isotopes that are unstable and disintegrate, or decay, at measurable rates by emitting radiation. Some elements have no stable isotopes and eventually decay to other elements."[2]

An atom of the same element will have the same number of protons but could have a different number of neutrons, and the sum of the number or protons and the number of neutrons will comprise its atomic number (carbon-12 has six protons and six neutrons, carbon-13 has six protons and seven neutrons, and carbon-14 has six protons and eight neutrons). Each element with a different number of neutrons is referred to as an isotope of that element. For this reason, all three carbon elements are referred to as isotopes. Some of these isotopes are stable and others are unstable.

For clarity, parent element will be referring to the unstable element, while the stable element will be referred to as the daughter element or child element. Since parent elements are unstable, they will revert to the child (stable) element, given sufficient time. This process is called *radioactive decay*. The measurement of this radioactive decay is the underlying basis for the process of radiometric dating.

Carbon-14 is a naturally occurring isotope on earth that is radioactive. The most common method of creating carbon-14 is by the sun's cosmic rays splitting a nitrogen-14 element into the carbon-14 isotope. As all living organisms utilize carbon in some form, carbon-14 is present in all living organisms. This continual intake of carbon stabilizes the ratio of carbon-12 to carbon-14 within the organism. Once that organism dies, it stops the intake of all carbon.

Given sufficient time, all the carbon-14 will decay back to nitrogen-14. This decay occurs by emitting an electron and an electron antineutrino, which turns into a proton. When carbon-14 decays, it yields seven protons and seven neutrons—the number of protons and neutrons in nitrogen-14. The amount of time needed for half of the sample's carbon-14 to decay back into nitrogen-14 is about 5,730 years. This is referred to as the half-life of the carbon-14 isotope. There are three naturally occurring forms of carbon on earth: Carbon-12 which makes up about 99 percent of all carbon on earth, Carbon-13 which makes up almost 1 percent of carbon on earth, and carbon-14 which makes up about 1.5 atoms per 10^{12} atoms of carbon in the atmosphere—so carbon-14 is very rare.[3]

Since carbon-14 is unstable and will decay, it yields scientists the opportunity to calculate the number of years since the organism's last intake of carbon in any form (*i.e.*, since it was alive). This results in an age referred to as the radiometric age of the deceased organism—namely, how many years it has been since the organism was alive.

❖ Radiometric Dating Methodology

Radiometric dating is premised upon three parts: 1) The current ratio is known between the parent element (in this example, carbon-14) to the daughter element (in this example, nitrogen-14), 2) The decay rate of the radioactive isotope is known, and 3) The original ratio of the parent element to the daughter element is assumed to be known.

Scientists presume that the ratio between carbon-12 and carbon-14 has remained constant over time, even though scientific research has shown that it does vary some over time.[4] The methodology of calibrating radiocarbon dates will be discussed later. It will reveal some variance, but the ratio is relatively stable for as far back as it can be calibrated.

Since the intake of carbon ceases upon the death of the organism, then the difference between the presumed beginning parent-daughter ratio, and the present parent-daughter ratio can be calculated, thus deriving an approximate number of years between the two points in time. Because organisms need to take in carbon to live, radiocarbon dating is limited to previously living organisms. Also, radiocarbon dating is limited to a maximum of 50,000 years. After 50,000 years (*i.e.*, almost nine half-lives for carbon-14), there is so little carbon-14 remaining that it can no longer be reliably dated. There have been some efforts to extend this limitation to about 56,000 years, but that is an experimental effort that is not fully trusted yet.

However, there are other parent–daughter elements that can be used for long-term dating—*i.e.*, millions of years long. So, there is a big gap between short-term radiometric dating and long-term radiometric dating, where there is little opportunity to calculate a radiometric date range. Overall, this is a minor issue, as the scientists are only interested in short-term dates and the very-long-term dates of paleontology (*i.e.*, the age of dinosaurs and before).

According to *NPS.gov*, scientists use different elements to calculate long-term dates, like potassium-40/argon-40 or uranium-235/lead-207.[5] And, while radiocarbon dating methods use the actual fossil, long-term dating must use the strata layers surrounding the fossil to date the fossil. Some of the time, the fossil lies in the strata layer. At other times, the strata layer just above the fossil's strata layer is dated. Consequently, the scientists are not dating the actual fossil, but the material around the fossil. This is a minor issue, so it will not be addressed further.

❖ Problems with Radiocarbon Dating

The main problem with radiometric dating is that the empirical evidence disproves the premises—namely the belief that the beginning ratio between the parent and daughter elements is known. Unfortunately, on the internet, radiometric dating errors are only discussed on Christian sources or those websites refuting Christian young-earth-creationists articles. So, this information is not readily available directly. Most of the time, one must read the Christian websites to find the Naturalists sources that admit these errors, since Naturalists are reluctant to acknowledge problems with their beliefs. Here is one example of a Naturalist website (*TalkOrigins*) attempting to explain why some radiocarbon dates were proven wrong but that the technique is still scientifically valid. Specifically, there have been times when the calculated radiometric age was proven to be wrong based upon the known death of the animal.

> For example, the apparent radiocarbon age of the Lake Bonney seal known to have been *dead no more than a few weeks was determined to be 615 +/- 100 years. A seal freshly killed at McMurdo had an apparent age of 1,300 years.* [citing Wakefield (1971)]

> [*TalkOrigins* response:] This is the well-known reservoir effect that occurs also with mollusks and other animals that live in the water. It happens when "old" carbon is introduced into the water. In the above case of the seal, old carbon dioxide is present within deep ocean bottom water that has been circulating through the ocean for thousands of years before upwelling along the Antarctic coast.[6] [Emphasis added]

There are two problems with this defense. First, decay should not matter where the element resides, so there should not be anything known as "old carbon." Second, and most serious, is the issue that radiocarbon dating is not reliable against known ages (the years since the animal was last alive). As shown, radiocarbon dating has some obvious errors and is unreliable. What happens if a fossil was dated without a known date of death? The error remains unchallenged. Accordingly, the obvious question is how prevalent are these errors in radiocarbon dating? Nobody knows.

❖ Problems with Long-term Radiometric Dating

But this problem is not limited to carbon-14 radiometric dating. It extends to long-term radiometric dating methods also. An article in *Earth and Planetary Science Letters* addresses this very issue, stating that "An Ar-Ar "dating" study of high-grade metamorphic rocks in the Broken Hill region (New South Wales) found widely distributed *excess 40Ar*. Plagioclase and hornblende were most affected, step heating Ar-Ar "age" spectra yielding results up to 9.588Ga."[7] [Ga is a billion years ago, Emphasis added.]

How do they know there is an excess Argon-40? It is because the results do not match their preconceived belief of the age of the dated material. To be specific, Naturalists believe the Earth is only 4.5Ga years old, so the results of 9.588Ga cannot be right because it exceeds the Earth's age. Here are other examples using a different long-term dating method, potassium-argon radiometric dating from the *Institute of Creation Research*.[8]

> [Ma is a million years ago]
> 1. Hualalai basalt, Hawaii (AD 1800–1801) 1.6±0.16 Ma; 1.41±0.08 Ma
> 2. Mt. Etna basalt, Sicily (122 BC) 0.25±0.08 Ma
> 3. Mt. Etna basalt, Sicily (AD 1972) 0.35±0.14 Ma
> 4. Mt. Lassen plagioclase, California (AD 1915) 0.11±0.03 Ma
> 5. Sunset Crater basalt, Arizona (AD 1064–1065) 0.27±0.09 Ma; 0.25±0.15 Ma"

❖ Determinative Factor in Dating Fossils

If radiometric dating is *not* reliable, then what is used to determine the reliability of the radiometric date? Geologist Frank Rhodes addresses this issue in his book *Geology*, stating that *"Fossils are the most important single method of correlation.* Fossils are the remains of, or direct indication of, prehistoric animals and plants. Although they are influenced by environment of deposition, similar assemblages of fossils generally indicate similarity of age in the rocks that contain them."[9] [Emphasis added] So, radiometric dating is used to date the fossils, which, in turn, are used to validate the results. This is the logic fallacy known as circular logic.

Let us see this absurdity in action, with the radiometric dating of the KBS Tuff.[10] This summary is sourced from a Creationist's viewpoint

(Marvin L. Lubenow), but the author references Naturalists' research in his discussion.

❖ KBS Tuff—Example of Radiometric Dating Circular Logic

In 1967, Richard Leakey found some archeological human artifacts and fossils. It was impossible to directly date the findings because the expected age exceeded the 50,000 years limit on radiocarbon dating. Yet, wanting to get an age, he sent in some random samples—rocks and such from the strata layer to be dated—from a layer of sediment just above the artifacts. This layer is referred to as the KBS Tuff. The results of these initial random samples produced dates ranging from 212–230 MYA (million years ago). The experts dating the samples concluded the following: "From these results *it was clear that an extraneous argon* age discrepancy was present."[11] [Emphasis added]. How do they know there is extraneous argon? It is because the calculated age did not match the fossil's estimated age of less than three million years ago—*i.e.,* after early humanoids evolved.

This began the debacle of attempting to date the KBS Tuff to fit the theory of evolution. They next selected numerous nonrandom samples (more than three hundred). Then, they subjected the samples to four different tests, and discarded any results that did not agree with the fossil evidence. This allowed them to settle upon a date of 2.6 MYA for the KBS Tuff, even though some of the samples were from a different sediment layer (dated to be 3.18 MYA) which was below the artifacts—which would be logical because lower strata layers are presumed to be older. After all this was done, the targeted layer containing the human fossils and artifacts had an estimated date of 2.9 MYA. This newly calculated date now agreed with the fossil evidence.

Soon after the results came back for an age of 2.9 MYA, a humanoid skull (KNM-ER 1470) was announced. This fossil was much too developed evolutionarily to fit an estimated date of 2.9 MYA. Again, there was a mad scramble to *prove* the second set of dating attempts were *also flawed*. This time, the Naturalists only had to adjust it by one million years, bringing the final date of the fossils to 1.9 MYA, which they "successfully" did.

Yet, the question remains—How do we know if the radiometric dating results are valid without utilizing any outside information like fossils or archeological artifacts? The answer is not encouraging. We cannot know their validity independently for long-term dating methods, but we can for *some* short-term artifacts. Thus, fossils or archeological artifacts always confirm or deny the results from radiometric dating methods. However, there is some method for the calibration of the results for the short-term radiocarbon dating. Even here, there are some severe limitations.

❖ Calibrating Radiocarbon Dating

How do scientists know the approximate short-term date of archeological artifacts? They compare an archeological artifact with written history. Almost every major civilization has kept a written history: the Egyptians, Assyrians, Babylonians, Persians, Greeks, and Romans, to name a few. One problem is that these records only span the time in which the specific civilization thrived. After that, the written record stopped and, either was lost or some portion of the record remained until modern times. So, archeologists will match a known event in one civilization's record with another civilization's record for the same event to patch together a contiguous timeline (chronology) stretching back through time, then adjusting it to fit the Gregorian calendar we utilize today.

Linking Civilization Chronologies

When the Persian kingdom, under Xerxes I, invaded the Greek nation and fought the Battle of Thermopylae in what we now consider 480 BC, each civilization captured that event in their respective historical records. Each civilization kept their records based upon known events, like how many years Xerxes I reigned prior to the invasion and Herodotus's record of the Greco-Persian Wars (Herodotus is a well-known Greek historian). This allows the historians to link each empire's chronology via a common event and translate it into today's common Gregorian Calendar we use today, creating an extended chronology that spanned both civilizations. This method allows scientists to link multiple diverse civilizations into a single chronology.

However, this technique is limited, as the written records only go back to circa 1000 BC before they become too disjointed to make a contiguous record, excluding the Bible. Note that at this point, one must remain skeptical of the alleged biblical chronology, until the reliability of the Bible has been evaluated. That will be done in the next part.

Limitations of Radiocarbon Dating

Let us review the limitations of radiocarbon dating. First, the assumed ratio of carbon-12 to carbon-14 varies over time and can only be calibrated back to about 1000 BC (even this span of time has some limitations). Furthermore, some Christian scholars believe that the worldwide flood in Genesis occurred approximately 4,350 years ago. If this flood did occur, then any radiometric dates prior to the worldwide flood would be unreliable due to the "reservoir effect" on species found in water. Thus, optimally, the calibrated radiocarbon dates only span about three thousand years of recorded history—from 1000 BC to AD 2023. This means that radiometric dating has a very limited range of providing reliable dates for the age of the fossil.

❖ Radiometric Conclusion

So, geologist Frank Rhodes was right. The presupposed approximate age of the fossil or archeological artifact *always* determines the final date assigned to the fossil. There is another unaddressed problem with radiometric dating that this book does not cover. The various long-term dating methods rarely provide the same calibrated age for the same strata layer. Thus, radiometric dating falls into the category of a pathological science, rather than an objective way to date fossils.

CHAPTER 12

POPULATION GROWTH

A nother way of evaluating the evolutionary theory is the population growth of modern humans, from their proposed advent to today's known worldwide population. Using a population growth model (*i.e.*, a mathematical formula), it can determine whether the proposed dating of the advent of homo sapiens is reasonable or not.

Scientists model population growth with mathematical equations. There are three types of population growth models: I) A linear growth model, 2) An exponential growth model, and 3) A logistic regression model. The first two models are limited to short term estimates, with the first model being a very short-term model, and the exponential growth model being usable until the population starts to encounter limited resources, like food. The logistic regression model factors in both the exponential growth of an early population with unlimited food supply and a regressed exponential slowdown as food supply becomes limited to the point of starvation. Therefore, the logistic regression population growth model will be used for this analysis.

What a logistic regression equation means is that in the early stages of growth, the population size will grow slowly because of the limited population size to build upon. As growth reaches its intermediate level, the population size grows very rapidly. And, as the population size approaches maturity, the *"carrying capacity"*—which is the population size that the resources can support—the population growth rate slows down until it reaches zero at the carrying capacity limit. Thus, the total population arrives at the maximum capacity and remains there until the carrying capacity changes. The results look like a sideways "S" curve. So, what does this have to do with Naturalism?

❖ Homosapien Human History

Naturalists believe that modern humans, *i.e.*, homo sapiens, first evolved about 200,000 years ago. This number changes frequently, with some claiming as much as 300,000 years ago. Whatever estimate Naturalists use, they have a big problem with mathematically calculated population growth rates, regardless of however many hundreds of thousands of years since the evolution of modern humans.

Working with the more conservative 200,000 years estimate, while applying the constraints given by Naturalists to the equation, will allow an approximation of the human population growth over the Naturalists proposed history to evaluate the accuracy of this assumed estimate. Upon application of the known facts, when combined with some basic assumptions, it will be found that the population growth should result in a much higher population size today than currently exists.

❖ Population Growth Model

Leonard Lipkin and David Smith, of *Mathematical Association of America*, states that a "biological population with plenty of food, space to grow, and no threat from predators, tends to grow at a rate that is proportional to the population -- that is, in each unit of time, a certain percentage of the individuals produce new individuals"[1] An unconstrained natural growth results in exponential growth, but resources are always constrained. Thus, carrying capacity starts to limit the growth, approaching zero population growth as the total population nears the carrying capacity. Lipkin and Smith go on to address the limitations of population growth, then moving into what is now known as the logistic regression population growth rate— aka the logistic population growth rate.

The following population growth equation was developed by P. F. Verhulst, a Belgian mathematician, in the nineteenth century to address both the exponential early growth rate as well as the tapered growth rate as the constraints start to make an impact, yielding the following formula.

$$\frac{dP}{dt} = rP\left(1 - \frac{P}{K}\right)$$

2 - Logistic Population Growth Equation

Where: r = growth rate; P = current population size; K = carrying capacity; and dP / dt = the population size for the given future period.

Rather than going into details on how to use the equation, the information will be entered into a spreadsheet and graphed, starting 200,000 years ago for the start of modern humans that is stipulated by the Naturalists, while cutting the graph off in 1900. This will plot out on the graph as ranging from -198,000 to +1900, which covers 199,900 years of human history. The final one hundred years were left off due to the discoveries in medical knowledge that resulted in an outlier of the normal growth rate compared to prior history.

In the early 1900s, medical discoveries distort the growth rate out of the norm because of the discovery of antibiotics, ways to keep food from spoiling, and other ways of preventing an early death (childbirth, infections/diseases, blood pressure medication, diabetes, cancer, etc.). So, to keep this distortion out of the graphs, only the average growth rate prior to the modern medical discovery period will be used, and the super growth rate period of the last one hundred and twenty years will be left off. Rather than discussing the calculation process, the resulting graphs will tell the story as they are easier to assimilate.

❖ Graph Inputs

There are a few basic assumptions that need to be stated for the model. For the human species to survive, the beginning population size must be two people, one male and one female. So, the beginning population size will be two. To keep the calculations few, the population size will be calculated every fifty years, rather than monthly or even annually.

Carrying capacity: Carrying capacity is the largest population that the entire planet will support with enough food for humans to survive. This capacity will change over time due to inventions, like farming and domestication of animals, the discovery of the use of metal, namely iron, and other inventions or discoveries that would likely increase the planet's carrying capacity. There are too many inventions to plot out for a simple plot, so only a few key inventions to allow a basic plot to be graphed will be used. Note that any changes to these carrying capacity estimates will not impact the overall conclusion, regardless of *any contortions* used—unless they stray into the *highly unrealistic* realm. One example of such an unrealistic realm is the assumption that the worldwide carrying capacity would only support 1,000 people prior to the invention of farming. And even this extremely unrealistic assumption would still falsify the presumption that modern humans evolved 200,000 years ago, as it would result in a higher worldwide population size than has been historically observed. So, again, regardless of *any contortions* used, the resulting data would show that homo sapiens could not have originated 200,000 years ago.

Carrying Capacity Assumptions:

I. *Initial capacity*: Prior to the invention of farming and domestication of animals, the worldwide carrying capacity for humans is assumed to be *ten million* people. This number is based upon a rural nation, the African nation of Mauritania, extrapolating its population size to the land mass of the world during the Ice Age (*i.e.*, land not covered in ice) that ended some 15,000 years ago. This is not ideal, but it does provide a beginning place that is not arbitrarily pulled out of thin air. The carrying capacity prior to the Ice Age is immaterial, as any population above the carrying capacity during the Ice Age would die off. Mauritania was chosen because it represents a country that is in between the two extremes—good hunting / harvesting areas and poor hunting / harvesting areas. Any variation from this initial assumption does not change the overall conclusions reached when viewing the graphed results. It only changes the "when and how long" aspect of the conclusion reached.

2. *Farming / domestication of animals capacity*: After farming and the domestication of animals was discovered, the worldwide carrying capacity for humans is assumed to have risen to *one hundred million* people. This was based upon the assumption that farming would increase food production ten-fold since hunters and gatherers would need significantly more land to survive than those people who had the same amount of food domestically produced near to their settlements.

3. *Iron Age*: After the Iron Age began, the worldwide carrying capacity for humans is assumed to have risen to *five hundred million* people. This was based upon the assumption that metalworking would increase the current food production by five-fold, since iron plows would hold up better than wooden plows, do a better job at turning the soil over, and thus increasing overall output. Note that the invention of the bronze age is not included, as the inclusion of the bronze age only worsens the outcome of the result for Naturalists.

4. *Trade age*: After trade began to proliferate, the worldwide carrying capacity for humans is assumed to have risen to *750 million* people. The assumption is that trade began having an impact on the planet's carrying capacity approximately 100 BC. This date is easily disputed, but a more realistic date would be even earlier—worsening the outcome for Naturalists in the population growth analysis. So, this is the most favorable constraint for the Naturalists' viewpoint.

5. *Early medicine*: The use of herbs and other concoctions to treat people has existed for thousands of years. However, the term "early medicine" is used to indicate the industrialization period of medicine making, which has been presumed to have occurred between AD 1700 and the 1900s. The exact date, and any disputes about that date, is immaterial to the overall conclusion as it would have little to no impact on the population growth curve. Therefore, after early medicine slowed disease, the worldwide carrying capacity for humans is assumed to have risen to *one billion people* between 1700–1900.

Again, these assumptions were only the starting point for graphing the population growth. Each of these assumptions were made to yield the most favorable outcome for Naturalists. Many adjustments were made to these basic assumptions, but every adjustment resulted in the same conclusion—that human history is less than 21,000 years old, regardless of the assumed carrying capacity. Next, let us review the facts from the Naturalists viewpoint.

Naturalists' Assumptions and Facts:

1. *Number of years*: Homo Sapiens evolved 200,000 years ago.
2. *Farming*: Farming and the domestication of animals began 12,000 years ago. To be conservative, 10,000 years ago will be used, which will appear on the graph as -8000 to represent 8000 BC. Moving the date further back in time, to the 12,000 years ago, only worsens the outcome of the resulting graph for Naturalists.
3. *Iron Age*: The Iron Age began about 1,000 BC, represented on the graphs as -1000. Experts estimate the Iron Age as occurring between 1200–1000 BC. The Iron Age occurred during different periods over the worldwide civilizations, but this date (1000 BC) is the most favorable for Naturalists.
4. *Worldwide population estimates*: The worldwide population estimates based upon *McEvedy and Jones's* estimates from the US Census will be used for the graphs.[2] There are other expert estimates available on the census.gov website, but the McEvedy and Jones's estimates are the most extensive. Furthermore, there is little overall variance between any of the experts' estimates on the website, so one estimate works about as well as any other.
5. *Growth rate*: Starting around 100 BC, records of censuses were recorded and still exist to some extent today, allowing population experts to extrapolate the limited data across the world. McEvedy and Jones's estimates were used to calculate the average growth rate during this period. This growth rate accounts for deaths caused by wars, famine, childbirth, pestilence, and all other factors that occurred from the AD first century to the early 1900s. The average growth rate was determined to be 5.90 percent per fifty-year period

from 100 BC to AD 1900. One callout is that the Black Plagues that swept the world during this period will have lowered the average growth rate over the history of census counts. If these plagues were left out, the average growth rate would necessarily be increased. Since it is possible that other, unrecorded, plagues impacted the worldwide average growth rate before this period, the average growth rate for the graphs was not changed. Again, this lower estimated growth rate favors the Naturalists postulate that modern humans evolved 200,000 years ago.

These parameters are very limited, but they will allow a skeletonization of the basic graph and the application of the equation into a graph. However, all that the inclusion of these smaller steps would do is to raise the carrying capacity in a series of smaller steps and incrementally raise the population curve even higher, resulting in an even more unrealistic outcome for Naturalists. None of the inventions left out in the carrying capacity assumptions would have a major impact on the worldwide population later—their inclusion only worsens the results for Naturalists because the graphs reveal that the earth's carrying capacity limits the population size.

If this carrying capacity limitation was raised earlier due to the addition of these interim inventions, then the worldwide population would incrementally rise also allowing the population to remain in the steepest part of the slope of population increase on the graphs until the carrying capacity started restraining the population size. This would result in an even higher population disparity than the graphs reveal. So, they were not used in reaching the overall conclusion. To summarize, all of the assumptions used were the most favorable, realistic assumptions sympathetic to the Naturalists' postulate to include in the population graphs.

Graphing the results: There are a few challenges to overcome when using almost any mathematical model. At the extreme ends of a mathematical model, the predictions can often yield illogical results. These extremes, when the mathematical curve begins and ends, are challenging because they defy obvious, logical conclusions. The table below gives one such example of an illogical extreme. It shows that the population size would remain under three people for 350 years, incrementally raising the worldwide population by just 0.12 people per fifty-year period. This is an illogical conclusion since humans typically live 120 years or less.

Age	Calculated Population	Growth Rate
198000 BC	2.00	5.90%
197950 BC	2.12	5.90%
197900 BC	2.24	5.90%
197850 BC	2.38	5.90%
197800 BC	2.52	5.90%
197750 BC	2.66	5.90%
197700 BC	2.82	5.90%
197650 BC	2.99	5.90%
197600 BC	3.16	5.90%

3 - Beginning of Population Growth Calculation

To compensate for this absurdity, the first cycle growth rate was adjusted from 5.9% to 290%, which pushed the population size to approximately six people in the first cycle (*i.e.*, the first fifty years) after humans evolved. Afterwards, the 5.9% average growth rate was kept constant to the end of the graph's period in AD 1900. On the graphs, 198000 BC will be shown as -198000, while AD 1900 will be shown as 1900.

Because of scale distorting, the resulting graph was split into three graphs, ending in the year AD 1900. The first graph covers the first 30,000 years of human population growth history. It is displayed to demonstrate the explosive population growth in the early years of human history. The "S-curve" in the graph can be seen between -186,000 and -181,000. The second graph covers the first 190,000 years of human history, including the first 30,000 years again, includes the s-curve in a smaller scale due to the increased scaling of the y-axis. The third graph covers the latest 9,800 years of human history, from 7900 BC to AD 1900.

Graph First 30,000 Years

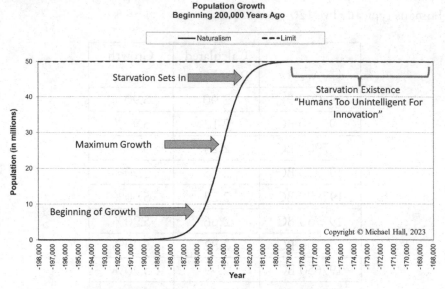

4 - Population Growth: First 30,000 years

Note the S-curvature of the graph near the middle of the graph, with a beginning of exponential growth, a maximum growth period, and a regressive growth period caused by limited food for population growth. One potential problem is that the graph shows population size for the entire world, but realistically, it is known that it takes time for the population to spread across the globe. However, this nuance would have limited impact, as populations tend to migrate to areas with more resources relatively quickly. Naturally, people would move to one "high food availability" place and, as constraints began to occur, others would migrate to another "high food availability" place. This would create a staggered shape to the S-curve, and it may take a few centuries longer to maximize the worldwide population to the carrying capacity level for the world. But eventually, population size would hit the limit of "starvation existence" for the entire world. The end results would be like what the graph shows—a species which Naturalism must assume to be "too unintelligent" to enhance their living standards with a few minor inventions like farming and the domestication of animals.

The next graph covers this same beginning period but extends the end period until just after the invention of farming and the domestication of animals, while adjusting the y-axis to allow for a higher population to be shown on the graph. The primary purpose of this graph is to show just how long humans had to remain (in the Naturalist's assumption) "too unintelligent" for even the simplest of inventions. Naturalists acknowledge that our intelligence capacity has not changed over time. So why did such a simple invention take 170,000 years to discover?

Graph First 190,000 Years

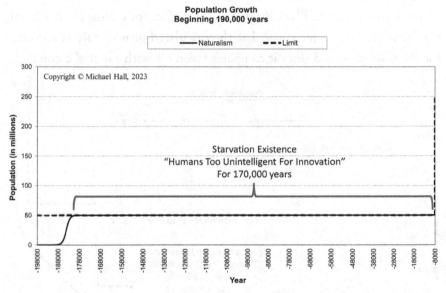

5 - Population Growth: First 190,000 years

How many people today would be content to watch their children die of starvation without trying everything in their power to help rectify the lack of sufficient food? History shows us that few people would tolerate such a situation.

Next, is the period in the graph from about 8000 BC to AD 1900. It is the final graph in the series. The graph axis scaling was adjusted to show the higher worldwide population size.

Graph 8000 BC to AD 1900

The last period covers the history of the last 10,000 years, including where population experts have been able to estimate a worldwide population—the last 3,000 years. These worldwide population estimates are represented as diamonds, while the calculated population is represented by a solid black line, and the maximum population size (*i.e.*, carrying capacity) is represented by a dotted black line. As seen on the graph, the calculated population line tracks above, but plots a similar curvature as the experts' population size. It is slightly different because the average growth rate does not adjust to factor in major events like the Black Plague that swept Europe during the Medieval era. This is a strong indicator that the calculated growth rate is accurate for the covered period since it compares favorably with experts' estimates.

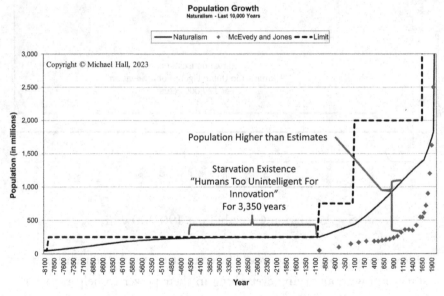

6 - Population Growth: 8000 BC – AD 1900

The calculated population always exceeds the experts' population size, which indicates that the early population sizes are too high. This is caused by one of two possible scenarios. One could be that the carrying capacity is too large. But, for this to be possible, it would require the worldwide population's capacity to be limited to an unreasonable low level of less than

100,000 people—even after the invention of farming and the domestication of animals. The second possible scenario is that the Naturalists' estimate of modern humans evolving 200,000 years ago is unreasonable. This is the most likely explanation.

The problem was also worked backwards to avoid any periods where the earth's worldwide population was in a starvation-existence situation, estimating when modern humans would have first evolved based upon this known growth rate, with the aforementioned adjustment to the first fifty-year period (of 290%). It predicted that early humans first appeared in history approximately 20,000 years ago—if all the assumptions are correct. Note that this 20,000 years ago limit also links into the empirical evidence of the dinosaur soft tissue (which limits dinosaurs having been alive 10,000 years ago or less). Further adjustments were made to test out the feasibility of the biblical age of the earth, and it was found to be possible with some adjustments.

For example, one would need to adjust for eight people as the starting population size after the worldwide flood about 4,350 years ago (based upon biblical chronology). And one would also need to assume an explosive growth for the early years, where explosive growth is a growth rate that materially exceeds the calculated 5.9% rate. This explosive growth rate is reasonable since one of the main growth rate limiters is the conflicts between neighboring societies and diseases passing through tightly packed populations. Without conflict (*i.e.*, wars) and tightly packed populations for disease to materially impact, then the growth rate would naturally be higher, until the population density rose high enough to cause conflicts and diseases.

❖ Population Growth Conclusion

By graphing the results, it is possible to observe the premise that modern humans evolved 200,000 years ago to be false. No explanation can resolve the difference between the population growth equation, which has been empirically verified many times, and the population experts' estimates for early human history.

CHAPTER 13

CIVILIZATIONS

C ivilizations arise when their population density reaches a level where they can move from survival mode into the arts and sciences. History teaches us that the earlier a settlement is established, the larger the settlement grows, until it becomes a city. As the city's sphere of influence grows, it becomes a nation, which grows until it becomes an empire, which is generally referred to as a civilization. Note that when looking at web articles on civilizations, they will often begin with the foundational population group, which may have nothing to do with the empire that arose in the same area later.

❖ Nation vs. Civilization

Early Native American Indians had numerous tribes which associated together to form nations. However, there is a significant difference between those nations and the current nation called United States of America (USA). The Indian nations had numerous conflicts and did not substantially impact any area outside their limited tribal lands. These nations were overrun by European settlers, who subsequently formed today's USA—which *has* had a mighty impact on worldwide politics and events.

Consequently, one needs to be careful to distinguish between a minor nation (or city-state) that had little impact on their surroundings and civilizations (or empires) that had a wide-reaching impact on the surrounding territory. More importantly, one must distinguish between the early inhabitants of the territory, and those inhabitants who eventually rose to form the empire. This chapter only considers those civilizations that had long-term and widespread impact on their neighbors—empires, although they will be referred to as civilizations usually.

❖ Early Civilizations

The Naturalists' current viewpoint is that modern humans first arose in Africa, and then spread out to the Middle East, and then to Europe and Asia. But tracing the expansion of the early civilizations tells an entirely different story. A major problem with tracing the expansion of any early civilization is placing them into a chronology.

Many of these civilizations have a problem with the dates given by experts, as they lack a historical link to known chronologies derived from written records—at least until the written records from those civilizations can be reconstructed to form a contiguous chronology linked to today's Gregorian Calendar. This chronology can only be traced back to about 1000 BC, with some problems even before that date in history. Between about 1000 to 600 BC, piecing together the chronology is partially guess-work because of survivability issues of the written records. All civilization dates within this chapter are derived from *History.com, Encyclopaedia Britannica, World History Encyclopedia,* or *World History Publishing.* Many of these are estimates without a link to known chronological history, but they will be used to demonstrate the problem without attempting to adjust them in any way.

One of the earliest civilizations was the Mesopotamia (Sumerian civilization) Empire, which originated in today's modern Iraq in the Tigris-Euphrates valley. Naturalists place a date on this civilization from approximately 4000 BC[1]. Another civilization was the Harappan Civilization (Indus Valley in India), with a date from 2500 to 1700 BC.[2] Ancient China is another civilization that is dated to 2070 to 1600 BC.[3] Another civilization is the Inca Civilization (South America), which is dated to AD 1000 to 1400.[4] The earliest Mayan Civilization (Central

America) is dated to 600 BC to AD 800.[5] All of these civilizations lack an established date to known history (*i.e.*, their records cannot be linked to known chronology), so there are many differing opinions from the experts on the dates for these civilizations. As a result, other expert opinions on their dates may vary from those given above.

Next are the civilizations with some written histories: Egypt (Early Dynastic Period in Egypt: 3150 to 2613 BC)[6], the Minoan civilization (Crete: 2000 to 1500 BC)[7], ancient Greece (Classical Period: 480 to 323 BC)[8], and finally Roman Empire (27 BC to AD 460)[9]. After 460, the Roman Empire split into two empires—falling outside the scope of this chapter.

Last, we find the civilizations of central and southern Africa. These are the Great Zimbabwe (AD 1100 to 1550), the Mali Empire (AD 1240 to 1645), and the Songhai Empire (AD 1460 to 1591).[10] Since the Egyptian Empire has already been addressed, they were not listed as among the African civilizations. Likewise, the Nubian kingdom (today's Sudan), which was often in conflict with Egypt—is likewise not mentioned as among the African empires.

❖ Spread of Civilization Conclusion

In this manner, visualizing the spread of civilizations on a map using their origination time, they seem to spread out from the Middle East area to surrounding countries or continents. The last ancient civilizations to be established were in central or southern Africa (*i.e.*, those civilizations not situated around the Mediterranean Sea or the Red Sea) and the Americas. If the Out-of-Africa theory were true, then the earliest civilizations should have been in central or southern Africa, not around the Middle East. Yet, the central or southern Africa region was among the last to see a great civilization. It is also noteworthy that the continents of South America and Central America (which is recognized today as part of North America) saw civilizations established about the same point in history as the southern region of Africa, even though humans had to cross an ocean to colonize the Americas. This is empirical evidence that counters the Naturalists' postulate that modern humans evolved in Africa and migrated across the globe.

CHAPTER 14

NATURALISM CONCLUSION

Naturalism is premised upon five major tenets. These are cosmology, abiogenesis, evolution, transitional species, and millions of years for evolution to occur. Every one of these tenets have been falsified by Naturalists specializing in the area where they published the empirical evidence falsifying the tenet. Since these tenets are considered research programs, these tenets are not subject to falsification by empirical evidence, according to Lakatos's concept of science.

In addition to the falsification of the five major Naturalists' tenets, there is even more empirical evidence against the Naturalists' worldview. These are 1) Evolution violates the Second Law of Thermodynamics, 2) Radiometric dating unreliability, 3) The population mismatch between calculated size and actual size, and 4) The spread of civilizations from the Middle East region rather than from the central/south African region postulated by Naturalists.

Worse is that none of these Naturalists' tenets are likely to be proven sufficiently enough to be considered a scientific law within the lifespan of anybody living today. Accordingly, one must have great faith when committing to Naturalism as a means of explaining the world seen today. Hence, Naturalists are effectively on their own one-yard line with ninety-nine-yards to go for a touchdown.

CHRISTIANITY

CHAPTER 15

ESTABLISHING A TESTABLE THEORY

Christianity does not have a proposed scientific theory behind it, so the first challenge is to establish a theory that can be empirically tested. After establishing a theory that is subject to falsification, it can then be tested against the empirical evidence available. Initially, only the Old and New Testament of the Christian Bible will be considered. Later, the other books that were either later included or not included in this definition of the Christian Bible will be addressed.

❖ The Theory of a Biblical God

The Bible lists many attributes of for its biblical God. However, only two of them can be empirically tested unless it is presumed the Bible is true, which is not an objective way of evaluating a hypothesis. So, the focus will be limited to these two attributes: God's omnipotence and omniscience. Omnipotence means all-powerful, while omniscience means all-knowing. These are two attributes that are widely accepted by most, if not all, Christians. Second, is the belief of Christians that the Bible is the Word of God. Last, empirical evidence must be provided that the Bible available today is the same Bible that existed as far back into time as can be realistically proven. Only after these three tenets can be proven empirically, can it be shown whether the biblical account is trustworthy.

❖ Problem with Past Prophecies

Many Christians will try to use the prophecies that were allegedly fulfilled in the New Testament manuscripts as empirical evidence to support the omniscience of God. Unfortunately, that falls short of the necessary level of objectivity in the quest for truth. Objectively, we cannot ascertain whether the New Testament books were written in such a way as to give the appearance of a prophetic fulfillment by giving falsified evidence to align to those prophecies in the Old Testament, or if the prophecies were written first and then they were fulfilled during New Testament times. Fortunately, new empirical evidence has been discovered in the last five hundred years to utilize during an objective analysis of the evidence, for or against the biblical record. Thus, we begin our dive into Christian apologetics.

❖ Meaning of Apologetics

Merriam-Webster defines *apologetics* as the "systematic argumentative discourse in defense (as of a doctrine)."[1] Generally, this defense is used by scholars as a defense of the Christian worldview from attacks by non-believers. It derives from the Greek term in 1st Peter 3:15, stating that one must be ready to give a defense of their beliefs. The Greek term in this passage that is translated as defense is "apologia," which comes from the Greek root words of "apo" (from) and "logos" (logical word).

Note that Greek words change their spelling for nouns and verbs, with the masculine words usually ending in an "s" and the feminine words frequently ending in an "a," which is why the word apologia is used, rather than "apologos." It is because apologia is considered a feminine word in the Greek language. Greek root words are always given as either masculine words or neuter words. Other languages, like Spanish, French, German, Hebrew, and Latin, have similar spelling differences between masculine and feminine words. A few English words change spelling based upon gender too, like Michael vs. Michelle and Samuel vs. Samantha. English is still trending away from neutered words following masculine spellings, like mankind is now referred to as humankind. Consequently, this is not an unusual practice.

The term logos is often applied to Jesus. Among many places in the Bible, the Greek term logos is found in John 1:1 "In the beginning was the Word [Greek: logos][2]." The English term logic is derived from the Greek term logos—hence logos, and any variants—could be better understood as "logical word," in contrast to babbling or nonsense. In 1st Peter 3:15, it is translated in a variety of words ranging from "give an answer", "give a defense", "make a defense", and "be ready to explain it"—among many other translations. A better rendering of this Greek phrase would be to "give a logical defense." This book is meant to equip all Christians to make a logical defense of their Christian beliefs utilizing empirical evidence that everyone can see and evaluate—without resorting to one's personal experiences, upbringing, or what their pastor may say, to justify their faith.

❖ Importance of Apologetics

Even Paul, who is attributed to writing much of the New Testament, utilized logic and empirical evidence in his presentation of the Gospel in the book of Acts.

> Then Paul stood in the midst of the Areopagus and said, "Men of Athens, I perceive that in all things you are very religious; for as I was passing through and considering the objects of your worship, I even found an altar with this inscription: TO THE UNKNOWN GOD Therefore, the One whom you worship without knowing, Him I proclaim to you: (Acts 17:22–23, NKJV).

Paul starts with a position that all his listeners would agree upon before he began to present the Gospel. This facilitated the acceptance of his message by his listeners. So, every Christian needs a firm foundation in apologetics if they want to witness to others—as Jesus commanded us to do.

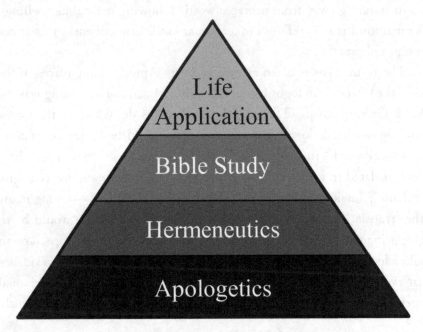

7 - Importance of Apologetics

The image above demonstrates the importance of apologetics for any Christian. Apologetics forms the initial foundation for one's belief system. For Christians, the next level up is hermeneutics, which is the translation and interpretation of the original language into modern English or other modern languages. Most Christians skip past these two important levels, jumping right into Bible study and life application. But they rarely question the underlying foundation. Anti-Christians work to undermine a Christian's faith by attacking their lack of a solid foundation in a Christian's life.

There are many different types of apologists. Some Christian apologists seek to counter the corruption of the Christian faith by liberal theologians. These apologists utilize a mixture of apologetics, combined with a strong dose of hermeneutics. This book will mostly focus on the apologetics foundation. It attempts to answer the question of "why trust the Bible in the first place," with limited clarification of the words in the original language (*i.e.*, hermeneutics).

❖ Purpose of Establishing a Theory

Not everyone viewing this information will agree with the objective conclusions reached by this book, since to do so would require some of them to admit they may be in the wrong. There are many philosophical sayings along the line of "every man is right in his own eyes," which originated from Proverbs 21:2. This section of the book was not written to force a person to accept any given conclusion. Instead, it was written for two purposes, I) Allow the empirical testing of the biblical God; and 2) To clear obstacles for the deepening of one's faith in the biblical God.

CHAPTER 16

AGE OF BIBLICAL DOCUMENTS

T here are many challenges with determining the age of the books of the Bible. However, scholars have devised a means of establishing a date of the initial writing of a manuscript, even when confronted with these challenges. So, what are the challenges and their solutions?

❖ Recording Materials

The recording of writing over time has used different mediums to accomplish the goal of passing information from the writer to the reader. The earliest written medium was stone. Then, it progressed to clay tablets (often referred to as cuneiform tablets) that were soft when written upon and subsequently hardened (*i.e.*, fired, or dried) into a rock-like substance.

The ancient Hebrews used skins from lambs, dried, stretched, and rolled up to record their writings. They are referred to as scrolls because of the way the material was rolled up for storage. During the era of the New Testament, the Egyptians used a substance called *papyrus*[1] (plural: *papyri*) which was made by creating multiple layers of the soft central part of papyrus stems (which were common along the Nile River), with each new layer laid on top at right angles. After the layering process, it was pressed and dried into a paper-like material. Later documents were on parchment (scraped and prepared animal skins, usually calfskins). Today we use paper and even electronic means.

Scrolls and papyri were used during the biblical age and were carefully hand-written over thousands of years. Because these mediums were organic, they tended to break down over time. To solve this issue, people carefully trained at writing (scribes) were tasked with copying these documents before the document was too worn to hand off to the next generation, as well as making copies for distribution to others. These written documents are called manuscripts. Today, the texts from these manuscripts are referred to as the books of the Bible.

❖ Dating Methods for Manuscripts

Manuscripts that were hand-written centuries ago and are still in existence today are referred to as *extant*[2] manuscripts. The closer an extant manuscript is to the original writing of the document, the more authentic scholars consider that manuscript to be. The term manuscript fell out of favor once the printing press was invented, since careful copying of text was no longer an issue. But extant manuscripts are vital in the evidence to support Christianity.

Dating manuscripts is difficult for several reasons. First, radiometric dating only gives a date range (usually too wide for manuscripts), not a specific date. Second, since the organic material used in manuscripts deteriorated quickly with use, the original manuscript never lasted long. Even stone, paper, and electronic records will deteriorate given sufficient time. Consequently, scholars developed alternative methods for determining the date a manuscript was originally written. This is composed of multiple factors, including information within the manuscript, the shape of the letters, etc. This process is called *paleography*. *Merriam-Webster* defines paleography as "the deciphering and interpretation of historical writing systems and manuscripts."[3]

If one watches a lot of movies, one will see a difference in the technology used within the various movies. Some movies include computers, while others do not. Some use rudimentary phones, rather than smart phones. Knowing when things were developed, one can closely determine the period in which the movie was made. For example, if one sees a movie with NYC Twin Towers standing in the background, one can logically presume the movie was made between 1973 (when they were built) and 2001 (when they were destroyed). Conversely, a film that is meant to portray an historical period, such as the US Revolutionary War, can often be called out by a mistake such as featuring an out-of-era prop (*i.e.*, the wrong flag or a plastic water bottle before water bottles were invented) or other technology that wasn't used at that time. Similar techniques are used in paleography. One must simply know intricate details of the history during which the manuscript was first allegedly written.

One last technique is cross-referencing—when was a manuscript first written about in scholarly or historical writings. Many church fathers (*i.e.*, the scholars of their time) would write something along the lines of "the disciple Mark wrote that 'The beginning of the gospel of Jesus Christ, the Son of God'." This would prove conclusively that the Gospel of Mark was written before this church father wrote about it in his writings—*i.e.*, within or before that scholar's lifetime. Since the Roman Empire ruled the area around where the early Church had its start, almost all (if not all) church fathers have years that are easily tied into the Roman Empire chronology. This in turn can be translated into the Gregorian Calendar years that we use today.

Paleography, using a variety of methods, allows scholars to reliably determine the date the manuscript was originally written. Paleography is more accurate than radiocarbon dating since it gives a narrower date range when compared to radiocarbon dating. However, radiocarbon dating is still important, as it can be used to sift out fake manuscripts and other archeological artifacts. For example, a forger could fake the writing style of a given period, but the medium could be radiocarbon dated and revealed to be a recent sheepskin (*i.e.*, medium). And forgers have gotten very good at faking "biblical artifacts," so paleography alone cannot be the sole determinative factor in deciding the age of a manuscript.

Old Testament

For this discussion, the term Old Testament will refer to the authoritative Hebrew and Aramaic texts of the thirty-nine books of the Hebrew Bible. The Deuterocanonical books are rejected by Jews and Protestants as being divinely inspired. As such, they will be discussed in their own section. Likewise, the *Septuagint* version of the Old Testament will also not be discussed, as it is a Koine (common) Greek translation made in the third and second centuries BC from the Hebrew Bible. Any translation of a translation, as would be needed if one were to use the Septuagint, has the potential of introducing errors in understanding. Since the Septuagint is a Hebrew to Greek translation, and the resulting English translation would be a Greek to English, then it falls into the category of a translation of a translation. The *Latin Vulgate* is, likewise, excluded for the same reason, albeit the intermediary language would be Latin, instead of Greek. The Latin Vulgate is a Roman Empire era translation of a mixture of the Septuagint (*i.e.*, Greek translation of Hebrew texts) and Hebrew manuscripts into the Old Testament text, combined with a translation of the four Gospels (in Greek) into Latin done by St. Jerome.[4] Other translators subsequently added to his work to include the rest of the New Testament books for the Latin Vulgate.

Today, there are two extant copies of the Old Testament manuscripts, the Masoretic Texts, and the Dead Sea Scrolls. The extant Masoretic Texts are reliably dated to between AD 501 to 1000[5], according to the editors of *Encyclopaedia Britannica. TheNIVBible.com* provides information concerning the Dead Sea Scrolls, saying "Carbon dating on some fragments suggested that they were from somewhere between roughly 2,400 and 1,900 years old. By analyzing the writing on those same fragments using paleography, scholars estimated they were between about 2,200 and 1,950 years old."[6]

The exact dates are not important, because the salient issue is that the universally accepted age for both sources is significantly older than five hundred years ago and that the Dead Sea Scrolls are from the time of Jesus—centuries before the Masoretic copies. All of today's Bible English versions are based upon the Masoretic Texts. We will compare these two Hebrew versions when we discuss the transmission of the biblical text in the next chapter.

New Testament

The earliest New Testament manuscripts were written almost exclusively on papyri. Papyrus does not take the environmental elements and usage well, so manuscripts written on them don't last long. The preferred medium for writing important documents was parchment (usually, calfskins). Parchment is also referred to as vellum. So, as Christianity became mainstream, its manuscripts transitioned from papyrus to parchment.

Vellum withstands the environmental elements and usage much better than papyrus, so more books on vellum remain today. However, there are still many incomplete New Testament manuscripts on papyrus. Some of the oldest papyrus fragments are Matthew ($\mathfrak{P}$104: AD 100–200), ($\mathfrak{P}$77: AD 100–300), ($\mathfrak{P}$103: AD 100– 300); John ($\mathfrak{P}$52: AD 125–175), ($\mathfrak{P}$90: AD 100–200), Mark ($\mathfrak{P}$137: AD 150–250); and Revelation ($\mathfrak{P}$98: AD 150–250).[7] These dates are from *Wikipedia's* webpage titled *"List of New Testament papyri."*

Complete papyrus copies of the New Testament did not survive, so the oldest complete New Testament books are on parchment and are dated as late as AD 500. Another reason these books on papyri do not exist today is the "wholesale destruction of the New Testament books by imperial command"[8] (*i.e.*, the Roman Empire) prior to AD 313.

Christianity.com states that the oldest extant manuscript written in Greek is the *Codex Vaticanus* (AD 350)[9] but it is missing the books of Hebrews and Revelation. *Encyclopaedia Britannica*[10] addresses another old, extant manuscript in Greek as the *Codex Sinaiticus* (AD 301–400) and contains the entire New Testament and part of the Old Testament. The *British Library Board* states that *"Codex Alexandrinus* is one of the three early Greek manuscripts that preserve both the Old and the New Testaments together" and that it was "Copied in the 5th century"[11] (AD 401–500). Modern translators today use these early copies as their foundation for translating today's Bibles. Some of these ancient copies were not available when the King James Version was translated in 1611.

In summary, the early New Testament manuscripts did not survive well, because of their material and because the Roman Empire tried to destroy all the Christian Scriptures, so the earliest complete manuscripts are from the fourth and fifth centuries. However, there are 5,839 extant fragments of the Greek New Testament manuscripts that have been catalogued, as per *Greek New Testament Dot Net.*[12]

Since the New Testament relies upon copies of copies, we need to look at how accurately these copies were passed through the ages. We also need to consider the accuracy of the transmission of the Old Testament down through the centuries.

❖ Biblical Document Age Conclusion

We have existing copies of the books of the Old Testament, some as early as 200 BC, and others as late as AD 1000. The earliest copies are known as the Dead Sea Scrolls, while the newer copies are known as the Masoretic Texts. The New Testament books consist of a few complete copies dating as early as AD 500, with some smaller fragments on papyrus dating to as early as AD 125. But most of the New Testament manuscripts are after AD 500. *Textual criticism* places the New Testament writings to have occurred within the first century (AD 1 to 100), although scholars will debate these dates based upon their personal interpretations. *Encyclopedia Britannica* defines textual criticism as "an ancillary academic discipline designed to lay the foundations for the so-called higher criticism, which deals with questions of authenticity and attribution, of interpretation, and of literary and historical evaluation."[13]

The important point from this chapter is that it is universally recognized by all sides that the oldest complete manuscripts of all the books of the Bible are more than five-hundred-years-ago, which is the critical component for the next step in our testing of the empirical evidence for the alleged attributes of God.

CHAPTER 17

ACCURACY OF THE TRANSMISSION OF BIBLICAL TEXT

A ll twentieth century Bible versions and later are based upon the Masoretic Text for the Old Testament. Masoretic Texts are over 1,000 years old. All twentieth century Bible versions and later are based upon the combined Greek manuscripts for the New Testament, of which the *Greek New Testament Dot Net* website states that currently "5,839 Greek manuscripts (fragments or complete) of the New Testament have been catalogued, of which 128 are papyri, 322 are majuscules, 2,926 are minuscules and 2,462 are lectionary manuscripts, i.e., manuscripts in which the text of the New Testament books is divided into separate pericopes."[1]

❖ Old Testament

Dead Sea Scrolls

The Dead Sea Scrolls, which are dated between 200 BC to AD 70, are numerous scrolls almost exclusively written on sheepskin that contain biblical writings, with most of them being non-biblical writings. The scrolls were preserved in such a way as to give the appearance that the scribes in charge of these scrolls were preparing for a long period of conquest, and that they needed to preserve their library for future generations. Specifically, each scroll was rolled up, wrapped in another layer of sheepskin, and then covered with tar, for preservation purposes. These tar-covered scrolls were then placed in pottery jars, which were then sealed, and stored in, presumably nearby, caves near Qumran—near the Dead Sea in today's land of Israel. It appears that the scribes were preparing them to be kept for several decades. However, it was thousands of years later that they were discovered, beginning in 1947.

Because organic material breaks down, the Dead Sea Scrolls began to deteriorate—despite the precautions taken by the preservers. The scrolls were placed in jars, which were then placed in the caves, leaving the scrolls standing on end. Often, the end of the scroll that was placed in the down position was the top of the scroll, which slowly deteriorated over the thousands of years. As a result of their storage efforts, the top few inches of each scroll broke down into fragments while the rest of the scroll remained intact for our generation to inspect and compare to other Old Testament copies. Many fragments could be reconstructed to fit into the intact remains of the scrolls, giving today's scholars the opportunity to compare the most ancient versions of the biblical manuscripts with the Masoretic Texts from a central date of AD 900—or about one thousand years of transmission of the Old Testament.

Per *TheNIVBible.com*, roughly 22 percent of the Dead Sea Scrolls contain biblical text ("among the more than 900 scrolls are over 200 copies of Old Testament books"[2]). The rest are various works, including scrolls of books of non-divinely inspired writing, and the minutiae of miscellaneous day-to-day activities recording things like the transfer of land from one person to another. Almost all the Hebrew biblical books, thirty-nine in all, are represented in the two hundred copies of the Dead Sea Scrolls—meaning that many books of the Bible have duplicates. The only missing book of the Hebrew Bible is the book of Esther, but even fragments of that book have been found recently, according to *The Torah.com*.[3] Among the duplicate writings, there are some minor variances.

The Hebrew language does not include vowels. This allowed the ancient Hebrews to record long books like Samuel, Kings, and Chronicles onto a single scroll. When these Hebrew scrolls were translated into a language that included vowels, the manuscripts became too long to fit onto a single sheepskin roll, and thus forced the scribes to split the manuscripts into a first and second manuscript, like the book of Kings was split into the books of First Kings and Second Kings, First Samuel and Second Samuel, and First Chronicles and Second Chronicles, that we see today.

Masoretic Texts

Masoretes ('Masters of the Tradition'[4], alternative spelling: Massoretes) were groups of Jewish scribes and scholars who worked from around the end of the fifth (AD 401–500) through tenth centuries to transmit the Bible accurately through the centuries. Thus, their writing became known as Masoretic Texts. The Masoretic Texts, circa AD 900, are slightly different from the Dead Sea Scrolls because of a minor change in how the Hebrew words were recorded. Around AD 500, the Hebrew language was ceasing to be an active language, and each new generation would struggle with how the Hebrew words were pronounced. To solve this issue, the Masoretes devised a vowel notation system by adding extraneous markings, like dots and dashes, to each Hebrew consonant to help future generations know how the Hebrew word was pronounced. These markings are called diacritics.[5] This did not change the original Hebrew language, because if these additional markings were ignored, the original writings were preserved unchanged.

The next question is how accurately they were transmitted from the earliest Dead Sea Scrolls when compared to the Masoretic Texts. Bible scholar Fredric Kenyon addresses that in his book, *Our Bible and the Ancient Manuscripts*.

> Besides recording varieties of reading, tradition, or conjecture, the Massoretes undertook a number of calculations which do not enter into the ordinary sphere of textual criticism. They numbered the verses, words, and letters of every book. They calculated the middle word and middle letter of each. They enumerated verses which contained all the letters of the alphabet, or a certain number of them; and so on. These trivialities, as we may rightly consider them, had yet the effect of securing minute attention to the precise transmission of the text; and

they are but an excessive manifestation of the respect for the sacred Scriptures which in itself deserves nothing but praise. The Massoretes were indeed anxious that not one jot or tittle, not the smallest letter not one part of a letter of the Law should pass away or be lost.[6]

So, 'Masters of the Tradition' went to extreme limits to preserve the Hebrew Bible. However, one should note that centuries passed between AD 123, when the nation of Israel was officially dissolved by the Roman empire, and the period when the Masoretes began their meticulous recording beginning around AD 401.

Dead Sea Scrolls Compared to Masoretic Texts

Therefore, let us compare the two versions of one book of the Hebrew Bible. Bible scholars Norman Geisler and William Nix did such a comparison in their 1968 book, *A General Introduction to the Bible*.

> The impact of this discovery is in the exactness of the Isaiah scroll (125 B.C.) with the Massoretic test of Isaiah (A.D 916) 1,000 years later.
>
> Of the 166 words in Isaiah 53, there are only seventeen letters in question. Ten of the letters are simply a matter of spelling, which does not affect the sense. Four more letters are minor stylistic changes, such as conjunctions. The remaining three letters comprise the word "light" which is added in verse 11, and does not affect the meaning greatly.[7]

With this information, one can conclude that the Old Testament has been handed down accurately for thousands of years. There is still some possibility that some additional changes occurred from when the first books of the Bible were scribed, around 1446 BC and before, and when the Dead Sea Scrolls were scribed. However, we do not have any empirical evidence to support this hypothesis, so we do not have a legitimate reason to doubt the overall transmission of the text, much less that there has been a significant meaning change in the text from which it was first penned until today's various versions.

Old Testament Contradictions

However, there are some legitimate contradictions in the Bible. For example, in describing the same event, two books of the Bible change the number of horsemen captured during a campaign by King David during a battle. The book of Second Samuel records that King David captured "seven hundred horsemen" (2 Samuel 8:4, KJV), while the book of First Chronicles records the number as "seven thousand horsemen" (I Chronicles 18:4, KJV). This is one indication of an error of transmission of the correct number. Second Samuel has multiple variations for the number of horsemen captured, depending upon the source. The "seven thousand" figure is recorded in the Dead Sea Scrolls, the Septuagint (a Hebrew to Greek translation by Jewish scholars circa 285–247 BC), and in First Chronicles. However, the Masoretic Text records the number in Second Samuel as "seventeen hundred," while the King James Version records it as "seven hundred." Most scholars today accept the seven thousand figure as the correct number of horsemen captured.

As shown, there are some subtle differences between these two sets of Old Testament Scripture. Nonetheless, does the differences between seven hundred, seventeen hundred, and seven thousand horseman really matter in the overall message? In my opinion, it does not. However, anti-Christians will use this empirical evidence to show that the Bible has changed over time. But they will be hard pressed to prove that a significant change occurred that distorts the fundamental message in the Bible.

❖ New Testament

Material

The New Testament was written after the crucifixion of Jesus in about AD 33 on papyrus. As previously mentioned, papyrus does not hold up to the environmental elements, nor does it maintain its forbearance when handled frequently by people who just want to read the manuscript. Therefore, any manuscript written on papyri will break down rapidly, historically speaking. In addition is a fact brought out by *Greek New Testament Dot Net*, where they address the deliberate destruction of any New Testament manuscripts by the Roman Empire.

> One of the worst incidents in the repeated persecutions that the early Christians had to undergo was the wholesale destruction of the New Testament books by imperial command, and by the rage of the pagans. Multitudes of the manuscript of the New Testament written in the first three centuries were destroyed at the beginning of the fourth, and there can be no doubt that multitudes of those written in the fourth and two following centuries met a similar fate in the various invasions of East and West.[8]

As a result, most of what we currently have of the New Testament papyri manuscripts are fragments. The parchment (vellum) manuscripts held up better to handling and have lasted through the millenniums to modern times for three reasons. First, they were written on a more lasting medium, second, they were written after the persecutions of the early Christians, and third, they escaped notice during the various invasions that saw some similar copies destroyed, which was likely just because they were more numerous compared to the papyri copies during these invasions.

There are over 5,800 fragments of the New Testament manuscripts written in Greek. There are a few whole books written on parchment hundreds of years after the time of Jesus that exist. This would lead a novice to conclude that not much could be made from just the fragments on papyrus. Yet, a paleographic scholar can do a lot with just a fragment of a manuscript.

Making Sense of Fragments

The reason they can make fragments useful requires a basic understanding of scribal work. First, a scribe copies the text as it is written, letter by letter. Second, scribes learn to write in letters that are consistently spaced—in today's vernacular, they used fixed fonts in their writing style. Thus, a line written in a manuscript would contain the same number of words *and* the same number of letters.

Thus, predictability occurs between copies of the same manuscript. So, when a fragment contains one or two letters on the first line in the fragment, four or five letters on the second line, and a few additional letters on the last line of the fragment, then scholars could often determine the manuscript from which the fragment came—if that manuscript was a copy of a previously known writing, like a biblical book.

If this book that you are reading was written in a fixed font, rather than a proportional font, you could take a fragment from anywhere in this book and determine that it came from this book based upon just a few letters on two or three lines. This lettering and spacing combination would eliminate almost every other book you've ever read. This is the general concept that paleographic scholars use to trace a fragment of a manuscript to a known manuscript of the same language. More important is the fact that there were far fewer manuscripts during pre-printing press days than there are now, so there would be fewer possible matches to consider.

Comparing the Fragments

Bible scholars decided to test the transmission of the New Testament manuscripts over the millennium that it's been handed down to us today using computers to compare the various fragments and whole manuscripts where available. Biblical scholar Terry Hall presented the findings in his book, *How the Bible Became a Book.*

> Computer analysis of all the known New Testament manuscripts reveal only 0.1 percent variance. That means that 99.9 percent of the manuscripts' contents are in perfect agreement. Most of the small percentage of actual differences are in spelling (such as the English "honour" versus "honor"), word order ("Paul the apostle" verses "the apostle Paul"), and grammar ("Father who art in heaven" versus "Father which art in heaven"). And none of the variations affects any basic doctrine.[9]

So, a comparison of *all* known Greek manuscripts reveal that they are nearly identical. Additionally, many early church fathers wrote about the biblical writings in their possession between AD 33 to 300. From these writings alone, we can confirm that the core beliefs in our New Testament Bibles today have not changed since the days of the church fathers. So, the overall conclusion is that the New Testament has been handed down over thousands of years very accurately, and the Bible we use today is almost identical to the earliest Bibles available.

❖ Accuracy of the Transmission Conclusion

Geisler and Nix wrote in their book *A General Introduction to the Bible, Rev. and expanded* the following about the Bible.

> Composed as it is of sixty-six books, written over a period of some fifteen hundred years by nearly forty authors using several languages and containing hundreds of topics, it is more than accidental or incidental that the Bible possesses an amazing unity of theme—Jesus Christ. One problem—sin—and one solution—the Savior—unify its pages from Genesis to Revelation. This is an especially valid point because no one person or group of men put the Bible together.[10]

Josh McDowell in his book *Josh McDowell's Handbook on Apologetics* wrote that "These sixty-six books were composed by more than forty authors, from a variety of educational and cultural backgrounds. Joshua was a general; Daniel was a prime minister; Nehemiah was a court servant; Amos was a shepherd; Luke, a physician; Paul, a rabbi; and Peter and John were fishermen."[11] So, we find that the Bible has a unified theme, even though it was done over fifteen hundred years, and it was written by a variety of writers with diverse levels of education. This is a strong indicator that someone other than the individuals scribing the text was the actual author of the Bible we have today.

Empirically, both the Old Testament and the New Testament have been passed down from their original penning to the earliest extant manuscripts with minor variances—none which affect the basic doctrines in the Bible. All modern versions of the Bible utilize these extant manuscripts in their translation process, with one slight exception—the King James Version. Its aberration will be addressed in a separate section.

There are many ways to translate one language to another language. A translation (*i.e.*, a version) could be word-for-word or thought-for-thought goal. And many words often have multiple interpretations. But we live in a very special age where if we have questions, we can look at all the alternative translations in our own language and come to our own conclusions as to what was meant by a particular passage. A blog post by Tiffany Nicole, writing for *Lavender Vines*, covers more details about the various Bible translations and has a handy chart that places several translations in a chart ranging from word-for-word to paraphrase.[12]

There are many tools online that can enable us to look at the original language word, its meaning and seek a deeper understanding of the meaning of the passage if we still have any doubts. Without endorsing either website, here are two such websites to help deepen your faith: *BibleGateway.com* and *BlueLetterBible.org*. There are many other tools available today, including smartphone apps, which will take you much further than any one book can do. Prior to the Information Age, this was not a possibility, so we are very fortunate to live in our modern era.

CHAPTER 18

OMNIPOTENCE OF GOD
(HISTORY AND SCIENCE)

Other popular religions have been founded for thousands of years. However, a long history and an accurate transmission of the writing does not constitute a validation of the beliefs. Instead, we must consider the attributes of the alleged deity, and compare these against what has been established empirically today—namely, what is in biblical writings that was not known then but is a fact that is widely accepted today.

There are three groups of facts found in the Bible to evaluate: history, science, and prophecy. In short, we will be attempting to prove that the ancient writings either falsify or verify the biblical God. This chapter addresses the omnipotence of God—specifically whether the books were written when they are alleged to have been written, and if the contents are scientifically accurate—that is, the universe's components and creation. The next chapter will address the omniscience of God.

❖ History

Any historical event recorded in the Bible does not prove the alleged deity of the biblical God. What it does establish is that the manuscript(s) were written during the period alleged in the manuscript(s), rather than after the facts became widely accepted. While there were many nations mentioned in the book of Genesis, four of these nations could be considered civilizations. Three of the four ancient civilizations mentioned in the book of Genesis were widely recognized by all parties throughout history. These were the Egyptian Empire (Gen 12:10), the Babylonian Empire (Gen 10:10), and the Assyrian Empire (Gen 10:11). This lends credibility to the idea that the book of Genesis was written in a period where these empires thrived.

In the 1800s, anti-Christians had enumerated a list of one hundred topics that they claimed proved the Bible to be false. Less than one hundred years later, every one of the so-called falsifications was demolished as new historical facts were discovered and the Bible was proven to be true. One of those alleged falsifications was shown to be inaccurate with the discovery of the existence of the Hittite Empire (Gen 10:15). There was no archeological record of any Hittite Empire in the 1800s, although French scholar Charles Texier found the first Hittite ruins in 1834.[1] Despite that, these ruins were not associated with the Hittite empire until the early twentieth century. *Wikipedia* goes into detail in the finding of the Hittite Empire, and its subsequent identification as the Hittle Empire, but as that is outside of the scope of this book, this history won't be addressed further.

The Hittite Empire was an ancient civilization that flourished in modern-day Turkey and is now considered by scholars to be one of the most influential and powerful civilizations of its time. Its control extended down into the area of today's modern Israel. The Hittite Empire was founded in the eighteenth century (1800 to 1701) BC. Following the biblical timeline, this would place its existence within the biblical account found in the book of Genesis.

However, Naturalists would—correctly—point out that historical validation does not prove the existence of an omnipotent and omniscient biblical God. All it can prove is that the original writings were done in the period in which they claim to have been written—*i.e.*, they were not passed down orally for thousands of years and then written down later. This refutes the claim of some that oral traditions from the early writings were passed down and then written down in approximately 800 BC.

❖ Science

Matter, Energy, and Time

Many Christians today do not recognize the importance of the first four or five verses of the Bible in the Book of Genesis. Most other religions start off with *esoteric* knowledge, with two exceptions—the Jewish religion and the Muslim (Islamic) religion. *Merriam-Webster* defines esoteric knowledge as "designed for or understood by the specially initiated alone."[2] In contrast, Genesis starts off with the creation of our universe in a manner that is consistent with the current scientific understanding of our universe—the creation of matter, energy, and time as coming from nothing.

If it is proven true, it establishes that the biblical God was omnipotent because He alone was able to create the universe from nothing. Second, it states that God created our universe in accordance with our current understanding in what is known today as *spacetime*. *Merriam-Webster* defines spacetime as "a system of one temporal and three spatial coordinates by which any physical object or event can be located."[3] Another way of stating spacetime is that the basic properties of the universe are matter, energy, and time, which is exactly how Genesis starts off its description of the creation of the universe.

> In the beginning God created the heaven and the earth *[matter]*. And the earth was without form, and void; and darkness was upon the face of the deep. And the Spirit of God moved upon the face of the waters. And God said, Let there be light *[energy]*: and there was light. And God saw the light, that it was good: and God divided the light from the darkness *[time]*. And God called the light Day, and the darkness he called Night. And the evening and the morning were the first day. (Genesis 1:1–5, KJV) [emphasis added].

So, God's first step of the creation of the universe is the creation of matter, energy, and time—our scientifically accepted properties of today's universe.

The classical elements of the universe proposed by most early civilizations were fire, earth, air, and water.[4] Later, a fifth one was added— the void.[5] Ancient Greeks passed these beliefs over to the Hellenistic (*i.e.,* Greek overseers) Egyptians. The ancient Indians (*i.e.,* people from India) also believed in these classical elements. "The Sicilian Greek philosopher Empedocles (c. 450 BC) was the first to propose the four classical elements as a set: fire, earth, air, and water. ... By the time of Antoine Lavoisier [1743–1794], for example, a list of elements would no longer refer to classical elements."[6] Only the biblical writings contradicted the belief in the classical elements. It could be argued that one scientific truth is insufficient to prove in a biblical God, so other evidence for the biblical God must be considered.

Plate Tectonics

The theory of plate tectonics, which is the movement and interaction of the earth's plates, is a scientific theory that is widely accepted today. It describes how earth's outer layer is divided into large and small plates that float over a softer layer in the earth. These plates include both the continents and the oceans of the planet. As documented in the *Encyclopaedia Britannica*, the theory was first proposed in 1912 by a German scientist named Alfred Wegener, who wrote two articles about continental drift.[7] It was accepted as a scientific theory in the 1960s, because it explained the many geological observations and sea floor spreading. The geologists observed that the Americas, when slightly contorted, would fit into the continents of Europe and Africa, and even the coasts of England would fit into continental Europe. The theory has transformed geology and the earth sciences, impacting wide ranging issues like history, paleoarcheology, evolution, and climate.

But when was plate tectonics first mentioned? In the book of Genesis. It does not mention the term plate tectonics because this scientific term is relatively new, so it couldn't appear in an ancient document. What the Bible does do is to describe an event, which was later assigned a term to categorize the concept. What does Genesis say about continental drift?

"And unto Eber were born two sons: the name of one was Peleg; for *in his* days was the earth ['erets] divided; and his brother's name was Joktan." (Genesis 10:25, KJV). The Hebrew term for "earth" is 'erets, which is defined by James Strong in his *Enhanced Strong's Lexicon* as "אֶרֶץ ['erets /eh·rets/] n f. I land, earth."[8] Thus, this verse is talking about the land dividing, not the people dividing, which is the Hebrew word [basar]. Basar is defined by James Strong in his *Enhanced Strong's Lexicon* as "בָּשָׂר [basar /baw·sawr/] n m. I flesh. IA of the body. IAI of humans. IAI of humans. IA2 of animals. IB the body itself. IC male organ of generation (euphemism). ID kindred, blood-relations. IE flesh as frail or erring (man against God). IF all living things. IG animals. IH mankind."[9]

So, the author writing about Peleg described the earth's continent as dividing. This was written thousands of years before even the idea of the continents dividing ever occurred to scientists, much less Naturalists. But the truth was in the biblical writings all this time. So, this makes two scientific facts found in the Bible well before these facts were discovered by modern scientists. Are there others? Yes, there are.

Spherical Earth

In the book of Job, the text describes the earth as a sphere. Let us begin with the passage, and then break it down for understanding. "He drew a *circular horizon on the face of the waters, At the boundary of light and darkness*" (Job 26:10, NKJV). So, how does a circle equate to the term sphere? To begin with, five concepts need to be established: I) The book of Job was written before anyone described the earth as a spherical shape, 2) When were the terms sphere and ball were first used, 3) How did the ancients described the earth without using the term sphere, 4) How the biblical word ball differs from circle, and 5) The flat earth theory.

Age of the Book of Job:

In the book of Job, the text itself does not directly identify its place in history. However, internal clues indicate that Job lived during the time of the patriarchs, which—according to the biblical chronology—is circa

2350 to 1750 BC. What are these clues? Some of these clues (#3 to #9) are identified in the *Amazing Bible Timeline with World History*.[10]

1. Job occurs in a pastoral setting, *i.e.*, shepherds and herdsmen, which is indicative of the patriarchal era.
2. The "land of Uz" is mentioned in the beginning of the book (Job 1:1). The name Uz is first mentioned in the book of Genesis (Gen 10:23), where Uz is identified as the son of Aram. In biblical times, nations were named after their founder—like Canaan, Israel, etc. So, the "land of Uz" is the area that the man Uz settled. Bible scholars place this land near modern day Kuwait. As time passes, these lands usually get renamed by new settlers, who take over from the natives. So, this implies that Job had to have been written shortly after Uz established his territory.
3. In the passages in Job, "Eliphaz refers to the flood as being in the past" in Job 22:16.
4. Job sacrifices to God as head of his family (a practice of patriarchal times that stopped with Moses) Job 1:5.
5. Job's daughters received an inheritance along with his sons Job 42:15—a patriarchal practice that also stopped with Moses.
6. Job's wealth is determined by flocks rather than money that is also consistent with patriarchal times Job 1:3, 42:12.
7. The kesitah or piece of money mentioned belongs to patriarchal times.
8. The musical instruments (organ, harp, and timbrel) are the instruments of early Genesis.
9. Job lived long enough to birth two families of ten children and raise them to adulthood then lived another 140 years. He lived at least 200 years and possibly longer. This is consistent with the ages of patriarchs prior to Abraham.[11]

No biblical scholar can place a definite time for the writing of the book of Job, but all Bible scholars agree that the book was written sometime before 1400 BC. And this is the important part, because no other scholars recognized the scientific facts found in Job for another 800 years or more.

First Use of Sphere or Globe:

Anti-Christians will be quick to point out that the text does not contain the term sphere, but this is a *strawman* logic fallacy. According to *Scribber,* a "Straw man fallacy is the distortion of someone else's argument to make it easier to attack or refute. Instead of addressing the actual argument of the opponent, one may present a somewhat similar but not equal argument."[12] The reason it is a logic fallacy is that the term sphere was first used in the 1300s, according to *Merriam-Webster.*[13] Thus, it would be impossible to use a new term in an ancient document. So, what words did the ancients use in place of the term sphere? They used terms like circle and circumference.

Describing a Sphere:

The ancient Greeks described the earth as a sphere beginning in the sixth century (600 to 501) BC. This hypothesis was further developed when the Greek Eratosthenes estimated its circumference around 240 BC.[14] However, the concept of a spherical earth was debated by both secular and Christian scholars, with parties on both sides taking opposing viewpoints— some advocated a flat earth, and some advocated a spherical earth.

Like the ancient Greeks, the book of Job also described the earth as a sphere, but it was written more than eight hundred years before the ancient Greeks. "He drew a *circular* horizon on the face of the waters, At the boundary of light and darkness" (Job 26:10, NKJV). The English term circular comes from the Hebrew word *chuwg. Enhanced Strong's Lexicon* translates the word as, "חוּג [chuwg /khoog/] v. I to encircle, encompass, describe a circle, draw round, make a circle. IA to encircle, encompass."[15]

As demonstrated, the boundary of light and darkness makes a circle on the earth. Given the fact that the sun moves across the earth's sky, then the only way that boundary could remain a circle is if the earth were in the geometric shape of a sphere. At any other point other than the sun being directly overhead, then the shape of the earth would be either an ellipse or a straight line. So, unless the earth was a sphere, the earth could not always be described as a circle at the boundary between light and darkness.

Imagine viewing a dinner plate. When viewed perpendicular to the plate, it would appear as a circle. When viewed slightly off perpendicular, the shape would appear as an ellipse. And when the dinner plate was viewed from its side, it would appear as just a line. Thus, the only valid shape of the earth described in the book of Job would be a geometrical sphere, even if that term did not occur prior to the last five hundred years.

Bible Uses the Term Ball:

Some anti-Christians may claim that the Bible does utilize a ball to describe an object. However, this is misleading, as the Hebrew word used in the verse also describes a circle. First, let us look at the verse in question, and then the *Enhanced Strong's Lexicon* on translation for the word translated as ball. "He will surely violently turn and toss thee like a *ball* into a large country: there shalt thou die, and there the chariots of thy glory shall be the shame of thy lord's house" (Isaiah 22:18, KJV) [Emphasis added]. The Hebrew word that was translated as ball in English is the word "דּוּר, כַּדּוּר [duwr /dure/] n m. 1 ball, *circle*. 1A *circle*. 1B ball."[16]. [emphasis added]. So, there is a word difference used here. A Hebrew verb is used in Job 26:10, while a Hebrew noun is used in Isaiah 22:18. Both can be literally translated to a circle. Bible translators understood what Isaiah was saying when he wrote "toss thee like a circle." Thus, this objection is incorrect.

Flat Earth Theory:

Many anti-Christians will claim that the Bible teaches a flat earth. While the ancients did debate this for centuries, most scholars had reached a consensus that the earth was a sphere around the AD third century (201–300). William DeLong addresses the modern flat earth theory, identifying it as a myth that was invented by an American writer, Washington Irving (1783 to 1859).[17] So very few scholars believed in a flat earth after the Medieval era and the Bible certainly does not teach such a concept.

Four Corners of the Earth:

Some anti-Christians will also argue that the Bible depicts the earth as flat, since it refers to the earth as with four corners, as in Isaiah 11:12—"gather together the dispersed of Judah from the *four corners* of the earth." Today, we also refer to the four positions of the earth. We call these four corners North, South, East, and West. So, this is just another misdirection (*i.e.*, a strawman logic fallacy) attempt by anti-Christians to cause a Christian to doubt the Bible.

Spherical Earth Conclusion:

To conclude, Job was the first writer who documented a circular earth around 2000 BC, well before the Greeks described it as a circle about 500 BC. It was not until the fourteenth century (1301 to 1400) before the term sphere[18] was first used, and the fifteenth century that the term globe[19] was first used. All these dates of the term's first use are documented in the *Merriam-Webster Dictionary*. However, Job's description of a "circle between light and darkness," combined with the apparent movement of the sun, can only be accomplished with the geometrical shape of a sphere.

Gravity

In Job 26:7, we see the earth suspended over nothing. "He stretches out the north over empty space; He *hangs the earth on nothing*" (Job 26:7, NKJV). Scientists have empirically found this to be true. The earth is suspended over nothing, pulled between two invisible forces: gravity and inertia. Gravity is the centripetal (inward) force that pulls the earth toward the Sun, while inertia is the centrifugal (outward) force that throws the earth away from the Sun. These two scientific forces balance each other out, leaving the earth suspended over nothing. Newton's Law of Gravity was first published in 1687.[20] Yet, approximately 3,600 years earlier, God described the earth as suspended over nothing.

❖ History and Science Conclusion

Christianity starts its Scripture off with the creation of the world that is empirically proven to be correct with today's historical and scientific knowledge. The universe's basic attributes are composed of matter, energy, and time. It has also been established that the books of the Bible are thousands of years old, which is before the latest five hundred years when scientists made key discoveries that validate the information contained within the biblical text. It has also been proven that the Bible has been accurately handed down to our current generation, with the New Testament books being analyzed by a computer and shown to be 99.9% identical in the words within each book. The Bible has been proven to be historically accurate, proving that its books were written during the period that they were allegedly written. The Bible has been proven to be scientifically accurate, with the discoveries of plate tectonics, gravity, and that the earth is spherical. So, there is plenty of scientific evidence that the biblical God is knowledgeable in the scientific principles guiding our universe. But does this God know the future as well? This is the key because it would prove the omniscience of God.

CHAPTER 19

OMNISCIENCE OF GOD

P rophecy is the foretelling of future events. It has been established that the Bible is several millennia (*i.e.,* thousands of years) old. Looking at events that occurred during biblical times does not provide empirical evidence, since one could never prove that the text was not manipulated to fit evidence to an Old Testament prophecy. For example, it cannot be proven that an angel told Joseph to go down to Egypt as it is written in Matthew 2:13-15, and they followed the angel's advice so that the prophecy from Hosea 11:1 would be fulfilled.

Therefore, to be objective, events are needed that are known to have occurred after the writing of the prophetic event in the Bible. Fortunately, we are living in such a period today. There are several events that have occurred during recent memory, *i.e.,* less than one hundred years ago, that were foretold within the text of the Bible. Everybody acknowledges that the current original language text within the Bible has not changed in the last five hundred years. Only two of these events will be considered, as the other events could be interpreted differently by biblical scholars on opposing sides of the debate.

❖ Israel's Rebirth

The first event is the rebirth of Israel—namely that after a long period of time in which the Israelites did not inhabit the Promised Land, they would reinhabit that land and reestablish their culture. The first to consider is what is meant by the Promised Land.

Promised Land

There are two main passages that link together to define the Promised Land. In Genesis, God promises Abram—later called Abraham—the land to the west of the Jordan and promised that land to Abraham's descendants forever. "Then Lot chose him all the plain of Jordan; and Lot journeyed east: and they separated themselves the one from the other. Abram dwelled in the land of Canaan, and Lot dwelled in the cities of the plain, and pitched his tent toward Sodom. ... For all the land which thou seest, to thee will I give it, and to thy seed for ever." (Genesis 13:11–12, 15, KJV). The land of the Canaanites was to the west of the Jordan River, and it was allotted to Abraham by Lot's decision. Lot was Abraham's nephew, and they traveled together from the land of Uz (Kuwait) to the area near modern day Israel. They concluded that their herds were too large to stay together, hence they decided to split up with Lot choosing the land near the Jordan River, and Abraham received the land to the west of the Jordan River. Subsequently, God promised Abraham this land west of the Jordan to Abraham's descendants forever. The promise was extended through Isaac in Genesis 28:13 and referred to by Jacob (aka Israel) in Genesis 50:24. This shows that each of Abraham's descendants recognized the land of the Canaanites (i.e., modern day Israel) as the Promised Land.

Later, Abraham's descendants fled the land of the Canaanites to the land of Egypt to avoid a famine in the land of the Canaanites. Abraham's grandson was initially named Jacob, but after Jacob had an encounter with God, he was renamed Israel ('he struggled with God') by God (Genesis 32:28 and 35:10). When Israel's descendants left Egypt with Moses, they eventually returned to Abraham's Promised Land.

And the LORD spake unto Moses, saying, Command the children of Israel, and say unto them, When ye come into the land of Canaan; (this is the land that shall fall unto you for an inheritance, even the land of Canaan with the coasts thereof:) . . . And the border shall go down to Jordan, and the goings out of it shall be at the salt sea: this shall be your land with the coasts thereof round about. (Numbers 34:1–2, 12, KJV)

As demonstrated, God reestablished Abraham's Promised Land to Israel's descendants when they left their captivity in Egypt. Israel's descendants divided the land between themselves, naming their territories after Israel's sons. One of the sons was named Judah and his descendants were allocated territory in the south of the Promised Land. This territory was called Judah. The inhabitants of this tribal land became known as Judeans or "Jews" for short. The Israelites (and Judeans) lived in the Promised Land from about 1446 BC until 123 AD, except for about seven decades during the Babylonian Captivity.

Demolishing the Nation of Israel/Judah

In AD 123, frequent rebellion in the land of Israel led the Roman Empire to abolish the nation known as Judah—the nation of Israel (the northern kingdom) met its demise centuries earlier in 722 BC. Prior to the conquest of the Canaanites' territory by the Israelites, the territory was split between the descendants of Canaan and descendants of other people. Some of these people were known as the Philistines.

Before Israel's conquest, the southern coastal territory was known as the land of the Philistines, but the Roman Empire misnamed it Palestine, by which the land is still recognized today. Biblically, the Philistines came from the lineage of Ishmael, the stepbrother of Isaac, son of Abraham. Some history scholars believe that the Philistines are thought to have come from some unidentified sea-going invaders from across the Mediterranean Sea and are unrelated to Abraham. With the rise of Islam around AD 600, the Muslims conquered the Promised Land and its surrounding territories. They kept the name of Palestine for this territory. Thus, the nation of Israel ceased to exist from AD 123 until 1948. This event, both the death of the nation and the rebirth of the nation (combined with a long period in between), was foretold in the book of Ezekiel.

Prophecy of Israel's Rebirth

Both the death of the nation of Israel in the Promised Land and Israel's rebirth in the Promised Land was foretold in the Old Testament book of Ezekiel. The prophecy was written in such a way that it was obvious that the nation of Israel would cease to exist for a long period of time, due to the description of the bones (an allegorical reference to the nation of Israel) as being very dry, and then it would be reborn after that long sojourn.

> The hand of the LORD was upon me, and carried me out in the spirit of the LORD, and set me down in the midst of the valley which was full of bones . . . they were *very dry*. And he said unto me, Son of man, can these bones live? . . .Thus saith the Lord GOD unto these bones; Behold, I will cause breath to enter into you, and ye shall live . . . Then he said unto me, Son of man, these bones are the whole house of Israel: behold, they say, Our bones are dried, and our hope is lost: we are cut off for our parts. Therefore prophesy and say unto them, Thus saith the Lord GOD; Behold, O my people, I will *open your graves, and cause you to come up out of your graves, and bring you into the land of Israel.* (Ezekiel 37:1–3, 11–12, KJV) [emphasis added]

Interpretation of Prophecy

From this prophecy, there are two specific facts: 1) Israel was gone from the Promised Land for so long that they had given up all hope of returning to the Promised Land, and 2) Israel's descendants would return to the Promised Land, including its original boundaries. There is some room for interpretation of this prophecy, as Israel returned to the Promised Land in 1948, but did not occupy its original boundaries. The original boundaries included the areas known today as the West Bank and the Golan Heights. This land was not occupied until 1967. So, was the prophecy fulfilled in 1948 or was it 1967? There is no definite answer to this. But it is beyond question that the prophecy's fulfillment was well after it was foretold in the book of Ezekiel for one of those two years.

❖ 666

The next prophecy is found in the book of Revelation. It has several parts, some of which have been fulfilled, and one which has yet to be fulfilled. The prophecy will be stated first, then it will be dissected, and each part will be addressed.

> And he causeth all, both small and great, rich and poor, free and bond, to receive a mark in their right hand, or in their foreheads: And that no man might buy or sell, save he that had the mark, or the name of the beast, or the number of his name. Here is wisdom. Let him that hath understanding count the number of the beast: for it is the number of a man; and his number is Six hundred threescore and six. (Revelation 13:16–18, KJV)

There are three parts to the prophecy. They are very specific, so there is no misinterpretation of the prophecy. First is that the mark is used for financial transactions, namely the buying and selling of everyday goods. Second is the mark is associated with the number of a human—this is in reference to the day Adam and Eve were created, the sixth day—so it could be interpreted as either 6-6-6 or 666. Third is the requirement that this mark be put on the right hand or on the forehead of every person on the planet.

UPC code

According to *Wikipedia*, the Universal Product Code (UPC or UPC code) is a code that is used ubiquitously across the world in our everyday lives to buy products from stores, and in a variety of forms for almost every product that we purchase today.[1] It was first used in 1974 in Troy, Ohio in the United States of America. It has since spread throughout the world for everyday transactions. Each UPC is unique and specific to a product, down to details like size and color. These codes are assigned by a nonprofit organization that represents the market for supply chain codes, called the Uniform Code Council. Each UPC code is a is a bar code symbol with a 12-digit number called a GTIN-12, or Global Trade Item Number 12 digits, to represent each product available for selling.

The UPC (technically refers to UPC-A) is composed of 15-sets of parallel bars, with 12-sets of the bars (marks) representing numbers for the product. The first, middle, and last set of bars are the same and are called guard patterns, dividing the mark into two groups of six sets of bars, hence the name UPC-12 (or UPC-A). The UPC-A's left-hand side digits have odd parity, while the UPC-A's right-hand side digits have even parity. The odd/even parity allows the scanner to know from which side to start the number sequence. Thus, with this parity/direction information, even an upside-down symbol cannot confuse the scanner. Furthermore, there are two sets of 5-digits under each side of the middle guard mark. These numbers are human-readable and are translated to the same unique number represented by the UPC-A code.

There are variations on the UPC codes, but they all can be translated back to the UPC-A version. For example, UPC-E (which has no guard patterns) can be translated back to a UPC-A format. *MarcoBarcode* describes the process of translating the UPC-E back to the UPC-A format, along with stating the advantage of doing such, stating that "UPC-A maintains full version of product information of the product which includes the full version of the manufacturer number and product number. It's easier to be decode by members in the supply chains."[2] So, all UPC codes have, directly or indirectly, included the 6-6-6 encoding in their bar codes (*i.e.*, marks).

UPC-12:

What is important about the UPC-12 code is the guard marks. A highlighted version of the UPC-12 code is shown below with an emphasis on the guard marks. The code used in this example does not represent any known product. It is a random number that uses the same set of numbers on both sides of the middle guard mark to show the difference in the marks on the left-side of the code from the right-side of the code, even as the same numbers are used on both sides. This image highlights the guard marks for easy identification purposes.

8 - Highlight of Guard Marks

We see a zero, followed by five digits, which is followed by five digits after the middle guard mark, which is finally followed by a single number. The first number is placed outside of the first guard mark, but the parallel bars (mark) associated with this number are inside of the beginning guard mark and slightly longer than the five-digit marks. The same is true for the check digit (the last digit and mark combination). The number for the check digit is outside of the end guard mark, while the parallel bars (mark) for the check digit are inside the end guard mark. The first digit and the check digit are encoded as longer marks than the main set of five digits marks. Last, notice that the marks for every number on the right side of the UPC code look different from the same number on the left side of the UPC code because of the odd or even parity issue.

The main callout here is that the guard marks for the UPC code are very similar to the right-hand mark corresponding to the number six. This can be seen in the image below, which highlights the guard marks and the right-hand mark for the number six.

9 - Highlight Guard Marks and Number Six

In the image shown, the #1 digit and the #3 mark correspond to represent the first digit of the 12-digit UPC number. Likewise, the #7 mark and the #9 digit represent the check-digit. Notice that the highlighted guard marks appear to be exact replicas of the highlighted right-side mark for the number six—they are spaced close together and they are two thin lines for each mark, exactly like the right-hand number six. Using this information, we can read the guard marks to represent the number 6-6-6. Accordingly, a mark that incorporates the number 6-6-6 within its code has been implemented for buying and selling merchandise. It is hidden, but it is there. How did John, who wrote the book of Revelation about AD 95, know that such a mark and represented number would be used for buying and selling during the End Times?

666 or 616

Some anti-Christians will try to discredit this prophecy by claiming that the original number was 616. However, an early church father called out this corruption, stating that *all* the known manuscripts with provenance from the disciples contained the number 666, rather than the number 616. This was addressed by the early church father Irenaeus in his manuscript *Against Heresies* written between AD 174 and 189.

I. Such, then, being the state of the case, and this number being found in all the most approved and ancient copies [of the Apocalypse], and those men who saw John face to face bearing their testimony [to it];

while reason also leads us to conclude that the number of the name of the beast, [if reckoned] according to the Greek mode of calculation by the [value of] the letters contained in it, will amount to six hundred and sixty and six; … I do not know how it is that some have erred following the ordinary mode of speech, and have vitiated the middle number in the name, deducting the amount of fifty from it, so that instead of six decads they will have it that there is but one. [*I am inclined to think that this occurred through the fault of the copyists*][3] [Emphasis added.]

So, Irenaeus states that all the "most approved and ancient" copies contained the number 666. This is in accordance with today's scientific standards of provenance. He then goes on to address the "616" discrepancy and ends with dismissing it as a likely copyist's error.

Block-Chain Digital Currency

Next, let us move on to the stipulation of "that no man might buy or sell" (Rev 13:17). Prior to the year 2000, this would be an impossible requirement to meet, as cash was king. What would prevent two individuals from conducting a transaction with cash? Nothing. However, a recent invention is block-chain digital currency. With this form of currency, the government could prevent anyone from conducting any financial transactions, unless both parties involved—individuals and institutions—were approved by the government. Thus, this invention provides the government with the means of control—who is authorized to buy and sell. Prior to this point, there would be no real means of such control. This is still in the implementation phase, but we all can see that it will be the future of all financial transactions.

Receiving the Mark

The final requirement of the prophecy is "he causeth all, both small and great, rich and poor, free and bond, to receive a mark in their right hand, or in their foreheads" (Revelation 13:16). The original means of verifying an electronic transaction was the signature of the person making the purchase. This was done by the person signing their name in cursive writing. However, there is now a trend away from learning how to write in cursive. So, vendors are going to look for a means to verify the purchaser is authorized to conclude the transaction. With the elimination of cursive writing, a unique code—like the 666 mark—is a possible replacement to today's need for a signature.

There is the problem of criminal activity, like drugs, identity theft, internet scams, and the issue of forgetting or losing your wallet. This same identifier could also carry other things as well, everything from your car insurance information, your health insurance information, your driver's license, and even miscellaneous things like photographs that you would like to review at a moment's notice. Imagine a world where everything you need from your wallet is contained by a mark, or possibly a Radio Frequency Identifier (RFID), containing the 666—all stored in a location that you could never leave behind, your hand. And, for those few individuals missing their right hand, the option of having the mark on the forehead would solve that problem as well. After all, you cannot leave your head behind.

666 Conclusion

Obviously, this prophecy has not yet been completely fulfilled at this time. But, with the move toward creating a mark with 666 encoded, more controlling and connected governments, the move to digital currencies, and the rise of internet, email, and phone scams, an encoded mark on the hand would be seen by many people to be a great improvement by most individuals in the world today. But, with these solutions comes the matter of control. What if the government decides that your religious views are heretical, and you are banned from all financial transactions. How would you be able to survive in today's interconnected world?

❖ Biblical Prophecy Conclusion

We have one part of a fulfilled prophecy, one part of a prophecy that is in process nearing fulfillment, and one part of a prophecy that is yet to be implemented but with all indications that it would be readily received by most people. These prophecies are much more detailed than any other alleged prophecies, like Nostradamus—the French astrologer in the 1500s. Nostradamus's prophesies are divided into 942 *quatrains*. Merriam-Webster defines quatrains as "a unit or group of four lines of verse."[4] How much detail can one provide in a mere four lines of verse for a prophecy? For those further interested in Nostradamus's prophesies, Ellie Crystal on *Crystalinks*[5] goes into more details of the prophecies of Nostradamus.

It appears that the entity that inspired the prophecies in the Bible knew what the future would hold, not just a vague and random guess of future events. Consequently, the Bible has been demonstrated to be inspired by an omniscient deity, who foretold the rebirth of Israel, the creation of the UPC code and the coming of digital currency. The last part of the prophecy is yet to be completed—the requirement of a mark, visible or not, upon a person's right hand or forehead in the event of a person missing their right hand. Yet, we can see the need for such a means of incontrovertible identification of a person, given the internet scams that steal people's money, impersonate other people, and other nefarious deeds conducted by criminals today. In addition, with a block-chain digital currency, any criminal financial transaction could be traced and reversed, providing relief to the person scammed. As follows, it can be readily expected that most people (*i.e.*, non-Christians) would fully embrace this last prophecy to prevent these criminal endeavors.

CHAPTER 20

CLASSICAL ARGUMENTS

There are five arguments that Christian Apologists have used historically to provide evidence of the biblical God. They were based upon the popular belief that logic and reason (aka rationalization) were the only things needed to determine true wisdom. These five arguments are known as the Cosmological Argument, the Teleological Argument, the Moral Argument, the Ontological Argument, and Pascal's Wager.

❖ Cosmological Argument

The Cosmological Argument is premised upon the belief that the spacetime universe had a beginning. It was first proposed by the ancient Greek philosopher Aristotle (384–322 BC) as the Unmoved Mover. Aristotle reasoned that if 1) every movement had a force initiating the movement, 2) that the mathematical concept of infinity is impossible, and 3) that our universe is moving, then the only logical conclusion is that our universe had an Unmoved Mover—something that existed before our universe was created that started all the movement that we see today. Christian apologist Thomas Aquinas (AD 1225–1274) stated it slightly different as the Uncaused Causer. It was also proposed by Islamic philosopher al-Ghazali (AD 1058–1111) as everything that has a beginning must have been caused and since the universe had a beginning, then there must be a Creator.

Nonetheless, this argument fails if one advocates that the universe did not have a beginning. Today, Naturalists are proposing scientific theories that postulate that the universe did not have a beginning. Some of these hypotheses include Hawking's string theory, the M-theory, and the multiverse theory.

Today's Christian should not be concerned about these new hypotheses because of two facts: 1) Scientific theories usually take 100 years or more before a consensus can be reached, and it becomes a scientific law, and 2) Finding empirical evidence for this non-beginning universe is near impossible because scientists can only observe and test in our own spacetime universe. This theory forces scientists to make observations in our universe and conclude things that are outside of our universe—leaving the probable outcome that other scientists will conduct testing and reach differing conclusions.

❖ Teleological Argument

The Teleological Argument looks at the intricate balance of life and the universe and attempts to answer the "Why so delicately balanced" question. It is known that the universe is in a delicate balance, and that even life on earth is in a delicate balance. If these delicate balances are modified in the least detail, then life as we know it ceases to exist. Hawking called out this delicate balance in his book *A Brief History of Time*.

> The remarkable fact is that the values of these numbers seem to have been very finely adjusted to make possible the development of life. For example, if the electric charge of the electron had been only slightly different, stars either would have been unable to burn hydrogen and helium, or else they would not have exploded. ... Nevertheless, it seems clear that there are relatively few ranges of values for the numbers that would allow the development of any form of intelligent life. Most sets of values would give rise to universes that, although they might have be very beautiful, would contain no one able to wonder at that beauty.

One can take this either as evidence of a divine purpose in Creation and the choice of laws of science or as support for the strong anthropic principle.[1] [Emphasis added]

The *anthropic principle* is defined by *Wikipedia* as "the hypothesis … that the range of possible observations that could be made about the universe is limited by the fact that observations could only happen in a universe capable of developing intelligent life in the first place."[2] As Hawking pointed out, one of the problems with this argument is akin to a Christian observing a two-story house-of-cards. Christians would conclude that only God could have created such a delicately balanced universe, while a Naturalist will be predisposed to reach the conclusion that this delicate balance is just a random chance event that must have occurred, else we would not be here to observe this balance. There is no objective way to reconcile this difference of opinions. Neither side will budge and both sides will remain convinced that their viewpoint is the correct viewpoint.

❖ Moral Argument

The Moral Argument recognizes that morals (like good vs. bad and beautiful vs. ugly) exist and attempts to answer the "How did morals develop" question. Christians argue that only humans have morals because God made us in His image, thus proving the existence of a Creator. However, there have been many attempts by Naturalists to show that animals have some sense of morals, too. They will point out incidents of a mother monkey dragging around her dead baby for three days because she *loves* her offspring. But to counter that, there have been some occurrences whereby the mother monkey has subsequently eaten her dead offspring. Another Naturalists' example is how a mother animal will often try to protect her offspring from predators. Yet, the mother will quickly give up her baby once the battle is lost. The Naturalist's response to these counterarguments is that animals do not have a big enough brain for a fully developed sense of morals. So, once again, the interpretation of the results will differ depending upon one's beliefs.

❖ Ontological Argument

The weakest rationalization argument is the Ontological Argument. It postulates that the idea of god exists, and that all ideas have some foundation. Hence, it attempts to answer the "Why do different societies all have an idea of god" question. Christian apologist Gaunilo of Marmoutier decisively addressed this argument in his work *On Behalf of the Fool*. He argued that one could imagine a perfect island. However, one could always imagine a bigger and more perfect island—until the whole earth was covered and the island could no longer be considered an island. Therefore, just because one can imagine a god, does not make a god possible.

❖ Pascal's Wager

Encyclopaedia Britannica covers the rationalization argument given by Blaise Pascal.[3] Pascal (1623–1662) postulated an argument that a person had two choices, atheism and God. If a person were to choose atheism, they would have a 50 percent chance of being right based upon the uncertainty of the future. The cost of investing in this system of belief would be finite (their life), its payout would be finite (their years on earth), and its expected return would be finite (whatever happiness they derived while living). Conversely, if a person were to choose God to place their faith in, they would have a 50 percent chance of being right, with a finite cost (their life), but that the potential payout would be infinite (eternity in heaven). Thus, the expected value of committing one's life to this system of beliefs would have an expected value of infinity. The table below demonstrates Pascal's Wager.

Bet	Chance	Cost	Payout	Expected Value
Atheism	50%	Finite	Finite	Finite
God	50%	Finite	Infinite	Infinite

10 - Pascal's Wager

Accordingly, Pascal's wager is showing that the smart choice would be to choose to follow God, as the cost is the same, but the payout is infinite reward. It is a strong argument, but it has the inherent flaw of all rationalization arguments.

❖ The Weakness of All the Classical Arguments

The major weakness of all these Classical Arguments is that they all strive to indicate that a god must exist, but they do not even attempt to prove the biblical God is that god. For this reason, the classical arguments (and most rationalization arguments) are inherently flawed.

❖ Classical Arguments Conclusion

The classical arguments are all rationalization arguments presented in the Age of Reasoning. They are inherently dependent upon a person's ability to reason. Individuals may find alternative solutions, like an endless existence to our universe by elements in our universe switching between alternative universes, and then being reborn in our universe. As a result, any conclusion reached is subject to the whims of the person doing the analysis. Worse, they never attempt to prove the existence of the biblical God, so any deity would satisfy their reasoning.

I believe that this fatal flaw is the reason that God uses empirical evidence in the Bible—to demonstrate that the messenger (*i.e.*, prophet or leader) was ordained by God to be His messenger. One can rationalize in many different directions, but empirical evidence can only be ignored or taken at face value.

CHAPTER 21

ISRAELITES IN EGYPT

T his topic delves more into a topic with limited support of empirical evidence, rather than established facts upon which all sides can agree—albeit there is some evidence to which all sides will agree. To complicate matters is the issue of the guesswork that establishes today's Egyptian chronology.

Many Christians will be confronted with the challenge from anti-Christians on the topic "There is no evidence of Israelites in Egypt nor evidence of their Exodus from Egypt, so the Bible cannot be trusted as authentic." This is the logic fallacy of *argument from ignorance*. *Wikipedia* defines the argument from ignorance as "that something is false if it has not yet been proved true."[1] The lack of evidence is just that—the lack of evidence. It doesn't support either side of the debate. Second, there is some evidence of the Israelites in Egypt, and their entrance into the Promised Land. The problem is that the available evidence is open to interpretation and debate. Since the purpose of this book is to provide all the evidence, and let the reader reach their own conclusions, this issue must be addressed. Before beginning this endeavor, a foundational understanding of the issues, terms, and such must be established. Since new Christians (and, in fact, many Christians) lack a basic understanding of biblical history, Biblical chronology needs to be addressed first.

❖ Biblical History Overview

Even though the Egyptian chronology is known to be inadequate, it will be used to some degree to help the reader get a grasp on the overall biblical history. Second, there is the problem with placing dates for certain events like the Babylon Captivity. The events were not a one-and-done issue. The Babylon Captivity was a war that spanned several decades, and there is still debate when those years occurred. Usually, most scholars agree within a few years, so the overview will still be helpful to some.

Biblical history can be viewed as several broad eras. The first is the *pre-patriarchal period*, which is the period between Adam and Abram (later renamed Abraham). This spanned from circa 4150 to 2090 BC.

Next was the *patriarchal period* (circa 2090 to 1526 BC), which included Abraham, Isaac, and Jacob (later renamed Israel). During Jacob/Israel's last days on earth, his family traveled to Egypt due to a famine in the land. One of Jacob's sons was Joseph. With Joseph's foresight, Egypt was prepared for this famine. Israel's family was in Egypt for a total of 430 years (Exodus 12:40), of which 400 of those years were in captivity (Genesis 15:13). Most of the years of the Hebrews in Egypt are not recorded in any book of the Bible. The only record of the Hebrews in Egypt comes right at the end of the book of Genesis, when Jacob/Israel entered Egypt and the beginning of the book of Exodus with the birth of Moses. Thus, it could be argued that the patriarchal period ended with Jacob's death. The book of Genesis covers from Creation (i.e., pre-patriarchal period) to the patriarchal period, although most biblical scholars believe that the book of Job also was written during the patriarchal period.

Next is the era of the *judges*, lasting from circa 1526 to 1020 BC. Exodus begins in 1526 BC with the birth of Moses—although Moses was the first judge, he is often set apart from the other judges. The period of the judges is characterized by an individual selected by God to lead His people while that individual lived, and later God would select another individual to lead. It encompasses the birth of Moses, and the confrontation with the Pharoah of Egypt when Moses was eighty years old (Exodus 7:7), which triggered the eventual Exodus in 1446 BC, based upon the calculations from *BibleArchaeology.org*.[2] Under Moses's leadership, the Israelites wandered in the desert of the Sinai for forty years, because of Moses's disobedience of God. After Moses passed away and the Israelites entered the Promised Land in 1406 BC, it then transitions to the commonly recognized period of the judges, which were God-appointed leaders for Israel. There were many judges, including Deborah, Samson, and Samuel. This era ended in 1020 BC when King Saul ascended to be king over Israel.[3] This era includes the books of Exodus, Leviticus, Numbers, Deuteronomy, Joshua, Judges, and the early parts of Samuel.

Next is the era of the kings of Israel, which are divided into two smaller sub-eras. The first sub-era was the united kingdom (spanning Saul, David, and Solomon from circa 1020 to 931 BC), while the second sub-era was the divided kingdom (931 to 586 BC).[4] The books covering the united kingdom are Samuel (later split into First Samuel and Second Samuel) and the early parts of Kings (later split into First Kings and Second Kings), ending with the death of Solomon in I Kings 11:42–43.

After Solomon, the nation of Israel became two separate kingdoms, with each side arguing over who was the designated king appointed by God. These two nations became known as the southern kingdom—Judea—with its capital in Jerusalem, and the northern kingdom—Israel—with its capital in Samaria. The southern kingdom was comprised of the tribes of Judah and Simeon, while the northern kingdom was comprised of the rest of the original Israelite tribes. The tribe of Levi is not included in either kingdom, as it became the priesthood during the forty-years of wandering in the wilderness under Moses (Exodus 32:26, Numbers 1:47–50). The book of Kings (later split into First Kings and Second Kings), starting in First Kings 12:1, records the history of the divided kingdom.

Some key events during the divided kingdom occurred that further characterized this period. The first is known as the Assyrian Captivity,[5] where the conquest of the northern kingdom began in 740 BC and ended in 722 BC with the capture of Israel's capital of Samaria. This conquest was allowed by God because the northern nation had rejected God as their God, transferring their worship to the gods of the Canaanites. Its people were dispersed throughout Assyria's kingdom, and the ten northern tribes ceased to exist after this point in history.

The southern kingdom, Judea—whose inhabitants were known as

Judeans or Jews for short—survived until 586 BC, although some of those years were during the Babylonian Captivity period.[6] Like its fellow tribes, Judea began rejecting God, so God eventually allowed Babylon to conquer them. The Babylonian captivity began in 605 BC, when the first Jews were deported to Babylon. Judea sporadically rebelled against the Babylonians, until Babylon decided to end their rebellion in 586 BC, conquering Jerusalem and carting its leaders into captivity. Approximately seventy years after the initial attack in 605 BC, Judeans were freed to return to their land of Judea sometime after Cyrus, the Persian king, conquered the Babylonians in 539 BC.[7] The Persian conquest of the Babylonians can be established to the date of 539 BC. However, we do not know how long after this conquest that the Jews were permitted to return to their lands. If the prophesied seventy years was strictly followed, then their return would have been in 535 BC.

Afterward, the Jews remained a captive city-state under the umbrella of different kingdoms—Persia, Greece and subsequently Rome. Rebellion against Rome finally prompted the Roman Empire to irradicate the nation of Judea in AD 123, renaming it Palestine.

A key detail is that during the patriarchal period, the book of Genesis refers to God's people as Hebrews. After the Exodus, the Bible refers to God's people as either Israelites or Judeans (shortened to Jews), depending upon the context. So, why are these two different terms (Hebrew or Israelite) used in the Bible to refer to the same group of people?

❖ Documents Containing the Phonetic "Hebrew" Word

According to *Encyclopaedia Britannica*, one of the earliest writing on earth is known as Akkadian language text, one of the writing systems of ancient Mesopotamia.[8] This writing is similar but different to Egyptian hieroglyphs. It was written on clay tablets—cuneiform tablets.

There are four sources of ancient texts on cuneiform tablets that are pertinent to this section, the Mari texts, the Ugaritic texts, the Hittite texts, and the Amarna Letters. They were found in today's Middle East and Egypt. They were all written during the biblical patriarchal period.

And they all contain an Akkadian word that has been loosely translated as Hebrew, with scholars on both sides of the issue debating their significance. There is some validity to this objection because (even if the translation is accepted) the word most likely did not just refer to God's People, but rather to all nomadic people in the area. This Akkadian word has been translated as *Habiru, Apiruma, Apiru, Hapiri,* and *Apiri.* All the variations of the word depended upon the ultimate language into which the Akkadian text was translated.

Mari Texts, found in Tell Hariri Syria, texts contain about 15,000 cuneiform tablets. They are written in the Akkadian language and contain references to Habiru. Further details about the Mari Texts can be found at *Encyclopaedia Judaica.*[9]

The Ugaritic texts were also found in Syria. They are cuneiform texts discovered in Ugarit (Ras Shamra) and Ras Ibn Hani. They contain approximately 1,500 cuneiform tablets and fragments. The official correspondence is written in the Akkadian language (approximately one hundred letters found), but many of the other tablets are in different languages, such as Sumerian and Hurrian cuneiform languages, Phoenician script, as well as Egyptian and Luwian hieroglyphs. They frequently reference a people-group called apiruma. Further details about the Ugaritic Texts can be found at *BiblicalTraining.org.*[10]

Some of the Hittite texts contain the official Akkadian language, as well as syllabic writing of Hittite words and Sumerograms—a long extinct language that is not related to any known language. These texts were discovered in modern day Turkey in the late 1800s but were not identified as belonging to the Hittite Empire until 1915. They also have a people-group called the Habiru. Further information about these texts can be found at *encyclopedia.com.*[11]

The Amarna Letters were found in Thebes, the ancient capital of Egypt. They were found by accident in 1887. They were written using Akkadian cuneiform logograms from Canaanite city-state rulers to the Pharoah in Egypt, usually asking for help. These rulers were from the outer reaches of the Egyptian Empire, from southern Syria and Canaan—today's modern Syria, Israel, and Gaza strip. They frequently reference a people-group called apiru. Further details about the Amarna Letters can be found at *BiblicalTraining.org.*[12]

Hebrew / Habiru Connection

All four of these sources complained to the Egyptian Pharoah about nomadic people groups committing acts of aggression against them. They utilized various spellings of the Akkadian designation for the nomads. These spellings all differ based upon the language used to interpret them. They are SA.GAZ (the Akkadian script), Habiru, Hapiri, Apiru, and Apiri, as per *BiblicalTraining.org.*[13] Many Bible scholars have pointed out the phonetics between these names and the biblical name of Hebrew.

During the time of the patriarchs, God's people were nomadic, traveling around with their sheep and goats. Furthermore, Abraham was described in a raider or war type of situation when he went with his men to rescue his cousin, Lot (Genesis 14:13–16). And there are other examples in the Bible (like Esau meeting Jacob on his return, Genesis 33:1). So, it is quite conceivable that the patriarchs would have been considered nomadic warrior groups by the established city-state rulers, and thus referred to as Habiru.

These texts also call out that some of these Habiru were friendly to the city-state rulers. Again, this fits with the biblical narrative as the biblical Hebrews were on friendly terms with the city-state rulers. Abraham, and the other patriarchs, were usually on friendly terms with the rulers of the neighboring city-states. The only time they appear in the Bible as being hostile is when they were attacked by other groups of people, like when Abraham rescued his cousin Lot (Genesis 14:13–16) and Jacob's sons getting revenge upon the defilement of Dinah (Genesis 34:13–29). As shown, there is the similarity of the name, the similarity of the description, and the period all align with the calling of God's people as Hebrews. However, it must also be noted that there were other groups of people that would also fit that description. For this reason, it is likely that the term Hebrew was more descriptive of the lifestyle, rather than the name of a people-group like the name of Israelite.

❖ Israelites

God's people became known as Israelites after they left the Egyptian Captivity around 1446 BC during the exodus of Egypt. Prior to that point in history, they were referred to as Hebrews. The Israelites are recorded as leaving Egypt and then wandering in the wilderness for forty years before entering the Promised Land about 1406 BC. This was long after Jacob (renamed to Israel) had died in the land of Egypt.

It is well known that there are twelve tribes of Israelites, one for each son born to Israel. What may be less known is that there were some changes in the twelve tribal names. For example, during the wandering in the wilderness after the Exodus, the tribe of Levi was renamed to a priesthood and was not assigned territory in the Promised Land (Joshua 13:33). Before Israel passed, Israel bestowed sonship to Joseph's two children born to an Egyptian woman (Genesis 48:16), giving these children a part of the inheritance in the Promised Land. These sons were named Manasseh and Ephraim, thus bringing the total tribes with land allocated in the Promised Land to twelve tribes (i.e., Levi and Joseph were removed, but Manasseh and Ephraim were added). The allocation of the Promised Lands to the twelve tribes is detailed in Joshua 15-19. So, are there twelve tribes or thirteen tribes? While Joseph's inheritance was passed on through his sons, he wouldn't be counted twice—once for himself and again through his sons. And are the people of Levi still considered to be a tribe? You need to decide this question, but in the end, it does not matter. They are all called Israelites and are part of God's Chosen People.

Almost all (if not all) historians acknowledge that the first mention of Israel was during the time of the Judges on what is known as the Merneptah Stele. The stele (a black granite stone monument with engravings detailing historical events) was discovered in Thebes, Egypt in 1896. The record is quite long, so only the pertinent part will be displayed here. Two quick callouts need to be made: 1) Some of the places are identified with a hieroglyph representing a city-state, but Israel is only identified with the hieroglyph representing a foreign people-group—i.e., not organized under a king, and 2) Israel's name in the stele is transliterated as "Isirar," but a consensus has been reached by both Egyptian and biblical scholars that the name represents the people of Israel. Here is the translation of the stele from *Expedition Bible*.

> Canaan is plundered with every evil;
> Ashkelon (city symbol) is conquered;
> Gezer (city symbol) is seized;
> Yanokam (city symbol) is made non-existent;
> Isirar *[Israel]* (foreign people group symbol) is laid waste,
> his seed is not.[14] [Emphasis added for clarification that
> Isirar is universally recognized as referring to Israel.]

Consequently, there is an extra-biblical source that identifies Israel as a group of people that is consistent with the biblical chronology in the first six books of the Old Testament. During this time, the Israelites did not have a king, nor did they have a capital. There are also later extra-biblical sources that mention the "nation of Israel", but those do not occur prior to the period of the united kingdom under Saul, David, and Solomon.

❖ Israelites in Egypt Conclusion

So, there is empirical evidence from Egypt that Israelites were in the land of Egypt. They were referred to as Hebrews (*i.e.*, a nomadic people-group) until they left Egypt and became known as a people-group named after their ancestor (*i.e.*, Israel). This occurred during the time of the Judges—*i.e.*, after the Exodus. At that time, they were a force to be reckoned with, but they had no established cities or king to lead them. Only after King Saul was anointed king of Israel did the Israelites become a city-state kingdom.

CHAPTER 22

DEFINING THE BIBLE
(CANON)

There is plenty of empirical evidence to support a Christian worldview, with the acknowledged extant records dating back thousands of years ago, historical accuracy, scientific accuracy, and the fulfillment of prophecy—although some of that is occurring before our eyes. To counter this evidence, many anti-Christians will attempt to sidetrack a person's faith in Christianity with various attacks. This chapter will address how the Bible was formed.

❖ Defining the Canon of the Bible

Anti-Christians will point out that many books were left out of the Bible because they did not conform to the ideologies of the early Christians. On the surface, this is true. But the fact that some books were left out of the Bible leads to the erroneous conclusion that authentic books were left out of the Bible. The validity of authenticity issue hinges on the widely accepted scientific concept of *provenance*. Collins English Dictionary defines this term as the "provenance of something is the place that it comes from or that it originally came from."[1]

Experts, whether academic scholars, archeologists, or other scientists, rely upon being able to prove any evidence presented to them. For historical evidence, it means that the experts must be able to prove the source of that evidence before accepting it as authentic evidence. The archeological field is rife with phony evidence that claims to be ancient, so that the phony evidence can be sold at a higher price. Likewise, biblical scholars must contend with safeguarding the authentic works from falsehood.

An example from Genesis will be used to demonstrate the importance of this issue, and how even a *minor* change can have dramatic impact on history. When Adam and Eve were in the Garden of Eden, God gave a commandment to not eat from the tree of knowledge of good and evil. Satan took this simple commandment and used people's inclination to add to the basic command to further protect themselves from inadvertently violating that command. Let us compare the two versions of this commandment. God's commandment was, "But of the tree of the knowledge of good and evil, thou *shalt not eat of it*: for in the day that thou eatest thereof thou shalt surely die" (Genesis 2:17, KJV). Meanwhile, Adam and Eve expanded upon that commandment to "But of the fruit of the tree which is in the midst of the garden, God hath said, Ye shall not eat of it, *neither shall ye touch it*, lest ye die" (Genesis 3:3, KJV).

Notice that Adam and Eve had added to God's prohibition of *eating* the fruit with an additional requirement of *nor touching* the fruit. Imagine being Adam or Eve, and you hear the command not to eat fruit. Isn't it logical that it be safer to add the additional prohibition of not touching it either? Then when Eve was tempted by the serpent, she reached out and touched it, and found that she did not die. Note that Adam stood next to her and did nothing to hinder her from her course of action, so he was equally guilty (*i.e.*, he was in complete agreement with Eve's actions). For this reason, it seemed reasonable to conclude that God's prohibition of eating nor touching would not lead to death. Consequently, the path to sin began. As the cliché states, one rotten apple spoils the barrel. This demonstrates the importance of sticking to exactly what God's Word states, without any additions to His commandments. So, how does this apply to which books were left out of the Bible?

Biblical Canon

Early New Testament church fathers were careful to keep a record of all the authentic manuscripts, *i.e.*, those known to have come from the author of the manuscript who had direct interaction with Jesus. This record is known as a *canon* (not the same as cannon, the large caliber gun). "[T]he term canon can be traced to the ancient Greeks, who used it in a literal sense: a kanon was a rod, ruler, staff, or measuring rod."[2] But what makes a book canonical? Norman L. Geisler and William E. Nix addresses this problem in their book *A General Introduction to the Bible, Rev. and expanded.*

> Underlying all the insufficient views of what determined canonicity is the failure to distinguish between determination and recognition of canonicity. ... Canonicity is determined by God. Actually, a canonical book is valuable and true because God inspired it. ... Canonicity is recognized by men of God. Inspiration determines canonicity. If a book was authoritative, it was so because God breathed it and made it so. How a book received authority, then, is determined by God. How men recognize that authority is another matter altogether.[3]

Norman L. Geisler and William E. Nix identify five criteria for determining whether a manuscript was included in the biblical canon in their book *A General Introduction to the Bible, Rev. and expanded,* for both the Old Testament and the New Testament. These were 1) "Was the book written by a prophet of God?"[4], 2) "Was the writer confirmed by acts of God?"[5], 3) "Did the message tell the truth about God?"[6], 4) "Does it come with the power of God?"[7], and 5) "Was it accepted by the people of God?"[8]

Universally, the Old Testament canon was determined by the Jewish leaders before the time of Jesus. But the New Testament was developed in the years after Jesus's crucifixion, as a church father received a copy of a manuscript that came from a recognized apostle or disciple of Jesus. However, not all early church fathers had the same set of manuscripts, so each father kept their own record of authentic manuscripts, along with a copy of the manuscript itself. However, there were challenges to keeping a manuscript that was deemed a threat to the Roman Empire.

"As late as 302/3 the Emperor Diocletian had decreed that all copies of the [New Testament] Scriptures be destroyed and those people having them in their possession be punished (often unto death)."[9] However, once Christianity became the de facto official religion of the Roman Empire during the fourth century (AD 301–400), an effort was made to collect these various canons into a single approved canon. This was started in the First Council of Nicaea in AD 325 and ended in AD 367, according to *Biblica, Inc.*[10]

> Within the New Testament itself may be seen the process of selecting and reading the prophetic and apostolic writings that were then being circulated, collected, and even quoted in other inspired writings. In support of this view of canonization, the apostolic Fathers may be cited as referring to all of the New Testament books within about a century of the time they were written. Individuals, translations, and canons show that all but a very few books were generally recognized as canonical before the end of the second century. During the next two centuries the controversy over those Antilegomena books gradually erased all doubts, and there was a final and official recognition of all twenty-seven books of the New Testament by the church universal.[11]

The term antilegomena is defined by *Merriam-Webster* as "the books of the New Testament whose canonicity was for a time in dispute."[12] This final canon, called the protocanonical or first canon, gives us what we recognize today as the Old Testament and the New Testament books of the Bible. But, what about the other books considered by the many council meetings? These other books are split into two groups, Old Testament era books and New Testament era books. Some of the Old Testament books were later deemed the Deuterocanonical books. All these books were originally deemed as *apocrypha*. *Merriam-Webster* defines apocrypha as "writings or statements of dubious authenticity."[13]

❖ Deuterocanonical Books

One of the first tasks of the many councils on the Bible was to identify which manuscripts belonged in the Bible. Another task was the translation of the manuscripts from their original language to the language in use at that time by the Roman Empire—Latin. The most notable translator was Jerome or St. Jerome.

St. Jerome also translated fifteen other manuscripts into Latin, including some books that he deemed to be apocryphal writings. He considered these as "books of the church," rather than "divinely inspired books." These books were written between about 400 BC and the birth of Jesus about 4 BC, so they are called Old Testament apocrypha books.[14] There were three reasons to doubt their authenticity. 1) The Jewish religious leaders dismiss them from their version of the canon, 2) They do not display any evidence of divine inspiration, like prophecy, and 3) They contained known historical inaccuracies.

For example, the book of Judith says that Nebuchadnezzar was king of the Assyrians, when he was actually a Babylonian king. "It was the twelfth year of the reign of Nebuchadnezzar, who ruled over the Assyrians in the great city of Nineveh. In those days Arphaxad ruled over the Medes in Ecbatana." (Judith 1:1, NRSV).

Another error is found in the Letter of Jeremiah, saying "Therefore when you have come to Babylon you will remain there for many years, for a long time, up to seven generations; after that I will bring you away from there in peace." (Letter of Jeremiah 6:3, NRSV). But when compared to the book of Daniel, the time span is recorded as seventy years. Daniel states "in the first year of his reign I, Daniel, understood by the books the number of the years specified by the word of the LORD through Jeremiah the prophet, that He would accomplish seventy years in the desolations of Jerusalem." (Daniel 9:2, NKJV). Seven generations would equate to 210 years of captivity, whereas it is widely recognized that the Israelites were released approximately seventy years after their captivity. So, the Letter of Jeremiah states a historically inaccurate span of captivity for the Israelites. Some may counterargue that the Letter of Jeremiah stated that their captivity could be "up to seven generations," not that it would be 210 years. The problem with that counterargument is that it assumes that God would vastly overstate a time span, "just to be on the safe side", which is unbecoming of an omniscient entity as an omniscient being who would know the exact number of years they were in captivity.

Seven of these books had their status changed in AD 1546 during the Council of Trent by the Catholic Church, which deemed them to be *deuterocanonical*—meaning second canon—books. However, other churches consider twelve of these Old Testament apocrypha books as deuterocanonical. The Protestant branch of Christianity split from both decisions and has rejected all fifteen of these books as divinely inspired. Likewise, the Jewish rabbis do not accept any of these books as being divinely inspired writings. The question remains, why did it take the Catholic Church twelve hundred years to reverse their prior decision that they were merely church writings, and not divinely inspired writings? What did they base this decision upon?

❖ Apocrypha Books

Apocrypha books fall into two categories—Old Testament apocrypha and New Testament apocrypha. There were fifteen Old Testament books that were considered apocrypha, twelve of which were subsequently changed to the status of deuterocanonical books by some churches. The three remaining books have remained out of any church canon.[15]

There are more than one hundred apocrypha from after the New Testament era. They are considered New Testament apocrypha because all of them were most likely to be written more than one hundred years after Jesus's time on the earth. They were all determined to be faked books trying to be passed off as authentic writings by one or more of the original disciples of Jesus. One of the most famous of these books is called the Gospel of Thomas. It will be used to demonstrate how and why the other apocrypha books were excluded from the final Bible.

Gospel of Thomas

The Gospel of Thomas is a collection of 114 sayings ascribed to Jesus. Many of the sayings parallel the Synoptic Gospels (*i.e.*, Matthew, Mark, and Luke). According to *Encyclopedia Britannica*, "The Gospel of Thomas is grounded in gnosticism, the philosophical and religious movement of the 2nd century CE that stressed the redemptive power of esoteric knowledge acquired by divine revelation."[16] It also contains illogical statements, like "the lion will become human" in saying number 7.2.[17] So, the Gospel of

Thomas is the mixture of truth (stolen from the Synoptic Gospels) and falsehood that is often used by Satan to deceive God's followers.

Most scholars date the Gospel of Thomas to the mid-second century. The earliest extant manuscript, written in Greek, is a few fragments of the gospel. It is dated between AD 132 to 200,[18] so it would have been written over a century after the death of Jesus. A nearly complete manuscript is dated to the late AD 300s. The four Gospels (Matthew, Mark, Luke, and John) were first canonized in AD 130 by an early church father, but the Gospel of Thomas was never canonized by any church father. The earliest mention of The Gospel of Thomas is found in *The Refutation of All Heresies* written by an early church father named Hippolytus between AD 222 to 235.[19] Hippolytus rejected the manuscript as heretical teachings, mixing Jesus's teachings with the Egyptian religious belief in Isis.

The priests, then, and champions of the system, have been first those who have been called Naasseni . . . they have styled themselves Gnostics, alleging that they alone have sounded the depths of knowledge.

CHAP. II.--NAASSENI ASCRIBE THEIR SYSTEM, THROUGH MARIAMNE, TO JAMES THE LORD'S BROTHER; . . .

This, however, is not (the teaching) of Christ . . . They assert, then, that the Egyptians, who after the Phrygians, it is established, are of greater antiquity than all mankind, and who confessedly were the first to proclaim to all the rest of men the rites and orgies of, at the same time, all the gods, as well as the species and energies (of things), have the sacred and august, and for those who are not initiated, unspeakable mysteries of Isis.[20] [emphasis added].

So, the Gospel of Thomas was apparently written by the Gnostics in the mid-to-late second century, which was well after the disciple named Thomas died. Thus, the provenance for the Gospel of Thomas was found to be too long after the crucifixion of Jesus to be considered authentic and is in part of the teaching of the Gnostics. The Gnostics are a widely recognized group of people who mixed various religions together to justify their leaning toward human pleasures. Consequently, it was categorized in a matter of decades as a fake manuscript by an early church father.

Often, phony gospels would be assigned to one of the disciples' names to increase the phony gospel's acceptance as authentic. So, early church fathers would call them out as heretical teachings as soon as they first found out about them. This was the core process by which the New Testament apocrypha books were rejected from inclusion within the biblical canon before the biblical canon was officially established.

❖ Genesis Authorship

Many people widely recognize Moses (circa 1446 BC) wrote the book of Genesis. This is both true, yet still misleading. Genesis is written in the Hebrew language, yet the Hebrew language was not the first language on earth. So, there is an apparent discrepancy in who authored the book of Genesis. Adding to this mystery is the fact that some mediums for writing were of very limited duration, as it would break down with use and over time, often in less than one hundred years. Stone and cuneiform could survive for a much longer time span. Couple this issue with the empirical fact that the earliest extant manuscript of any biblical book was about 200 BC, and one readily sees a very big gap to fill between these two dates.

Genesis Tablet Theory

Early researchers of this dilemma proposed that the Bible was orally handed down for generations and only recorded in either 1446 BC by Moses or much later, around 800 BC. Yet, no empirical evidence, neither internally nor externally, supports this viewpoint. Rather, the internal evidence supports a different theory, namely that Moses merely translated other written documents into the book of Genesis into the Hebrew language from then existing historical tablets (most likely in the Akkadian language as that was the language for official government business during that period). This viewpoint explains many oddities found in the book of Genesis.

A casual reader of Genesis will not realize that there are separations within the book of Genesis. But these separations provide the empirical evidence to conclude that the book was written by people living at the time of the events, and subsequently translated by Moses into a single book, most likely translating them from the Akkadian language into the Hebrew language. Let us look at these twelve separation points.[21]

1. In the beginning God created the heaven and the earth. (Genesis 1:1, KJV)

2. These are the generations of the heavens and of the earth (Genesis 2:4a, KJV)

3. This is the *book* of the generations of Adam (Genesis 5:1a, KJV) [Emphasis added]

4. These are the generations of Noah (Genesis 6:9a, KJV)

5. Now these are the generations of the sons of Noah, Shem, Ham, and Japheth (Genesis 10:1a, KJV)

6. These are the generations of Shem (Genesis 11:10a, KJV)

7. Now these are the generations of Terah. (Genesis 11:27a, KJV)

8. Now these are the *generations of Ishmael*, Abraham's son (Genesis 25:12a, KJV) [Emphasis added].

9. And these are the generations of Isaac, Abraham's son (Genesis 25:19a, KJV)

10. Now these are the *generations of Esau*, who is Edom. (Genesis 36:1, KJV) [Emphasis added]

11. And these are the *generations of Esau* (Genesis 36:9a, KJV) [Emphasis added]

12. These are the generations of Jacob. (Genesis 37:2a, KJV)

Note that almost all these separation points state something like "these are the generations of." Generations give the historical lineages of the person writing the document. This gives some limited evidence that they were written records (*i.e.*, cuneiform tablets), rather than oral traditions.

We all know that Adam could not have witnessed the creation of the universe, as he was created after everything else was created. So, this would mean that this had to be a story that was passed on to him, rather than him being an eyewitness. However, there are two accounts of Creation, each of them slightly different. Why are there two differing accounts? In my opinion, the first account was told from God's perspective, while the second account was told from Adam's perspective. Adam's perspective would, necessarily, minimize the parts that he did not personally witness, while focusing on the parts that he *did* witness. Adam only put the parts of Creation that were pertinent to his version of the event, while God's perspective would be more holistic.

Adam's Account

The first thing that stands out in Genesis 5:1 is that it specifically states that it is a *book* of generations. Why is the term book so important, yet it is only called out one time? Before we delve into this issue, let us seek the Hebrew words and their meanings before continuing.

The Hebrew word translated to the English word generation is defined by the *Enhanced Strong's Lexicon* as "תּוֹלְדוֹת [tolâdah /to·led·aw/] I descendants, results, proceedings, generations, genealogies. IA account of men and their descendants. IAI genealogical list of one's descendants."[22] So, loosely translated, the Hebrew word "tolâdah" means an account of one's life and descendants. Next, we look at the Hebrew word that is translated to the English word book which is translated by the *Enhanced Strong's Lexicon* as "הַתְפֹס, רְפָס, רְפָס [cepher, ciphrah /say·fer/] I book. 2 missive, document, writing, book."[23] So, the Hebrew word for book is a written document. Thus, Genesis 5:1 clearly states that it is a written record, rather than an oral history passed down through time. But could Adam write?

According to experts, the earliest writing began about 5,500 years ago. Joshua Mark, writing for *World History Encyclopedia* addresses this issue, stating that "Written language, however, does not emerge until its invention in Sumer, southern Mesopotamia, c. 3500–3000 BCE. This early writing was called cuneiform and consisted of making specific marks in wet clay with a reed implement."[24]

Assuming the earth, and Adam, was created approximately six thousand years ago, and that Adam lived 930 years (Gen 5:5), then Adam lived between 4000 to 3070 BC. These years would need to be adjusted by about 140 years because the calculated biblical age of the earth is 6,140 years, but that issue will be covered in the next section. Regardless of the dates used, Adam would have been alive when writing was invented. But why does the first tablet (*i.e.*, a separation point) state that Adam's genealogy was a written record, while all the other records do not? We have all had the experience of buying new technology during our lives. One of the first things people do with recent technology is to brag about it. However, once it is considered old technology, then people quit calling it out. The same would likely be true during Adam's era. He would have bragged about his new-found technology, but his predecessors would have considered it old technology, and would not have mentioned it.

Other Oddities of the Accounts

There are two mystifying issues with the account of Esau. The first issue is that Esau's account has two beginnings—one in Genesis 36:1 and another one, with a slightly different beginning, in Genesis 36:9. This issue could be explained with thoughtful consideration over the issue. Over time, it is quite possible to lose an important document. So, you would restart that document so that you do not lose your history, and then you find the original document. This appears to be the case for Esau. And since Moses had two separate tablets for Esau—he would not have just discarded one— he would include both in his compilation of the "beginnings," which is what the term genesis means.

The other mystifying issue is due to the inclusion of Esau's history in Genesis for any reason. If one were to look at the various accounts written down in Genesis, every person's lineage is a direct trace from Adam through to Israel—except for Esau and Ishmael. So almost every record would be needed to trace the Messiah's lineage from Jospeh and Mary, back to Adam and Eve. But, Esau's lineage, his entire history, is a dead-end branch that makes no sense to include in the writing of Genesis—unless one concludes that Moses recorded Esau's account simply because he was translating all the recorded lineages that he had in his possession.

This same point could be made about the lineage of Ishmael in Genesis 25:12. Why include them in the first place, if their lineage had either ceased to exist or was nearly extinct in 800 BC? It still could be argued that Moses wrote them down around 1446 BC, as they still existed in the 1400s BC, but why include them at all if they were cut off from the lineage to the Messiah (*i.e.,* Jacob/Israel)? There were thousands of dead branches that split off from the link between Adam and Jacob/Israel, so why include these two and not the others?

The last oddity in Genesis is the length of the account of Jacob. Most of the accounts contained within Genesis are short accounts, spanning five chapters or less. The one exception is the account of Jacob (Israel), which spans thirteen chapters in Genesis (37–50). Why is this account so much longer? In my opinion, it was written on a different medium, possibly sheepskin. The other accounts would fit within the size of a cuneiform tablet's typical size of smaller than today's typical sheet of paper—8.5 x 11 inches. But Jacob's account would need multiple tablets or be on a different medium.

Genesis Authorship Conclusion

If nothing more than oral traditions were passed down to Moses, we should not see these oddities. They should be all uniform, stating something to the effect of "these are the generations of" and only a single version for each person and only for those individuals needed to trace the lineage of the coming Messiah. Yet, we do not see this happening. Thus, I believe that the only possible conclusion that explains these identified issues is the Genesis Tablet theory—which holds that Moses compiled and translated twelve then-extant tablets (and one possible sheepskin) into the book Genesis and that the tablets he used did not survive to the modern era. Furthermore, I believe that Moses would have translated other tablets if he had access to them, but since he did not have them, they do not appear in the book the beginnings—*i.e.,* Genesis.

❖ Biblical Age of the Earth

Dating Artifacts

The age of a fossil, manuscript, paleoarcheology, or other artifact is assigned by one of three methods. The first method is based upon a written historical record. For example, we know from the written record when George Washington lived, died, and was the president of the United States. Other methods fall into the so-called scientific category. These include radiometric dating, which has been shown to be fallible, *dendrochronology* (*i.e.*, counting tree rings, with each set of rings indicating a summer/winter passage of time), and some other methods. Some of these scientific methods are dependable, while others seem to be little more than guesses. Sometimes, the assigned date is a mix between one of the two categories and is a *guestimate* (*i.e.*, a calculated guess). Anytime guesswork is included, the reliability is questionable.

6000-Years of Biblical History

Naturalists dismiss the validity of the written record of the Bible, claiming that its "6000-year history" has been falsified by science. Where did this 6000-year history assignment come from in the first place? A Bible scholar calculated the 6000-years back in the late 1800s. A casual reading of the Bible does not appear to support this conclusion. But careful reading, combined with other written historical records in the known chronology, does support this approximate date. The most important of the written historical records is Egyptian chronology—which is confusing when one gets into the details.

Egyptian Chronology and Its Problems

Manetho's List: The primary source that archeologists use for basing the Egyptian chronology is the history from Manetho's work *Aegyptiaca* (History of Egypt). Manetho was an Egyptian priest who lived around 200 BC.[25] There are several salient points all Egyptian experts acknowledge. 1) Manetho's original list has not survived to modern times, 2) His list was used and abused by other scholars in a rivalry to prove which civilization was the oldest—Egyptian, Greek, or Jewish, 3) His list also included legends and fanciful stories, 4) His list is contradictory with extant Egyptian artifacts that were contemporaneous with the events that they recorded, like those found within the tombs of the Pharaohs, 5) The further back in time from

Manetho's time, the less accuracy of the history recorded, 6) Many Egyptian scholars acknowledge the need to revise the Egyptian chronology, but they are at odds with how to accomplish it accurately.

Manetho's list only records the Pharaohs' names and the number of years that they reigned. Despite its many flaws, Manetho's list is the only comprehensive record of Egyptian chronology, so scholars use it as a foundation for every published Egyptian chronology and then try to link all other historical records to that Egyptian chronology. Another critical point about Egyptian chronology is that none of the extant contemporary Egyptian archeological evidence, including those found in the various tombs of the Pharaohs, can be completely reconciled with any other extant archeological record—including Manetho's list. Some names appear in multiple contemporary lists and Manetho's list, but they often skip over many other names found in Manetho's list and even in other contemporary tomb lists.

Egypt's Genealogy: Another problem with Egyptian chronology is that Egypt is named in the Bible as a son of Ham, the son of Noah. Although the name does not look the same, the *Enhanced Strong's Lexicon* translates the same Hebrew word as the English names "Mizraim" and "Egypt"— "מִצְרַיִם [mits·rah·yim]. AV [Authorized Version aka: King James Version] translates as "Egypt" 586 times, "Egyptian" 90 times, "Mizraim" four times, and "Egyptians + 1121" once. I a country at the northeastern section of Africa, adjacent to Palestine, and through which the Nile flows adj Egyptians = "double straits". 2 the inhabitants or natives of Egypt."[26]

On that account, this Hebrew word is only translated by today's Bible versions four times as Mizraim, but all the other times it is translated as Egypt. This is important because Mizraim is listed in the Bible as the son of Ham, who is the son of Noah (Genesis 10:1, Genesis 10:6). So, if Egypt was the grandson of Noah, then Mizraim / Egypt must have been born after the flood, and he could not have established his land thousands of years before the worldwide flood in Genesis.

In conclusion, using Manetho's list for dates prior to about 1000 BC should be taken with a grain of salt and any dates between 1000 to 500 BC should be seen as a close approximation. Thus, the provided dates for Egyptian chronology are approximations, not exact figures. Second, the

Bible lists Egypt as being the grandson of Noah, which means that the foundation of Mizraim / Egypt could not be dated prior to the worldwide flood. Therefore, one must be very careful with accepting the Egyptian chronology given by Naturalists.

Biblical Chronology

Certain chapters in the Book of Genesis, namely chapters 5 and 11, give a lineage with the age of the father when the son is born. "And Adam lived an hundred and thirty years, and begat a son in his own likeness, after his image; and called his name Seth" (Genesis 5:3, KJV). This means that 130 years passed between Adam's creation and his son through whose lineage is traced to the Messiah. If one were to add up all the years to the first son of each father that creates the traced lineage in Genesis 5, one would reach a total of 1,556 years of history. Doing this for each of the relevant number of years in the Bible, one could almost determine the age of the earth. The problem is after the book of Genesis, the years are summarized to selected periods, and then cease to exist in any form thereafter. However, what does appear in the Bible is an accounting of the years in Exodus, and then to the fourth year of Solomon's reign, which then can be linked to the Egyptian chronology (with its known problems), and thus to Jesus's birth in 4 BC. The table below calculates all the biblical history, displaying the various years and its biblical verse, and summarizing the total years.

Genesis 5	1,556 years
Genesis 11:11–26, Genesis 21:3, Genesis 25:26, Genesis 47:9	680 years
Exodus 12:4	430 years
1 Kings 6:1	480 years
Fourth year of Solomon to Jesus's birth in 4 BC	968 years
4 BC to AD 2022	2,026 years
TOTAL	6,140 years

11 - Bible Chronology of 6,140 years

These numbers are estimates only. The reasons are complex. First, a son is rarely born on a father's birthday. So, when the Bible states that Seth was born when Adam was 130 years old, it could mean that Adam was 129 ¾ years old or it could mean that Adam was 130 ¼ years old. Second, the years given in Exodus and First Kings could be similar estimates, rather than exactly "429 years and 365 days" for the Exodus years. Last, the Egyptian chronology is unsure prior to about 580 BC, and its earliest dates conflict with biblical chronology and all contemporary Egyptian records.

However, the biblical chronology's margin for error is going to be slight. So, when a 6,150-year history is calculated, one must realize that the date is an approximation that could have variances up to 5 percent of its stated age. The website *Answers in Genesis*[27] may have slightly different calculations, but any differences are within the margins for error. *Answers in Genesis* is not as succinct as this book, but it does go into a lot more detail about the problems with Egyptian chronology.

Biblical Age of the Earth Conclusion

Today's attempts to establish the age of the earth is convoluted at best unless one places some reliance upon the information in the Bible. Egyptian chronology is known to be hyperinflated and is not dependable much earlier than when Manetho's List was produced in 200 BC. Still, by utilizing Egyptian chronology and the written history of the Bible, one can determine that the earth is approximately 6,140 years old, ±308 years.

❖ Defining the Bible Conclusion

Only the books proven to be authentic by early scholars were included in today's Old and New Testaments. The Catholic Church included an additional seven books in AD 1546, after 1200 years of rejecting them as divinely inspired. Other books, called the Apocrypha, were excluded either because they were written long after Jesus had been crucified, or they showed no signs of being divinely inspired writings. And some of the manuscripts have been shown to be historically inaccurate—something an omniscient God would never do.

Most likely, the book of Genesis was translated by Moses into the Hebrew language from existing cuneiform tablets, likely written in the Akkadian language. This explains the various discrepancies in Genesis, like Adam's account was stated that it was a *written* account while all the others do not. Likewise, there are two accounts for Esau, and both Esau's and Ishmael's accounts serve no purpose in tracing the Messiah's lineage through Jacob/Israel to Adam. And there is the excessive length of Jacob's account of thirteen chapters of the fifty chapters in Genesis.

The biblical age of the earth is approximately 6,140 years, based upon today's widely recognized date of King Solomon's fourth year of reign being 967 BC. In the 1800s, a Bible scholar announced the biblical Age as 6,000 years, but more than one hundred years have passed since his announcement, and people have not adjusted his original calculations from this original 6,000-years calculation.

CHAPTER 23

NON-CHRISTIAN EVIDENCE FOR JESUS

There were two non-Christian historians who lived shortly after the time of Jesus's resurrection who recorded Jesus has having lived, been crucified, and rumored to have risen from the dead. This is empirical evidence for three things: 1) Jesus lived and was executed by the Roman Empire, 2) Jesus's body disappeared from the most powerful government of that era—despite attempts to prevent that disappearance, and 3) There were rumors of Jesus's resurrection.

The easiest way to quelch the rumored resurrection of Jesus would be to produce His body. Since the rumors persisted, it is empirical evidence that His body did disappear from their control, and that they were unable to recover it, despite the motivation that would have prompted a major search for the body. In the Roman Empire's eyes, any person declared to be superior to Caesar would have threatened the stability of the empire. In fact, history suggests that the consequences of this perceived failure cost Judea's governor his life. Historical data suggests that the governor of Judea, Pontius Pilate, lost his position in AD 36, and shortly afterwards, his life, approximately three years after Jesus's crucifixion.[1]

So, shortly after Jesus's death, Pilate's world fell apart, leading to his death. *Biography.com* records that the "circumstances surrounding Pontius Pilate's death in circa 39 A.D. are something of a mystery and a source of contention. According to some traditions, the Roman emperor Caligula ordered Pontius Pilate to death by execution or suicide. By other accounts, Pontius Pilate was sent into exile and committed suicide of his own accord."[2] Consequently, Pilate would have known the potential repercussions of Jesus's rumored resurrection upon his career and his life, and he would have put every effort into squelching the rumor. Therefore, we can conclude he put his best effort into it, yet he still failed.

❖ Flavius Josephus

Flavius Josephus was a Jewish priest, scholar, and historian. He wrote about Pilate's failure in his history of the Jews, *Antiquities*, including the rumor of Jesus's resurrection. It is stipulated as a rumor because Josephus was not alive when Jesus was crucified, and Josephus could not have personally witnessed His resurrection. But, rumor or fact, it is a fact that Pilate would have done any and everything possible to find the body of Jesus to put an end to this threat to the Roman Empire and his reign as governor. Yet, he was unable to do so. William Whiston, writing for Tufts University, translated Josephus's *Antiquities of the Jews* which stated the following about Jesus.

> [63] Now there was about this time Jesus, a wise man, if it be lawful to call him a man; for he was a doer of wonderful works, a teacher of such men as receive the truth with pleasure. He drew over to him both many of the Jews and many of the Gentiles. He was [the] Christ. And when Pilate, at the suggestion of the principal men amongst us, had condemned him to the cross, those that loved him at the first did not forsake him; for he appeared to them alive again the third day; as the divine prophets had foretold these and ten thousand other wonderful things concerning him. And the tribe of Christians, so named from him, are not extinct at this day.[3]

So, Josephus recorded the common rumor that 1) Jesus performed miracles, 2) Jesus was crucified by Pilate, and 3) that Jesus rose from dead. Josephus had no ulterior motives to perpetuate this rumor, as he was a Jewish historian and not a follower of Jesus. And Josephus would have written *Antiquities of the Jews* decades after the events, which is a strong indicator that it was common knowledge circulating throughout the people of Israel and beyond.

❖ Cornelius Tacitus

The second reference to Jesus was by a Roman Senator name Cornelius Tacitus (circa AD 56–120) who wrote *The Annals* circa AD 116. In his historical account, he complained about a "most mischievous superstition" that broke out in Judea and even in Rome, the center of the Roman Empire.

> But all human efforts, all the lavish gifts of the emperor, and the propitiations of the gods, did not banish the sinister belief that the conflagration *[of Rome]* was the result of an order. Consequently, to get rid of the report, Nero fastened the guilt and inflicted the most exquisite tortures on a class hated for their abominations, called Christians by the populace. Christus, from whom the name had its origin, suffered the extreme penalty during the reign of Tiberius at the hands of one of our procurators, Pontius Pilatus, and a *most mischievous superstition*, thus checked for the moment, again broke out not only in Judaea, the first source of the evil, but even in Rome, where all things hideous and shameful from every part of the world find their centre and become popular. (*The Annals, XV. 44*).[4] [As translated by MIT's The Internet Classics Archive.] [Emphasis added]

We cannot empirically prove what this "most mischievous superstition" was, but it is likely that Cornelius was talking about Jesus's resurrection, since Cornelius states that Jesus was put to death during the reign of Tiberius by Pilate just before mentioning the superstition. This indicates that Jesus's reputation was known even to the emperor of Rome, and that it was troubling to the Roman Empire. Tacitus would not be motivated to encourage this rumor. In fact, he would likely want to suppress this rumor given the fact that Tacitus was a senator of the empire, and that by spreading the rumor, he was encouraging the rumor to spread—a direct threat to the empire. That he would write about it at all indicates that the rumor was so well known that it was beyond anyone's ability to suppress the rumor. So, the only conclusion that could be reached from these facts is that Tacitus conceded that any suppression was impossible and that he was just recording a well-known fact.

❖ James Ossuary

In 2002, an archeological artifact was discovered that instigated a brouhaha, with opponents on both sides issuing conflicting opinions on the artifact. It is important because it appears to imply that it was associated with a first century Jesus (first century BC–AD 70). Its authenticity was debated in several publications of the *Biblical Archeological Review* journal, starting in its November / December 2002 edition.[5] It also hit the major news media at the time, so it became an international sensation for months before it faded from the major news sources.

In ancient Israel, from the times of Abraham until mid-first century BC, the deceased were laid in a family tomb. However, beginning in the mid-first century BC until the time of Israel's destruction in AD 123, a slight variation occurred in this practice due to a limitation of space within the tombs surrounding Israel. The deceased's remains were laid in the tomb until their bodies were reduced to a skeleton, and then the bones were gathered and subsequently placed in a bone box, called an ossuary. Prior to its use, the ossuary was molded in clay, inscribed with the deceased's name, and then hardened (dried or fired). This process caused the deceased's name to appear in the center of the front of the ossuary, while other designs may have been placed upon the back of the ossuary.

Discovery

Many people in Israel tend to search for archeological artifacts to sell on the black market for antiquities. The Dead Sea Scrolls are one such discovery, albeit only the initial scrolls were discovered in this manner while the rest were discovered in official archeological digs—which provided the archeologists the necessary provenance required for their authenticity.

What is now known as the James Ossuary was discovered in an illegal search for antiquities for the black market, sold on the black market, and its buyer subsequently discovering its enhanced value. Like most ossuaries on the black market, the bone box was empty of any bones. There are hundreds of ossuaries that pass through the black market before archeological scientists get hold of them for research. What made this discovery unique is that the empty box appeared to be for the remains of someone named "James" the brother of "Jesus." Before going any further in this discussion, some mistranslations in the Bible need to be addressed so that the discovery of the James Ossuary can be better understood.

Two famous mistranslations in the English Bible are the names known as Jesus and James. The direct Hebrew-to-English translations for Jesus and James would be Joshua and Jacob, respectively. Masculine Greek names always ended with the Greek letter translated as the English letter "s." And the Hebrew language does not have the letter "J." Thus, the Hebrew letter yod [׳], which is silent, became the English letter "J." So, Jesus came to be spelled as Yeshuas in Greek, which in turn was translated as Jesus in English. John Wycliffe (1328 to 1384) completed the first English translation of the Bible. While translating the New Testament, he mistranslated the Greek name for Jacob, which was "Yakobus," into the English name James. This mistranslation for the New Testament has been enshrined into today's modern English Bibles. So much so, that whenever Jesus's brother's name (Jacob) is used in modern English, it is translated as James, not the correct translation of Jacob.

One additional piece of information needs to be addressed in the James Ossuary discovery. When archeological artifacts such as this are discovered, the finder or buyer often cleans up the artifact to assess its value before attempting to sell it on the black market. The importance of this practice will become apparent later.

Inscription

Hebrew and Aramaic words are written in a right-to-left orientation and utilize the same letters. Meanwhile, English is written in a left-to-right orientation. So, all Hebrew and Aramaic lettering will appear in a right-to-left orientation, while the English will be reversed. In English, the inscription states "James son of Joseph brother of Jesus" on the bone box. If authentic, this gives evidence of a historical Jesus during the AD first century.

Tracing the Hebrew Letters in the Inscription:

The image below is the Hebrew and Aramaic lettering found on the James Ossuary. It was obtained by tracing the engraving on the ossuary to highlight the actual lettering.

12 - James Ossuary Inscription

Using a computer font, while adding spacing between the words renders the script into a more modern looking language, shown below. From these computer fonts, the engraved letters can be recognized. The words are then translated below using the *Enhanced Strong's Lexicon*. Note that some of the words are in Hebrew, but others are in Aramaic, which is an indication of the mixed use of both languages during Jesus's time on the earth.

עושיד יזחא פסוי רב בוקעי

יעקוב [yah·ak·obe]	Jacob[6]
בר [bar]	son (Aramaic word)[7]
יוסף [yo·safe]	Joseph[8]

אחי [awkh]0	brother (Aramaic word)[9]
ד [di]	of
עשי [yeh·shoo·ah (Yeshua)]	Jesus[10]

Because of the potential importance of this artifact, the Israel Antiquities Authority stepped in to investigate the matter, as per the norm for all alleged artifacts from historical times.

Israel Antiquities Authority Investigation

Upon the announcement of the discovery, the authorities became involved. Their first goal was to determine if the artifact was authentic. So, they established three committees tasked with that objective. Although there were three committees, only the findings of two of these committees will be addressed in this book. The reason for only presenting the two committees is that it appears that an *a priori* (preconceived) conclusion was reached before the research was even started. This resulted in contradictory findings, yet with the same overall finding—*i.e.*, that the artifact was a fake.

The first committee, the Ossuary Inscription Committee, was tasked with examining the inscription itself to determine if the inscription was authentic, specifically it addressed the issue "was the Hebrew lettering in the style that was used during the first century AD." All languages change over time, sometimes in the spelling, sometimes in the way the letter is formed. So, this committee was composed of paleographists—specialists in how these Hebrew letters and spelling changed over time.

The second committee, the Materials Committee was tasked with determining if the *patina* was authentic for the alleged age of the artifact. The *Cambridge Dictionary* defines patina as "a thin surface layer that develops on something because of use, age, or chemical action."[11] When objects are stored in a wet, underground area, like a tomb, patina will develop on the outside of the object. Successful forgers of ancient artifacts have developed methods of falsifying this patina covering to make the artifact appear authentic. So, the Materials Committee was tasked with determining if this patina was real or fake.

Findings of the Committees:

The Inscription Committee

Dr. Tal Ilan: "Even if the ossuary is authentic, there is *no reason to assume that the deceased was actually the brother of Jesus.*"[12] [Emphasis added].

Prof. Roni Reich: "The inscription does not exhibit a combination of configurational or substantial effects that would imply a forgery. But *I was convinced that the inscription is a forgery when presented with the findings by the Materials Committee.*"[13] [Emphasis added].

The Materials Committee

Jacques Neguer: "The ossuary is authentic. It's inscription is a forgery. ... *The inscription cuts through the original Patina and appears to be written by two different writers using different tools.*"[14] [Emphasis added].

Ms. Orna Cohen: "The first part of the inscription is new, cuts through the original patina ... *The end of the inscription "brother of Jesus" appears to be authentic,* in some places there seems to be remains of old patina."[15] [Emphasis added].

Analyzing the Announced Findings

All the specialists on the committees were convinced the ossuary was fake. However, when one looks at their reasoning, one finds aberrations that are too illogical to explain. They are opining an opinion that is outside their area of expertise, or they are basing it upon another committee's findings, or a similar illogical reasoning.

On the Inscription Committee, Dr. Ilan opined that the inscription was authentic, but it was unknown if it was linked to Jesus the Christ. That was not his assigned task. His only job was to determine if the lettering was authentic for the period from which the artifact allegedly originated. Professor Reich, also on the Inscription Committee, found the inscription to be authentic, but was convinced it was a forgery because of the findings by the materials committee. Again, that was not his task. His task was the inscription alone, not to use another committee's conclusion to determine his opinion. The committees were deliberately separated so that each committees' conclusions could be reached independently. So, to summarize the findings of the Inscription Committee, they found no evidence that the inscription was fake. Their opinions rested solely on their opinions formed before undertaking the investigation.

On the Materials Committee, Jacques Neguer found the ossuary to be authentic. His callout that the inscription appears to cut through the patina could be a valid point. However, let us review what we know about this ossuary: 1) It was found and sold on the black market, 2) It had an unknown provenance, and 3) the antiquities dealer cleaned the face (*i.e.*, the inscription) to clarify the inscription to determine its value for a subsequent selling on the black market. So, it would not be unusual for the patina to be removed during the cleaning process around the inscription area, especially around the name of the deceased. Then, Neguer opines in an area that is not his area of expertise—the inscription itself. The Inscription Committee was assigned to the inscription authentication. They found that the inscription was authentic, *i.e.*, *not* "by two different writers with different tools" as determined by Neguer. So, it appears that Neguer was searching for any excuse to dismiss the artifact as a fake. Ms. Orna Cohen, also on the Materials Committee, found that the patina at the beginning is new, while the patina around the words "brother of Jesus" to be authentic, stating "in some places there seems to be remains of old patina" in the words "brother of Jesus."

Again, this is consistent with the buyer cleaning the name of the deceased to better read the inscription. And why would anyone bother to write "brother of Jesus" almost two thousand years ago without writing the name of the deceased on the ossuary at the same time? So, the Materials Committee found that the ossuary was authentic and the critical part of the inscription, brother of Jesus, contained authentic patina.

In summary, the committees were separated to provide independent viewpoints, yet they discussed their findings before settling on a conclusion as to its authenticity. The inscription is authentic, the ossuary itself is authentic, and the end of the inscription has two thousand years of patina covering it, yet—somehow—they still deemed it to be a fake.

James Ossuary Conclusion

Almost a decade after the June 18, 2003, analysis by the Israeli Antiquities Authority, many archeology scholars have pushed back upon the IAA's initial findings, with most advocating that both the bone box and the inscription are authentic to the AD first century. Additionally, a press release by the *Biblical Archeological Review* in June 2012 suggests that only 1.7 men would meet the qualifications contained on the James Ossuary.

In conclusion, both the twenty-inch-long James Ossuary and the inscription are likely authentic. At one time, it did contain the remains of a man named Jacob (*i.e.*, James), who was the son of Joseph, and the brother of Joshua (*i.e.*, Yeshua or Jesus). Most ossuaries only contain the name of the deceased and the deceased's father's name. Only a few contain the name of a relative and when a relative was named, the relative was famous. Joshua (*i.e.*, Yeshua or Jesus) was a common Hebrew name for biblical times. With the given constraints of 1) James (Jacob); 2) Fathered by a Joseph; 3) With a famous brother named Jesus (Joshua); and 4) In the first century, it really narrows the potential matches down quite a bit (*i.e.*, 1.7 possible matches). But it is still open to some debate whether this box contained the remains of the brother of Jesus the Christ—and more importantly if this Jesus performed miracles and rose from the dead.

❖ Non-Christian Evidence for Jesus Conclusion

So, contrary to many anti-Christian claims, there are non-Christian historians who were contemporary to the generation of people who witnessed Jesus's resurrection and reported about Jesus's miracles in their writings. And there is the acceptance of the authenticity of the James Ossuary for the evidence of a historical Jesus in the first century. As a result, almost all historians accept the conclusion that a historical Jesus did exist and that He was crucified by Pontius Pilate in circa AD 33. Where the difference of opinion occurs is whether this Jesus was resurrected and is the Son of God.

CHAPTER 24

BIBLE DIFFICULTIES

Anti-Christians will also try to confuse a Christian, causing them to doubt their faith, with seemingly contradictory issues found in the Bible. However, once the issue is researched thoroughly, the contradictions are resolved. This chapter addresses many of these seemingly contradictory issues.

❖ Once Saved, Always Saved

One of these apparent discrepancies is the concept of "Once Saved, Always Saved." There is evidence on both sides of this issue. But, when viewed in the proper light, it becomes apparent that this is a *false dichotomy* logic fallacy. *Logical Fallacy* states that a "False Dichotomy is a formal fallacy based on an "either-or" type of argument. Two choices are presented, when more might exist, and the claim is made that one is false, and one is true"[1] What does Scripture says about this issue? There are many verses on the side of assurance of salvation. Here are four of them.

I.   That if thou shalt confess with thy mouth the Lord Jesus, and shalt believe in thine heart that God hath raised him from the dead, *thou shalt be saved.* (Romans 10:9, KJV) [Empasis added].

2. He that hath the Son hath life; and he that hath not the Son of God hath not life. These things have I written unto you that believe on the name of the Son of God; *that ye may know that ye have eternal life, and that ye may believe on the name of the Son of God.* (I John 5:12–13, KJV) [Empasis added].

3. My Father, which gave them me, is greater than all; and *no man is able to pluck them out of my Father's hand.* (John 10:29, KJV) [Empasis added].

4. For I am persuaded, that neither death, nor life, nor angels, nor principalities, nor powers, nor things present, nor things to come, Nor height, nor depth, nor any other creature, *shall be able to separate us from the love of God,* which is in Christ Jesus our Lord. (Romans 8:38–39, KJV) [Empasis added].

So, the Bible does seem to indicate that once a person is saved, they cannot lose their salvation. All that appears to be required is to confess a belief in Jesus as Lord and Savior. But sound doctrine is not based upon a few select verses. Rather, it is based upon the entirety of the Bible. So, the next question is—Can you lose your salvation?

I. And ye shall be hated of all men for my name's sake: but he that *endureth to the end shall be saved."* (Matthew 10:22, KJV) [Empasis added].

2. But he that shall *endure unto the end, the same shall be saved.* (Matthew 24:13, KJV) [Empasis added].

3. [Parable of the seeds] Some fell upon stony places, where they had not much earth: and forthwith they sprung up, because they had no deepness of earth: And when the sun was up, they were scorched; and because they had no root, they withered away. . . . But he that received the seed into stony places, the same is he that heareth the word, and anon with joy receiveth it; Yet hath he not root in himself, but *dureth for a while:* for when tribulation or persecution ariseth because of the word, by and by he is *offended.* (Matthew 13:5–6, 13:20–21, KJV) [Emphasis added].

For clarity's sake, let us look at the final passage, focusing on the Greek word "offended." This word is translated with the following English definition. "Offended: σκανδαλίζω [skan·dal·id·zo] v. I to put a stumbling block or impediment in the way, upon which another may trip and fall, metaph. to offend. IA to entice to sin. IB *to cause a person to begin to distrust and desert one whom he ought to trust and obey.*" [2] [Emphasis added] So, all three passages here seem to indicate that you can lose your salvation unless you believe until the end of your life (or Christ returns).

The real answer lies in the middle. Viewed from God's perspective (*i.e.*, outside of time), you cannot lose your salvation because there is *no time left* to change your mind because you are standing at the Judgment Seat for judgment. Viewed from a Christian's perspective (*i.e.*, inside of time), you have plenty of time to change your mind in following Christ. Since your salvation does not happen until the Judgment Seat, you are not technically "saved" until then. But what is the meaning of salvation and how do Christians use the term today?

Meaning of Salvation

There are three terms used in Christian circles to describe a person's salvation. Therefore, to fully understand this issue, one needs to distinguish between the three terms. 1) *Actual salvation* is when you are standing before the Judgement Seat and Jesus stands as your advocate, and God states that you may enter heaven, 2) *Promise of Salvation* is the assurance that a follower of Jesus will be saved, as long as the person continues to follow Jesus throughout their life—this promise never ends, and 3) *Work of Salvation* is the process by which you draw closer to Jesus throughout your life. It doesn't end. Every time you defeat one sin in your life, another sin that has been in your life all along is revealed to you to work on. Just for clarification, this definition is not to be interpreted as an indication that one is saved by their works, but that salvation is a process—always drawing closer to Jesus. Salvation is by the grace of God.

Once Saved, Always Saved Conclusion

Scripture clearly states that no person can *steal* your salvation from you. Thus, Satan cannot *take* from you what Christ has given to you, a choice.

Consequently, Satan tries to influence your decision to follow Christ by putting up obstacles that will encourage you to change your mind. And you are free to change your mind at any time. Christ will not force a person to go to Heaven. Hence, the correct solution is that the answer is "both"—you cannot lose your salvation *if* you keep your faith until the end of your life. You are also still safe in that no one, including Satan, can force you to renounce your faith in Jesus. However, there are those that Satan does succeed in convincing them to renounce their faith in Jesus (*i.e.*, as demonstrated in the parable of the seeds).

❖ The Trinity—How Can God be Three-in-One?

Anti-Christians tend to mock Christians due to their belief in a Triune God. They will posit that this concept grew out of a pagan belief system, inspired by the Councils of Nicaea (there were multiple meetings in Nicaea over the defining of modern Christianity). Many Christians have heard of this concept, but they may not understand where in Scripture this idea is found. So, let us explore this issue, find the supporting verses, and the empirical evidence from the word to support this, apparently, outrageous idea. Then, we will look at other evidence to see that it, too, operates as a trinity—just like the Triune God.

Plurality of God

In God's creation account, God identified himself in both the singular and the plural. Let us begin with the Hebrew word for "God"—in the singular. In Genesis 1:26, the Hebrew word for "God" is "אֱלוֹהַּ" [el·o·ah][3]. Note that the Hebrew lettering is read from right to left, while the transliteration in English letters is read left to right. But God continues his statement, referring to himself in the plural form later. He states, "Let us," a plural form. He goes on to say, "in our image," again in the plural form. And finally, "after our likeness," again in the plural form.

So, from the beginning, God considered Himself to be a plurality that functioned as a singular person. "And God said, Let *us* make man in *our* image, after *our* likeness." (Genesis 1:26a, KJV) [Emphasis added]. Many opponents of this plurality advance the claim that the plurality is due to the usage of terminology known as the "royal-we" concept, whereby a king refers to himself in a plural form. However, the royal-we usage did not come into usage until the 12th century. As *Wikipedia* states "William Longchamp is credited with its [royal we, majestic plural] introduction to England in the late 12th century, following the practice of the Chancery of Apostolic Briefs."[4] By the same token, Bible scholars also recognize the Lord's use of "Us" as implying the Trinity. In his book, *The Moody Handbook of Theology*, Enns makes the following connection between the plurality of God's pronouns and the Trinity by writing, "The Lord's transcendence and immanence is evident (Gen. 11:7). He who is distant "came down" to see what the people were doing. The Trinity is also implied in the statement, "Let Us go down.""[5]

But this does not address the root of the problem. Is Jesus a part of that plurality? And is the Holy Spirit part of that plurality?

Jesus and God, the Father

First, we need to establish that Jesus, Himself, claimed to be the same as God. "I and my Father are one." (John 10:30, KJV). When Moses asked God His name, God responded with "I AM." "And God said unto Moses, I AM THAT I AM: and he said, Thus shalt thou say unto the children of Israel, I AM hath sent me unto you." (Exodus 3:14, KJV). In the Gospels, Jesus also claims the name "I AM."

> But he held his peace, and answered nothing. Again the high priest asked him, and said unto him, Art thou the Christ, the Son of the Blessed? And Jesus said, *I am*: and ye shall see the Son of man sitting on the right hand of power, and coming in the clouds of heaven. Then the high priest rent his clothes, and saith, What need we any further witnesses? Ye have heard the *blasphemy*: what think ye? And they all condemned him to be guilty of death. (Mark 14:61–64, KJV) [Emphasis added]

There are two things to note about this passage. First, Jesus did not say "I am xyz", He simply stated "I am"—the name of God, the Father stated about Himself (note, that while modern versions of the Bible have capitalization and punctuations, the original Hebrew and Greek text had no such additions). Moreover, the High Priest recognized that Jesus was claiming the name of the "I AM" because he accused Jesus of blasphemy. The *Merriam-Webster* defines blasphemy as "the act of claiming the attributes of a deity."[6] Jesus also claimed to be one with the Father, saying "I and my Father are one." (John 10:30, KJV). Therefore, we can find empirical evidence in the Bible that Jesus claimed to be the same as God.

The Holy Spirit, Jesus, and God the Father

But, what about the Holy Spirit? In the King James Version Bible, the term "Holy Spirit" is translated as "Holy Ghost." Other versions translate the Greek words for this term into Holy Spirit. There are passages whereby Jesus claims that the Holy Spirit is equal to Himself and God. "Go ye therefore, and teach all nations, baptizing them in the name of the Father, and of the Son, and of the *Holy Ghost:*" (Matthew 28:19, KJV) [Emphasis added]. The Gospel of John also affirms that concept. "But the Comforter, which is the Holy Ghost, whom the Father will send in my name, he shall teach you all things, and bring all things to your remembrance, whatsoever I have said unto you." (John 14:26, KJV). So, we have empirical evidence from the Bible that the Holy Spirit is a part of that plurality.

Early Church Recognition

And the Apostle John affirmed the concept of the Trinity in his Gospel when he wrote "In the beginning was the Word, and the Word was with God, and the Word was God. The same was in the beginning with God." (John 1:1–2, KJV). So, the early Christians knew about the Trinity. What is less clear is how well they understood the concept. But that is immaterial to the anti-Christian's hypothesis.

Other Trinities in Everyday Life

If you look throughout Scripture, God always provides empirical evidence to His followers to accept Him as their Lord and Savior. Why did God provide Abraham a ram to sacrifice in lieu of Isaac? To provide empirical evidence that God is in control. Why did God have Moses part the Red Sea? Why did God send the prophets to His Chosen People? Why did God say, "This is my beloved Son, in whom I am well pleased." (Matthew 3:17, KJV)? Why did Jesus rise from the dead? All of these are examples of God providing empirical evidence for His doubting followers. God has always provided empirical evidence that the message came from God. This provision of empirical evidence is true on this issue, as well. Our universe is composed of trinities everywhere.

We observe trinity concepts every day of our lives, even if we do not grasp that idea as a trinity. What is ice, water, and steam but a trinity? We have three phases of the same compound made up of two atoms of hydrogen and one atom of oxygen, forming the compound called H^2O. Our universe is composed of a trinity, too, composed of "matter, energy, and time," called spacetime. All of them are different components of the universe, yet without one, the others could not exist.

Humans are also made as a trinity, but we call that trinity a "body, mind, and soul." There is an earthly body, which is made from the elements of the earth. Then, there is the mind (sometimes called the spirit), which are the electrical impulses that keep the body alive. And last, there is the soul, which remains after death and faces the Judgement Seat of God. As Scripture states, "And the LORD God formed man of the dust of the ground, and breathed into his nostrils the breath of life; and man became a *living soul.*" (Genesis 2:7, KJV). [emphasis added] Scripture does not say "became a living soul" about any other animal on earth, only humankind— we are, after all, made in His image.

Heresies — Modalism and Partialism

Many will attempt to argue these attempts to explain the Trinity are some form of heresy. However, when they do, they fall into the trap of heresy of

Traditionalism. In essence, if they cannot explain it in their own words, then it must be some heresy. And, then they throw out names that have been traditionally associated with heresies. One of the reasons that these explanations are not a heresy is the fact that they show trinities exist in our created universe, rather than being directly applied to the Triune Godhead. An equivalent concept is Jesus's telling of the "Parable of the Seeds." The logic of "This is a heresy" would be the equivalent of claiming that Jesus said, "people are plants." Obviously, Jesus was using an analogy, rather describing people.

One of these attempts is the heresy of modalism, which teaches that one God merely manifests Himself in three various ways. The correct view of the Trinity is "there are no three individuals alongside of, and separate from, one another, but only personal self-distinctions within the Divine essence [Berkhof, *Systematic Theology*, p. 87.]."[7] In addition, the "three Persons have distinct relationships"[8] and the "three Persons are equal in authority."[9]

Charles Johnson in *Christianity.com* explains his objections to modality by saying, "Christians believe God is three separate, eternal Persons with unique roles. Modalists believe God is one entity who changes modes as He sees fit. Hence, He was God the Father in the Old Testament, shifted into God the Son (Jesus Christ) in the New Testament, and now operates as the Holy Spirit. It logically follows that no divine mode can be eternal or distinct."[10]

The H_2O analogy has these elements given by Enns in his *The Moody Handbook of Theology* within them. They are self-distinctions within the same essence (compound), have distinct relationships, and are equal in authority. And, unlike Johnson's objections, all the H_2O does not change into ice, water, or steam at the same time. They always co-exist. Thus, the H_2O does not meet the criteria of modalism.

Another of these attempts is the heresy of *partialism*. "According to partialism, each Person of the Trinity is 100 percent divine in nature, but God is only God when, where, and if all three Persons are unified. ... Since partialism is fairly obscure and open to such wide interpretation, it is rarely named among the major false views of the Trinity."[11]

In the body, spirit, soul example, we all know that the body and spirit will die, while the soul faces judgment, so they are destined for separation. In the matter, energy, and time analogy, it doesn't claim that these components are divine in nature. Consequently, the claim of the heresy of partialism is a misapplication or misunderstanding of the heresy. Furthermore, why would a person advance the claim of partialism when it is obscure and open to such wide interpretation?

The primary reason these examples are not heresies is in their application. These examples are applied to objects found in the natural world, rather than trying to apply them to the supernatural world (i.e., the Triune Godhead). They are the difference between looking at an online influencer's photo, where she is looks her best with make-up, filters, and the setting "just perfect." Then assuming that this is the real person. If this mirage was applied to the Triune Godhead, it would be considered a heresy. On the other hand, if a painting of this same woman was made, without makeup, improvements to her setting, and other artificial improvements to her looks, this would be the equivalent of the allegories found in this section, whereby objects found in nature are compared to the Triune Godhead to demonstrate God designing our universe with trinity concepts. We get an image, not a clear reflection of the Trinity.

The Triune Godhood Conclusion

The Bible is rife with God providing empirical evidence to His followers of His divine nature. One part of His nature is His trinity. The biblical text shows that Jesus claimed to be the same as God the Father, and that the Holy Spirit was the same as they. Furthermore, the biblical text shows that the disciples of Jesus also were aware of this confusing concept. And today's scientific knowledge provides us with empirical evidence that the trinity exists in nature itself. The most obvious is the element H^2O, which we recognize its three phases as ice, water, and steam. Even our universe is a trinity, composed of matter, energy, and time. And last, humankind—which is in God's image—is also a trinity of body, mind, and soul. None of these examples can exist without the original entity (i.e., ice cannot be "ice" unless it retains the H^2O compound). Therefore, a triune godhood should be expected.

❖ Free Will vs. Predestination

Another topic that tends to divide Christians in their interpretation of Scripture is the concept of "Free Will" or "God Called" (*i.e.*, referred to as predestination among Christians). Some anti-Christians have attempted to use this issue to encourage division among Christians. Once again, it is a False Dichotomy logic fallacy at the root of the perceived controversy. Both sides have support from Scriptures on their preferred interpretation on the topic. As a result, both are true while both being false at the same time. Again, it is simply a matter of viewpoint—God's viewpoint or an individual's viewpoint. There are many verses that support both sides of the debate, so only a few will be provided on each side of the debate. The first three verses will appear to support the viewpoint that we are called by God, and thus have no choice in the matter, while the latter verses will appear to support the viewpoint that we, alone, make the decision.

Predestination viewpoint:

1. For whom he did foreknow, he also did *predestinate* to be conformed to the image of his Son, that he might be the firstborn among many brethren. (Romans 8:29, KJV) [Emphasis added]
2. Having *predestinated* us unto the adoption of children by Jesus Christ to himself, according to the good pleasure of his will (Ephesians 1:5, KJV) [Emphasis added]
3. In whom also we have obtained an inheritance, being *predestinated* according to the purpose of him who worketh all things after the counsel of his own will (Ephesians 1:11, KJV) [Emphasis added]

Note that the first verse supporting predestination is the most explanative of those supporting the viewpoint for predestination. The passage lays out the required steps for God's calling—namely, He *foreknew* His children before He *predestined* them to become His children. What did He foreknow? Remember that God is outside of time. He knows every choice you will ever make in your life—before you are ever born. He knows your good choices and He knows your failures. He also knows if and when you will make the decision to follow Him as Lord and Savior. If you choose *not* to follow Him, then He is not going to *force* you to follow Him. Everybody is free to decide if they want to spend eternity with or without the presence of God in their life.

The major problem with the predestination viewpoint is that when one takes the concept to its final logical conclusion, it contradicts many of the Bible's other verses. Essentially, it stipulates that an individual was created in God's image—with free will (as demonstrated when God created our world)—but the person is still just a robot for God to control without a choice in this issue. Hence, we must consider the Free Will side of the dilemma.

Free Will viewpoint:

I. And if it seem evil unto you to serve the LORD, *choose you this day whom ye will serve*; whether the gods which your fathers served that were on the other side of the flood, or the gods of the Amorites, in whose land ye dwell: but as for me and my house, we will serve the LORD. (Joshua 24:15, KJV) [Emphasis added]

2. Behold, I stand at the door, and knock: if any man <u>hear</u> my voice, and *open the door,* I will come in to him, and will sup with him, and he with me. (Revelation 3:20, KJV) [Emphasis added]

3. And when he had called the people unto him with his disciples also, he said unto them, Whosoever will come after me, let him deny himself, and *take up his cross,* and *follow me.* (Mark 8:34, KJV) [Emphasis added]

The passages that indicate that every person must make a choice to follow Christ are told from an individual's viewpoint. We do not have the ability to step outside of time to know if we will choose to follow Him at some point in our life. In short, we are blind to our future. Thus, it becomes imperative to make the decision sooner in life, rather than later. Why? It is because we do not have the foresight to know if we will even be alive to make that decision tomorrow morning. Therefore, from the individual's perspective, the sooner the better. And the sooner you make your choice, the better for God as well because once we make our decision, we become useful for the service of Christ.

The major problem with the free will viewpoint is that when one takes the concept to its final logical conclusion, it contradicts many of the Bible's other verses. Essentially, it stipulates that an individual alone makes the decision of where he spends eternity—not God—therefore God is not omnipotent nor omniscient. Consequently, what's the solution to this quandary?

Predestined vs. Free-Will Conclusion

Contrary to the false dilemma which seems to be presented to us, this issue is easily resolved when we look at it from the two differing perspectives of the participants—God and the person. God knows of your decision whether to follow Him and thus can predestine your outcome based upon that knowledge. You, however, do not know it. Therefore, you are left with the free-will choice to follow Him or not. As shown, this false dichotomy is resolved with the answer of "both are true," when viewed appropriately.

❖ Lake of Fire (Hell)

The question of "Why doesn't God just take His followers into Heaven, while allowing non-followers to simply perish without suffering the everlasting torment of 'hell'?" is often asked of Christians from non-Christians. Another version of stating this issue is "Why would God send people to everlasting torment?" This argument implies that God is evil.

But the underlying issue is what does the Bible mean by hell. There are two terms in the original Greek language that is translated as "hell" in some English versions of the Bible, so we need to differentiate between these two terms. The first term is sometimes interpreted as "Sheol," which comes from the Hebrew word "seol." Some English translations use the term "grave," since the original term meant the abode of the dead. Other English translations use the term "Hades" or "Hell" because that is the Greek term for the abode of the dead. Almost everybody will go down to the grave at the end of their life. No one is really worried about this destination because we all accept it as inevitable. Our only concern with going to the grave is the *when* part of the issue.

The Bible distinguishes between these two destinations, as well. It states that death and the grave will be cast into the lake of fire. It refers to the lake of fire as the second death. This is the one that worries people. "And death and hell were cast into the lake of fire. This is the second death. And whosoever was not found written in the book of life was cast into the lake of fire." (Revelation 20:14–15, KJV). To understand this issue requires us to look at the book of Genesis, using the two differing viewpoints of the creation of humans by God, the first in Genesis 1 and the second in Genesis 2.

What is the Lake of Fire

God's viewpoint: "So God created man in his own image, in the image of God created he him; male and female created he them." (Genesis 1:27, KJV). Adam's viewpoint: "And the LORD God formed man of the dust of the ground, and breathed into his nostrils the breath of life; and man became *a living soul.*" (Genesis 2:7, KJV). We are told that we were created in God's image. It has already been established that God exists outside of our spacetime continuum, and thus He is outside of time. In Genesis 2:7, Adam wrote that God breathed life into humankind and humankind became a *living soul.* This implies that God placed in us a tiny "seed" of Himself and that we have the capacity of living outside of time as well. Part of this capacity was taken from us (Genesis 3:22) when humankind was kicked out of the Garden of Eden. But at the end of this age, we will face the Judgment Seat of God. In Revelation 20, it is written that our souls will be with God in Heaven. So, our earthly bodies cannot exist outside of time, but our souls can and will exist outside of time. "... and I saw the souls of them that were beheaded for the witness of Jesus ... and they lived and reigned with Christ a thousand years. But the rest of the dead lived not again until the thousand years were finished. This is the first resurrection." (Revelation 20:4–5, KJV). This implies that our souls, whether we are followers of Christ or reject Him, will live forever. But what exactly is God?

We do not have the ability to fully comprehend God, but First John gives us enough to use to explain the concept of the lake of fire. "And we have known and believed the love that God hath to us. *God is love*; and he that dwelleth in love dwelleth in God, and God in him." (I John 4:16, KJV). So, God is *love*. This means that if we reject God, we reject any kind of love, including *self-love*. Right now, we are sustained in God's love every living moment of our lives. We are so thoroughly enmeshed in His love that it is as natural as breathing air, so we do not even recognize it. But after the Judgement, we will not have that love in our life—unless we are in Heaven. Imagine being somewhere without *any* love—not even self-love. We would be in a universe filled with hate, hate for ourselves, others pouring their hate on us, while we pour our hate on them.

I cannot imagine a worse fate for eternity. I would not want my worst enemy to experience that level of hate for even one second, much less for eternity. But God gives us the choice to live with Him in eternity or live without Him in eternity. Unfortunately, some will choose any existence, as long as it is without serving God.

Why does God kill people?

Again, this is a matter of one's perspective. Viewed from a Naturalist's view, once we die it is all over. Nothing is left. As a result, dying is among the worst things that could happen to a person. But from God's perspective, things look much different. Since our *real* life is in eternity, then our life here on earth is something akin to being in school during our childhood. As we go through school, we are aware that, eventually, we will get out of school, and enter the workforce. Likewise, we all know that eventually we will die. This *dying* is not the bad news that Naturalists believe it is.

From the Christian perspective, dying is a graduation from our trials (*i.e.*, our time of learning) here on earth to transition to our real lives in eternity. Viewed from this perspective, then the matter of when a person dies is really a matter of when the person has learned all the lessons they will ever learn here on earth and are now ready for eternity. Those that God knows will reject Him, no matter what circumstances He puts in their life, are bound for the Lake of Fire. Why prolong their training here on earth if they have learned everything they will ever learn in life? Likewise, a person who has already chosen God as their Lord and Savior is destined for eternity with God, regardless of any further trials here on earth. Most of these people will be useful to God by teaching others about Jesus. Others will be of better use to God by dying a martyr's death—because they will stand fast in the ultimate test before others and inspire others to follow Jesus Christ. God knows the limits that a person can take and will use that person's suffering to bring all His children to Him (I Corinthians 10:13).

Lake of Fire Conclusion

The image of the lake of fire is the best illustration of the eternal torment that a person endures when they are forever separated from the love of God. God does not force a person to follow Him but rather allows that person to spend eternity within His love or totally separated from all love. God does not send a person into torment forever. Rather, it is every person's choice of where they will spend eternity—with God or without any love, forever.

❖ Dinosaurs

One of the challenges that a Christian has is the evidence of dinosaur fossils in museums. This seems to stump many Christians in their faith. Yet, there is evidence for dinosaurs in the Bible and in archeological artifacts. *Merriam-Webster* states that the first known use of the term dinosaur was first used in 1842, so it won't be found in the Bible.[12] However, we do find a term in the Bible that likely refers to a dinosaur—namely a sauropod—the *behemoth*.

Dinosaurs in the Bible

> Behold now behemoth, which I made with thee; he *eateth grass* as an ox. Lo now, his strength is in his loins, and his force is in the navel of his belly. He *moveth his tail like a cedar*: the sinews of his stones are wrapped together. His bones are as strong pieces of brass; *his bones are like bars of iron*. He is the chief of the ways of God: . . .Behold, he *drinketh up a river*,

and hasteth not: he trusteth that he can draw up Jordan into his mouth. (Job 40:15–19, 23, KJV) [emphasis added]

Job describes the behemoth as a herbivore (eats grass), that is very strong, its tail sways like a tree, its bones are like iron, and it is not challenged by a large river (*i.e.*, can drink a large volume of water). No known animal on earth fits such a description, except for sauropods—like the brontosaurus. Sauropods were very large animals, too large to be concerned with the rushing waters of a mighty river. Few known animals have a tail large enough to sway like a cedar tree. One of them is the crocodile, but it is a meat-eater. A hippopotamus is a large animal, and it is an herbivore, but it has a tiny tail. Likewise, an elephant is a large herbivore, but it too has a tiny tail. This seems to narrow the possible candidates for this animal down to some sort of sauropod.

Dinosaurs in Art

There are also dinosaurs found in the art of ancient civilizations. For example, an Iguanodon seems to match an engraving on King Nebuchadnezzar's Ishtar Gate.[13] And, the North American Anasazi Indians have an engraving of what appears to be a brontosaurus. "One evolutionist wrote, 'There is a petroglyph in Natural Bridges National Monument that bears a startling resemblance to a dinosaur, specifically a Brontosaurus, with a long tail and neck, small head and all.' (Barnes, Fred A., and Pendleton, Michaelene, *Prehistoric Indians: Their Cultures, Ruins, Artifacts and Rock Art*, 1979, p.201.)."[14]

There is also evidence of large, long-necked, long-tailed animals entwined in combat. These are found on the Narmer Palette, in Hierakonpolis located in the south of Egypt.[15] There is also a 3000 BC cylinder seal of Uruk with serpopard design found in Mesopotamia that has similar depictions.[16] Naturalists claim these animals are mythological creatures that are a mix of serpents and leopards—called Serpopards. But how would such a large creature come into one's imagination in the first place and across many different cultures? Did these creatures represent the same animal that is called a sauropod today?

Dinosaur Conclusion

Empirical evidence of dinosaurs is found in many places, in the Bible and in ancient art. Even evolutionists recognize these facts. This evidence appears to contradict the "millions of years since dinosaurs existed" postulated by Naturalists. There is also evidence of dinosaur soft tissue found by Naturalists, which is scientifically proven to last less than 10,000 years. Is this evidence accepted by all? No. However, the evidence can be evaluated by anyone. Is the dinosaur soft tissue related to these images? Are these images serpopards or sauropods?

❖ Worldwide Flood

There are many Naturalists who dispute the Genesis account of the worldwide flood. However, there is much evidence for this event. Most ancient cultures have a worldwide flood account. The Naturalists dispute this evidence by claiming that they were only recording a massive, localized flood, rather than a worldwide flood. So, let's look at the undisputed evidence of a worldwide flood.

Let us look at what the Bible recorded concerning the flood. "In the six hundredth year of Noah's life, in the second month, the seventeenth day of the month, the same day were all the *fountains of the great deep* broken up, and the *windows of heaven* were opened." (Genesis 7:11, KJV) [Emphasis added]. So, the water came from two sources, underground and from the sky. Two questions are spawned from this claim, 1) Is there sufficient water in the earth's crust to supply the necessary water when combined with the water trapped in the clouds, and 2) Where did this alleged water go after the flood? For the first issue, let us look at evidence of water trapped in the "fountains of the great deep" from the *New Scientist* article in 2014, stating that a "reservoir of water three times the volume of all the oceans has been discovered deep beneath the earth's surface. The finding could help explain where earth's seas came from."[17] So, this proves there is plenty of water on earth to completely cover the earth with water and drown all life not found on the alleged Noah's Ark. But if the waters covered the earth, where did that water go afterwards? Before we delve into this matter, let us consider the state of the earth before the flood.

We know that mountains would have formed when the tectonic plates shifted and uplifted the plates to form the mountains. But were the mountains as high before the flood? We don't know the answer to this question. As a result, let us assume that the mountains were as high as they are now, since that will address the most skeptical view of the floodwaters. An article in *Geology. com* concerning the Mariana Trench stated that "In 2010 the United States Center for Coastal & Ocean Mapping measured the depth of the Challenger Deep at 10,994 meters (36,070 feet) below sea level with an estimated vertical accuracy of ± 40 meters. If Mount Everest, the highest mountain on earth, were placed at this location it would be covered by over one mile of water."[18] Keep in mind that the mountains we see today are certainly higher than the mountains of old, since the shifting of the plate tectonics occurred after the flood, and would lift the land mass even higher than they were before the flood. Even in the worst-case scenario (which assumes the mountains are at their current height), the highest mountain could still be covered by over a mile of water by the Mariana Trench, and this factoid does not include the possibility of the water returning to the "fountains of the great deep" mentioned in the *New Scientist* article. Because of this, there is sufficient water to cover the earth in water, and there are sufficient valleys in the oceans' deep for that water to subside after the flood. As such, there is no justifiable reason to doubt the authenticity of the biblical account of a worldwide flood.

Gilgamesh Flood

Many anti-Christians will point to the Epic of Gilgamesh, tablet XI— about a worldwide flood—as evidence that Christians borrowed the flood story from this story. Granted, there are many similarities between the two stories. But let us look at the facts found on *Answers In Genesis's* webpage titled *The Background of the Gilgamesh Epic* before we compare the two stories.[19]

The Epic of Gilgamesh has two recognized versions. "Heidel states, "It has long been recognized that the Gilgamesh Epic constitutes a literary compilation of material from various originally unrelated sources, put together to form one grand, more or less harmonious, whole."[20] So, unlike today's literature, in the earliest times scribes not only took dictation for the work, but they also added to the work as they saw fit. This fact alone should cause one to question the reliability of the Epic of Gilgamesh story. The oldest version is the Old Babylonian Version, and it is in a fragmentary state. It appears to date about the second millennium, which is older than the extant biblical texts. However, it does not contain the important tablet XI, which contains the flood story. A later Assyrian version, called the Standard Version, is more complete and includes tablet XI. It is dated to around the thirteenth century (1300 to 1201) BC. Concerning the inclusion of tablet XI (aka tablet 11), *Answers In Genesis* quotes William Moran in his work *The Gilgamesh Epic: A Masterpiece from Ancient Mesopotamia* as saying,

> It is generally conceded that the Flood was not part of the original epic, which may have referred to it, but only briefly. The long account in Tablet 11 seems to be told for its own sake. It seriously interrupts not only the flow of dialogue between Utnapishtim and Gilgamesh but the otherwise smooth and natural transition from the end of the Tablet 10, where Utnapishtim tells Gilgamesh about the assembly of the gods after the Flood, to Utnapishtim's rhetorical question.[21] [in Tablet 12]

This implies that it was an insertion into the original story by a creative scribe, rather than one making the effort to record history as it was passed down to him. But who was William Moran? *Wikipedia* states that he was a professor of Assyriology at Harvard University who "was respected as a rigorous and learned teacher of the Akkadian language who could easily discuss problems in Biblical lexicon and literature."[22] So, he was very knowledgeable on the languages of Gilgamesh and the overall history of the area.

Most scholars view the book of Genesis to be a historical work, while most scholars view the Epic of Gilgamesh as a mythological account. If the Genesis Authorship is viewed as coming to Moses via twelve tablets, who then translated them into the book of Genesis, then the Genesis Flood story predates the flood story in the Epic of Gilgamesh and not the other way around.

Additionally, there are several differences between the two stories.[23] In the Genesis flood, the boat is rectangular, while in the Gilgamesh flood, the boat is square. Engineering tells us that a rectangular boat could survive in an ocean, but a square boat would not survive because the four corners could not be strengthened sufficiently to take the ocean's pounding of waves—which is why all ships today are rectangular in shape. This is because the ocean's waves would toss the boat around, stressing the members (the boat's ribs and strakes) until they begin to separate at the corners of the boat, and the boat would sink. Thus, a square boat is impractical, while a rectangular boat is practical, making the Gilgamesh story impractical.

Another difference in the stories is that the water comes from both the ground and the sky in the Genesis account, but in the Gilgamesh account the water comes from the sky alone. The atmosphere cannot contain enough water to flood the surface of the earth, so again the Gilgamesh story lacks credibility.

Both stories have the boat landing in the same general vicinity in the Middle East, but about three-hundred-miles apart. The Genesis account has the boat landing on Mount Ararat, while the Gilgamesh story has the boat landing on Mount Nisir. Therefore, though the two stories are similar they do have recognizable differences, with the biblical story reading more like history than myth, while the Gilgamesh Epic reads more like a myth.

Dinosaurs Covered by Flood Waters

Almost all dinosaurs are found in sedimentary strata layers. This means that the dinosaurs—even the largest sauropod—died and then were covered over by flood water conditions—rapidly. It is postulated that when a dinosaur died, it was slowly covered in sediment. There are two problems with this hypothesis.

One problem is that any life form decays rapidly, geologically speaking. If a dinosaur died, most of its remains would be destroyed or broken down by the elements within a year or less. However, many dinosaur fossils have been found relatively intact. They also have been found with fossilized skin and internal organs. An article in the journal *Science* reported researchers found internal organs that should have decayed before it could become fossilized, stating "Using ultraviolet (UV) light from an ordinary UV lamp, Ruben was able to identify the outlines of the intestines, liver, trachea, and muscles of an incredibly well-preserved 100-million-year-old Scipionyx, a raptor or small meat eater."[24] Likewise, an article found in the *Natural History Museum* quoted researchers saying, "In the case of dinosaurs we have their skeletons, but we also have other evidence that can give insight into their daily lives, including preserved gut contents, eggs, nests, footprints, skin impressions and even dinosaur poo."[25]

Last, an article in the journal *Scientific Reports* show researchers even found skin impressions, stating that "The internal soft-tissue morphology of the sauropod tail is unknown, despite several specimens with preserved skin impressions."[26] If a long-geological period had passed between the dinosaur's death and its covering with sediment, then the dinosaur's skin and organs would have been eaten or decayed into nothing. We see this happen all the time when an animal is killed alongside the road—it rapidly breaks down.

The evolutionary premise is that it takes hundreds of thousands of years to create a strata layer. Yet, the empirical evidence suggests that these dinosaurs died in a flood-like condition *and* were rapidly buried by sediment. How could many dinosaurs, including a large sauropod, be covered quickly with multiple sedimentary layers before they rotted away?

The second problem is that almost all dinosaur fossils are found in sedimentary strata layers. Sedimentary layers are formed when flood waters carry sediment down river to cover lower levels with the sediment within the waters. As the water flow slows, it deposits the sediments. Only a small percentage of dinosaur fossils are found outside of sedimentary layers. A recent article on the website *Phys.org* stated the following, "Dr. Nick Longrich, from the Milner Center for Evolution at the University of Bath, led the study, which was published in Cretaceous Research. He said, "What's surprising here is that these are marine beds. It's a shallow, tropical sea full of plesiosaurs, mosasaurs, and sharks. It's not exactly a place you'd expect to find a lot of dinosaurs. But we're finding them.""[27]

The evidence indicates that a worldwide flood did occur, drowning dinosaurs—including even the largest dinosaurs on the planet. After an animal drowns, its body will naturally float for some time before sinking into the depths. After they drowned, the settling of the water and the shifting of the soil would allow for the burial of all species, even the largest, by sediments. Combining this information with the discovery of abundance of dinosaur soft tissue seems that a flood did, in fact, occur and is the only likely explanation of dinosaur's remains—outside of bones—of surviving the animal's burial by sediment.

Worldwide Flood Conclusion

We have the empirical evidence in the Bible that a worldwide flood occurred. We also have legends of a worldwide flood occurring, like the Gilgamesh flood story which appears to have been stylized after other historical accounts. We have depictions of dinosaurs in artform across the world. We also see the rapid death and burial of large and small dinosaurs, preserving skin impressions and many internal organs. This leads to the conclusion that the dinosaurs died in a flood, sank to the bottom after floating for a period, and then were rapidly buried by the disturbed silt caused by the waters settling into today's oceans. As demonstrated, all the evidence points to the occurrence of a worldwide flood.

❖ Bible Error: Rabbits don't chew cud

This is a misconception that a person will often encounter when debating anti-Christians. It stems from the Levitical Laws given to Moses about which animals could and could not be eaten because some of them were considered unclean. However, once a person delves into the issue, the apparent error is revealed to be a misconception caused by man's changing definitions of animals, rather than a biblical error. First, let us look at the passage that identified rabbits or hares as chewing the cud.

> Nevertheless these shall ye not eat of them that chew the cud, or of them that divide the hoof: as the camel, because he cheweth the cud, but divideth not the hoof; he is unclean unto you. And the coney, because he cheweth the cud, but divideth not the hoof; he is unclean

unto you. And the *hare, because he cheweth the cud*, but divideth not the hoof; he is unclean unto you. And the swine, though he divide the hoof, and be clovenfooted, yet he cheweth not the cud; he is unclean to you. (Leviticus 11:4–7, KJV) [emphasis added]

Part of the issue is a difference in understanding of the phrase "chews the cud." Cud is defined by *Merriam-Webster* as "food brought up into the mouth by a ruminating animal from its rumen to be chewed again."[28] A ruminating animal, like a cow, has four stomachs, the first stomach is called the rumen, hence the name "ruminating". The cow regurgitates partially digested vegetation to rechew the vegetation, aiding in the animal's digestive process. Following this definition, camels are not ruminants taxonomically, physiologically, or behaviorally because they do not have a rumen. Yet, even current government regulators have placed them in the category of ruminants. Camels are in the suborder/family of *"Tylopoda/Camelidae,"* while cattle are in the suborder/family of *"Ruminantia/Bovidae."* Ruminantia animals have four compartments to their stomachs while the camelidae have three compartments. Accordingly, the government is in the wrong on this identification, too. Yet, both categories of animals (cattle and camels) regurgitate their food to rechew it. Thus, the problem stems from a recent reclassification of animals involving those that "chew the cud."

The Swedish botanist, Carolus Linnaeus (1707–1778), is known as the Father of Modern Taxonomy—the classification of animals. He developed his classification system in 1758.[29] When he was developing his classification system, he defined the coney (aka: rock badger or hyrax)[30] and the rabbit[31] as ruminants (animals who chew regurgitated cud). All the animals in the Bible's unclean list as chewing the cud (camel, coney, and hare), move their jaws in such a manner as to appear to be chewing cud. In addition, rabbits rechew their partially digested food. Rabbits produce *cecotropes*, which are passed through the intestines and subsequently are reingested for added nutrients in a process known as *refection*.[32] *Merriam-Webster's* medical definition of refection is "the eating of feces especially by the animal producing them."[33] So, the discrepancy is caused by how society decided to change its classification system for animals, not that the Bible is scientifically wrong.

CHAPTER 25

TEXTUAL CRITICISM

One of the challenges in translating the New Testament manuscripts is that there is some variance between the thousands of copies. This variance is less than one percent, but scholars are at odds as to which version should be used when these differences arise. This area of biblical scholarship is known as textual criticism, which attempts to determine what the original text contained compared to what is available to us today.

Berean Patriot writes that "There are three major competing Greek sources to use for translating the New Testament: the Critical Text, the Majority Text, and the Textus Receptus."[1] He then goes into detail on how textual criticism plays a role in determining what the original author wrote, how the variants from that original writing most likely came to occur, and—most importantly—the significance of those variants.

All the variants are from what will be referred to as the *Original Text*, to differentiate between the variants. Since these early manuscripts were often purged by the Roman Empire (see Biblical Canon section), none of the Original Text exist. However, these twenty-seven manuscripts spawned over 5,800 variants over the last two thousand years—all with less than 99 percent variance between all of them, so that indicates a very high accuracy in the transmission of the text. With that said, there are four groups of variants in these copies, the Byzantine Majority Text, the Textus Receptus (which is partly based upon the Majority Text), the Alexandrian Text, and the Critical Text (which is mostly based upon the Alexandrian Text).

❖ Majority Text and Textus Receptus

As the name implies, the *Byzantine Majority Text* represents the majority of the New Testament Greek texts available, with most estimates between 85–90 percent of all Greek text manuscripts belonging in this group. The *Textus Receptus* is loosely based upon the Majority Text. "That the Textus Receptus (TR) resembles the majority text is no accident, since in compiling the TR Erasmus simply used about a half dozen late manuscripts that were available to him."[2] The first version of the Textus Receptus was from Complutensian Polyglot in 1514, although Desiderius Erasmus usually gets the credit for the Textus Receptus due to his publication of five versions between 1516 and 1535. Later versions of the Textus Receptus included the version by Elzevir 1624, and a later version by Scrivener in 1894.[3] Those that advocate for the use of the Majority Text premise their advocacy based upon the number of copies that exists for the Majority Text.

Writing for *GB Times – The Spirit Magazine*, Emma Miller writes the following about the Textus Receptus version of the New Testament.

> The Textus Receptus played an important role in the Protestant Reformation, as it provided a Greek text of the New Testament that could be used to challenge the authority of the Roman Catholic Church. Protestant reformers used the Textus Receptus to translate the New Testament into vernacular languages, such as English, so that people could read and interpret the Bible for themselves.[4]

The term Textus Receptus means "received text," but its name is very misleading. In fact, it was a compilation of printed editions of the New Testament mostly done between 1516 to 1633, for a total of twenty-seven versions coming as late as 1894.[5] In addition, it was not called Textus Receptus until 1630, when the Latin blurb "This is the text that is received by all"[6] was placed in an advertisement for it.

Erasmus began his printing process of the Greek version using three manuscripts. The last leaf of the book of Revelation was missing, so Erasmus utilized his defective copy of the Latin Vulgate to translate the Latin into Greek for the last six verses of Revelation. In his efforts, "he created twenty new textual variants that have not been found in any other manuscripts."[7] Even after he finished his publication, Erasmus admitted that he was not pleased with his rushed publication, and that he never liked it. "In the late 1800s, Frederick Scrivener said that there was no book that he had seen with as many errors as Erasmus's first edition of what is referred to as Textus Receptus."[8] The later editions attempted to correct the errors found in the earlier versions.

❖ Alexandrian Text and Critical Text

The copies of the New Testament manuscripts which did not fall into the Majority Text are referred to as the *Alexandrian Texts*, which were found in Alexandria Egypt. The difference between the Majority Text and the Alexandrian Text are minor—less than one percent variation.

The use of the Majority Text as the authoritative source of the New Testament text in modern Bible changed with the discovery of two early Greek manuscripts, the Codex Sinaiticus and the Codex Vaticanus. The first was found in 1844, while the latter languished in Vatican Library, possibly appearing in the library's earliest catalog of 1475.[9] These findings changed biblical scholars' thinking on how to determine what the Original Text contained, from basing it upon which group had the most copies (i.e., weight) over to which group was oldest (*i.e.*, earlier is better). Geisler and Nix advanced the case for the use of the *Critical Text* in their book titled, *A General Introduction to the Bible, Rev. and expanded.*

The ancient manuscripts are the most important witnesses to the autographs and, by the method of textual criticism ..., they form the basis for the modern versions of the Bible .... Some early modern versions were based on medieval versions ...; however, since the discoveries of the great manuscripts of the New Testament and other miscellaneous items, most recent versions and translations are based on the latter. These discoveries form the basis of the critical Greek text rather than the so-called Received Text used as the authority of the earlier modern versions. In the minds of most modern textual scholars, that so-called "critical" text represents an objective attempt to reconstruct the autographs. It is a scientific approach to the question of integrity, and it concludes that the present Greek text (after the Nestle/United Bible Societies text) is probably over 99 percent accurate in reproducing the exact words of the autographs. Others maintain that the Received Text, or "Majority Text," is preferred.[10]

These discoveries spawned a revolution between Bible scholars around biblical textual criticism—Should the Bible use the Majority Text or the Critical Text? While this is still debated today, most modern Bible translations have moved to the Critical Text as their underlying foundation for the translation of the Greek New Testament books, as Luke Wayne wrote for *CARM.org*.

Most modern translations are based on a modern Critical Text platform often known as the Nestle-Aland/UBS (NU) platform. This is an eclectic text compiled from diverse manuscripts, but one that often gives weight to the earliest manuscripts even when they are in the minority. Thus, the NU often differs with the M-Text, but almost always based on how early and/or diverse the testimony for the minority reading is.[11]

So, there are differences between the two major versions, Textus Receptus and Critical Text. These differences number in the thousands, but why? Here's an example of how one simple error can magnify into dozens or even hundreds of variants. Note, this example is based upon an example from Berean Patriot's webpage titled *Majority Text vs. Critical Text vs. Textus Receptus – Textual Criticism 101*.[12] Let us suppose the following variant gets introduced early in history (i.e., AD 600), whereby the Original Text stated "But we were *gentle* among you, even as a nurse cherisheth her children:" (I Thessalonians 2:7, KJV). Our example is partially fictitious in reference to the number of copies. The next word is a minor variation, but it is copied by other scribes later in history: ēpioi (Greek: gentle) verses nēpioi (Greek: little children).[13] If the Original Text version is copied twenty times before the second variant is made by a copyist's error, but that error is then copied "as is" for another one hundred copies over the next thousand years, then you have twenty "correct" variants out of a total of 120 variants. But only one error was made, and it doesn't significantly impact the meaning. Yet, the Majority Text weighting process (i.e., more copies indicate Original Text) demands the interpretation of "little children" over the original text of "gentle". Meanwhile, the Critical Text method places more weight on when the manuscript was written, and since the one hundred variants occurred after the twenty earlier versions (with "gentle"), it rejects the "little children" as the Original Text, yielding the translation of "gentle" as the correct text.

In conclusion, most modern Bible versions utilize the Nestle-Aland (Critical Text) as the foundation of their Greek New Testament translation, while the King James Version and a few others (like Young's Literal Translation) still use the Textus Receptus version for their Greek New Testament translation.

CHAPTER 26

KING JAMES VERSION
(AUTHORIZED VERSION)

During the Medieval Era, the Church was going through an upheaval over the interpretation of certain passages of the Bible and other church issues like the infallibility of the Pope. One of these conflicts was over the translation of the Bible from the church's Bible in Latin into a translation of the modern language. Several translations were spawned during this conflict. One of the most well-known translations is the King James Version (also known as the Authorized Version). However, few people know of the challenges the translators of the King James Version faced in their translation process. These challenges resulted in today's conflict over the King James Version Bible, and the numerous errors found in the King James Version of the Bible.

❖ Protestant Reformation

The Protestant Reformation was initially perceived as a means of correcting what biblical scholars perceived as the Church's erroneous thinking. Coupled with that were new inventions by Europeans. One of the inventions that was new to European people was the printing press, which was invented in China but further developed Johannes Gutenberg in the 1400s.[14] Some Medieval church leaders wanted to use this device to translate the Bible from its current translation of the Latin Vulgate into modern languages so that anyone could read and interpret the Scriptures themselves. These differences resulted in the split of the Church into two separate branches— known today as the Catholic Church and the Protestant Church. The Catholic Church kept to the traditional ways, using the Latin Vulgate as its official Bible. Meanwhile, the Protestant Church began experimenting with translating the Bible into modern languages, including English and German. A part of this effort included using a printed version called Textus Receptus as their source for the translations of the Greek New Testament text.

❖ Textus Receptus

There were many attempts to translate the Bible into modern languages, including the German Luther Bible, the New Testament into English by William Tyndale (1526), Myles Coverdale's Bible (1535), Matthew's Bible (1537), The Great Bible (1539), The Geneva Bible (1557–1560), and The Bishops's Bible (1568). The most recognized version of these efforts is known today as the King James Bible. The King James Bible translation was started in 1604 and finished in 1611. It got its name because it was sponsored by the English monarch, King James. Like the previous efforts to translate the Bible into a modern language, it too used the Textus Receptus as its foundation in translating the New Testament into English. The main problem with the King James Version is the numerous variants introduced due to the use of the Textus Receptus as its source for the New Testament text.

Adulterous Woman Caught in the Act

One of the more famous new textual variants created by the Textus Receptus is the passage found at the beginning of John chapter eight, where a woman was caught in the act of adultery.

> Jesus went unto the mount of Olives. And early in the morning he came again into the temple, and all the people came unto him; and he sat down, and taught them. And the scribes and Pharisees brought

unto him a woman taken in adultery; and when they had set her in the midst, They say unto him, Master, this woman was taken in adultery, in the very act. Now Moses in the law commanded us, that such should be stoned: but what sayest thou? This they said, tempting him, that they might have to accuse him. But Jesus stooped down, and with his finger wrote on the ground, as though he heard them not. So when they continued asking him, he lifted up himself, and said unto them, He that is without sin among you, let him first cast a stone at her. And again he stooped down, and wrote on the ground. And they which heard it, being convicted by their own conscience, went out one by one, beginning at the eldest, even unto the last: and Jesus was left alone, and the woman standing in the midst. When Jesus had lifted up himself, and saw none but the woman, he said unto her, Woman, where are those thine accusers? hath no man condemned thee? She said, No man, Lord. And Jesus said unto her, Neither do I condemn thee: go, and sin no more. (John 8:I–8:II, KJV)

This passage is not found in any of the early Greek manuscripts. However, I personally like it because it encapsulates the teaching of Jesus in one simple story. Throughout Scripture, God's message to His followers is to "Repent and sin no more." It is found in the Old Testament (I Kings 8:47 and Ezekiel 14:6, among others) and it is found in the New Testament (Matthew 4:17 and Luke 5:32, among others).

The New Testament term "repent" comes from the Greek word "μεταμέλομαι" [metamelomai][15], which *Enhanced Strong's Lexicon* defines as "I to change one's mind, i.e. to repent. 2 to change one's mind for better, heartily to amend with abhorrence of one's past sins."[16] So, this short story may not be in the original manuscripts, but it still cuts to the heart of Jesus's teachings. However, one must be careful of "adding or subtracting" words from the Bible. This is my personal opinion, and some people may prefer to keep to the original text for their Bible translation rather than use a version with acknowledged corruptions in the text.

However, there are other variants that were introduced as well. One of them is found in First John. "For there are three that bear record *in heaven, the Father, the Word, and the Holy Ghost: and these three are one. And there are three that bear witness in earth*, the Spirit, and the water, and the blood: and these three agree in one." (I John 5:7–8, KJV). The highlighted words are additions to the Original Text and are known as the Johannine Comma. "The passage appears to have originated as a gloss [a brief notation] in a Latin manuscript around the end of the 4th century ... and subsequently entered the Greek manuscript tradition in the 15th century ... The comma is absent from the Ethiopic, Aramaic, Syriac, Slavic, Armenian, Georgian, and Arabic translations of the Greek New Testament."[17] To summarize, it was not a part of the original Greek text, but was a Latin note added by a scholar, and then was subsequently added to a Greek text less than one hundred years before the King James Version was published.

Another problem with the King James Version is that the reader must overcome the translation of Old English into Modern English. One example is the passage which states that "So David slept with his fathers" (I Kings 2:10a, KJV), which is understood today to say that "So David died." In today's vernacular, "sleeping with someone" implies sexual immorality.

❖ King James Version Conclusion

The King James Version was a good attempt at translating the original language into English. However, it is written in Old English, rather than today's modern English. For its time, it was a well-written translation. However, much has been learned since then about translating the original languages. Additionally, the King James Version utilized the Textus Receptus (which added twenty variants not found in any other Greek manuscripts) for the New Testament. It was cobbled together, including using a translation-of-a-translation for a few verses of its final form. There is no major harm in using the King James Version, if one realizes the limitations of this translation attempt.

CHAPTER 27

CHRISTIANITY CONCLUSION

C hristianity has two branches, one of which has included some books of doubtful authenticity. It can be proven that the books in the Old Testament were passed down as manuscripts that can be validated as being accurately transmitted over the millennium from the Dead Sea Scrolls to the Masoretic Text that scholars use today to render the Old Testament. Likewise, it can be proven that the books of the New Testament have been passed down 99.9% accurately to today's versions of the Bible.

The Catholic Bibles include the Deuterocanonical books as divinely inspired, even though they were not considered to be divinely inspired historically. There are no issues in reading books that are not divinely inspired writings, until that person starts to apply their teachings to guide their beliefs toward truth.

There are numerous attempts by anti-Christians to cast doubt upon the Christian faith, many of which have been discussed in this book. For any challenge to the Christian faith, one must consider the empirical facts, and one must view the issue from both their own viewpoint and God's viewpoint. These two viewpoints are often widely disparate in thinking, so it takes a special effort to see it from God's perspective.

One of the most common attacks on Christianity is about the numerous versions of the Bible. One must realize that some translations seek a word-for-word translation to "remain true to the original writings," (*i.e.,* New American Standard Bible) while others seek a "thought for thought" translation (New International Version). Both versions have their own merits. Still other translations seek to utilize modern ideas to translate the Bible. While this may be admirable, it can lead to a dangerous corruption of the actual meaning. The use of the King James Version is not necessarily dangerous, if the reader understands that some passages were inadvertently added to the original text of the divinely inspired Word of God. When in doubt, consider several different versions of the Bible to seek the message God intended for His followers. You can utilize experts for guidance and clarity, but do not depend exclusively upon any one expert. Utilize online resources to seek out the meaning of the word in the original language, if necessary. The focus should be on the application of God's Word to your life as He *intended* it to be interpreted. To utilize the cliché, "practice makes perfect." So, study often, seek advice, and dig into His written Word.

OTHER RELIGIONS

❖ Introduction

There are hundreds of religions other than Naturalism and Christianity. This book will only address some of the more popular religions, limiting the discussion to a brief overview of Judaism, Islam, Buddhism, and Hinduism.

❖ Judaism

Judaism utilizes the same books for its holy writings as those contained in the Old Testament Bible. As such, much of the empirical evidence presented in the case for Christianity is applicable to Judaism also. The main difference is that Judaism does not recognize the New Testament as holy scripture.

In my viewpoint, this weakens their faith, given that one of the prophecies presented in this book was from Revelation, which is found in the New Testament. If this prophecy is indeed a foretelling from God, then Judaism does not include all of God's evidence that would be needed to determine the bullseye of the truth target.

❖ Islam

Islam is like Christianity and Judaism in some areas, so there is some empirical evidence for Islam. Nonetheless, Islam selectively rejects most of the Protestant Bible. Islam includes parts of the book of Genesis but rejects other parts—specifically the part that declared Isaac as the anointed line through which God's blessing would pass. The primary scriptures for Muslims (*i.e.*, followers of Islam) is the Koran (aka Quran).

Muslims believe that their god Allah did not send down the Quran all at once but sent it down as a series of wisdom teachings over a period of 23 years. They also believe that Muhammed was Allah's chosen prophet to give his message to Allah's followers. Allah did this by sending teachings to Muhammed. For a time, these teachings were memorized, but eventually several scribes, like Zaid bin Thabet, undertook the task of recording these teachings during the life of Muhammed.

These teachings (*ayats* or verses) were compiled into chapters, called *Surahs*. After Muhammed's death in 632 AD, Islam leaders began the process of compiling these ayats into a single book, which is called the Quran. The first to undertake this mission was Abu Bakr Siddiq, who tasked companions with the project.

"The factor that helped the companions to compile the Quran was writing down each verse and surah that Allah revealed on different materials such as stones, papers, palm leaves, and pieces of leather. On the other side, the companions had a *strong memory* that helped him to retain many Quranic verses."[1] So, some of these ayats are based upon memory only. Later, the compilation work was handled by Umar Ibn Al Khattab, and even later by Umar's daughter Hafsah, who "was one of the most prominent contributors to compiling the Quran during her father's reign."[2] Compilation of the Quran continued under the reign of Usman bin Affan.

During the compilation of the Quran, Muslim conquests added other nations to their empire, which was divided into Caliphs. But this conquest had the impact of adding non-Arab speaking foreigners to the Islamic faith. Thus, these Surahs needed to be translated into their language for them to follow Muhammed's teachings. This created conflict in the Muslim community, with each party arguing which version was the authentic message from Allah. So, Usman bin Affan undertook the effort to compile the various teachings into a single book. "This version of the text, also known as 'Mushaf 'Uthman' in fact constitutes the ijma` (*consensus*) of the sahaba, all of whom agreed that it contained what Prophet Muhammad (peace and blessings of Allah be upon him) had brought as revelation from Allah."[3] Then, Usman bin Affan ordered all other versions of Muhammed's teachings burned.[4] This final version of the Quran is divided into 114 Surahs with varying numbers of ayats.

There are several main problems with the Islamic religion. First, is that it is a compilation reached by consensus and biases would—necessarily—be included in any such consensus. Second, any version except those blessed by the "ijma` of the sahaba" were burned, so no further verification can be made in modern times. Third, these teachings are instructions on how to live a proper life. Thus, there is no evidence of any attribute of a deity within the Quran. Fourth, which I think is the most damaging, is an ayat that explicitly defines Mary as a part of the Triune God, which is a falsehood. "And ʿon Judgment Dayʾ Allah will say, "O Jesus, son of Mary! Did you ever ask the people to *worship you and your mother as gods* besides Allah?"[5] (Surah 5:116). [emphasis added].

In my opinion, the lack of empirical evidence for any attribute of a deity, combined with empirical evidence of the fallibility for the so-named deity, destroys any hope that this religion is founded upon anything but the wishful thinking of people.

❖ Buddhism

Buddhism was founded more than 2,500 years ago in India by a man named Siddhartha Gautama, who subsequently became known as the Buddha. There is no single collection for all of Buddhist beliefs and traditions. Instead, there are three Buddhist Canons: the "Pali Canon" of the Theravada tradition, the "Chinese Buddhist Canon" used in East Asian Buddhist tradition, and the "Tibetan Buddhist Canon." The oldest extant Buddhist manuscript dates from the first century BC to the AD third century.

There are many different views and traditions of Buddhism, along with many interpretations of his teachings. At the core, Buddhism is a path to seek the truth, called "nirvana" or an enlightened state. To guide the Buddhist seeker, Buddha gave four "truths." These are that 1) suffering exists, 2) suffering is caused by ignorance and human cravings, 3) this suffering can be overcome, and 4) the way to end the suffering is to follow the "Noble Eightfold Path." This path consists of eight aspects, guided by one's views. These are known as the "right view," the "right intention," the "right speech," the "right action," the "right livelihood," the "right effort," the "right mindfulness," and the "right concentration." Last, there are three guides for a Buddhists to seek, "Budda, the teacher," "the Dharma—the teachings and truth," and the "Sangha" or the community of followers of Buddhism.

The core problem is that Budda never displayed any attributes of a deity. His guide may be useful for living a better life, but what empirical evidence is there to support such a belief system?

❖ Hinduism

Hinduism is one of the religions with the longest history, stretching back for several thousands of years, to around 1500 BC. It is possible that Hinduism got its start in the Harappan Civilization (Indus Valley in India). Hindu texts contain "universal truths" through symbolism and mythology. The primary source for the Hindu faith is the "Smriti Literature," which refers to memorized or remembered poetry and epics. They are popular because they are easy to understand and contain beautiful and exciting stories. The three most important texts of the Smriti literature are the "Mahabharata," the "Bhagavad Gita" and the "Ramayana."

The Mahabharata is the world's longest poem written between 900–701 BC. "That this is "a date not too far removed from the 8th or 9th century B.C." is likely."[6] It details a dispute between two important families, the Pandava and the Kaurava. The Bhagavad Gita is called the "Song of the Adorable One" and "According to the Indologist Arvind Sharma, the Gita is generally accepted to be a 2nd-century-BCE (200–101) BC text."[7] The Ramayana is a story about a royal couple named Ram and Sita and is about adventures in their lives. "Scholarly estimates for the earliest stage of the available text range from the 7th to 4th centuries BCE, with later stages extending up to the 3rd century CE."[8]

The core issue is that Hinduism does not display any attributes as coming from a deity. Thus, there is no empirical evidence to support it as a "truth" that one can base their life upon. It may bring a sense of peace to the reader, but why value it over any other literature written throughout history?

❖ Other Religions Conclusion

While Judaism has very strong support, it deliberately ignores other writings as divinely inspired, namely the book of Revelation found in the New Testament, which has empirical evidence as originated from God.

Islam attempts to hijack select writings for its own use, but it befouls its goal through its efforts. By selecting portions of the Old Testament, it seeks to claim itself as a God-based faith. Yet, by the rejection of complete manuscripts, it sets itself up *as god* with the ability to define what is authentic and what is not authentic. If one desires objectivity in seeking truth, one must accept manuscripts that have been empirically shown to be divinely inspired, even if that evidence no longer exists today.

One should also have a healthy sense of skepticism and not blindly accept any writings as divinely inspired truth without one's own testing for some empirical evidence of them being divinely inspired words. Thus, Islam goes off the rails in its arbitrary selection of parts of Genesis, while rejecting other parts of Genesis. Islam's weakness is revealed when its "scripture," the Quran, is demonstrated to have obvious errors contained within it. Thus, one is left with the conclusion that it is a human-inspired faith, rather than a God-inspired faith.

Buddhism and Hinduism do not claim to be divinely inspired, but a means to seek ultimate truth through wisdom from historical figures. Their faith may inspire a person to live a better life, but for what purpose? They lack facts to support their beliefs, so how can one be confident that they point toward the "truth bullseye?"

CONCLUSION

Naturalism is the only religion which has its tenets presented in a fashion that is testable. Yet it lacks validation for any of its core tenets. There is still a possibility of it leading to truth, but its analogy is a football team being on their own one-yard line with ninety-nine-yards to the touchdown. So, it takes a lot of faith to subscribe to that system of beliefs. Yet, most of its acolytes are blind to its shortcomings. Other religions, except for Christianity, lack any evidence for a deity and/or creator of the universe that we can observe with our own eyes.

Of all the religions on earth, Christianity is the only system of beliefs that is supported with empirical evidence. Its analogy is being on the defense's one-yard line, with only a single yard to the goal line. Yet, many modern churches today fail to teach this evidence to their congregants, leaving the average Christian leaning heavily upon blind faith in their efforts to follow Jesus Christ as their Lord and Savior.

My hope is that this book will strengthen fellow Christians in their walk with the One True God of this universe, that it clears the obstacles in the ground for people open-minded enough to consider the Christian faith, and (*maybe*) convince some Naturalists to consider Christianity more seriously. From my own experience, I know that people *never* change their worldviews overnight. For me, it was a twenty-five-year journey. But I hope my research will be of help to some struggling in their walk with the God of the Bible.

MY PERSONAL ENCOUNTER
WITH GOD

In the introduction, I intimated that I had a personal encounter with God that changed my life. This is somewhat misleading, as I didn't have just one encounter, but a series of encounters that spanned about a three-year period. Explaining these encounters are going to be difficult for two reasons, 1) there will be many doubters / mockers who will not believe me, and 2) the "spirit world" is vastly different than our "spacetime world." And the encounters were almost always an interaction between these two worlds.

God has many names within the Bible—Comforter, Lord God Almighty, The Most High God, Lord, Master, Jehovah, The Lord My Banner, The Lord That Heals, The Lord Our Righteousness, The Lord Who Sanctifies You, The Everlasting God, Jealous, The Lord Will Provide, The Lord is Peace, The Lord of Hosts, I Am who I Am, Judge, and Savior are just some of His many names. In the spirit world, all these names apply simultaneously. Imagine if we were to replace every occurrence of the words "Lord" or "God" throughout the Bible with all these names. The Bible would become excessively long and cumbersome to read. This is somewhat equivalent to describing interactions between our spacetime world and God's spirit world.

To simplify this communication challenge, I am going to capitalize words which apply to the spirit world, and you will need to understand that these few words would need to be expanded by many other words just to convey the proper meaning. Likewise, I will italicize words that I want to emphasize in our spacetime world. Using these two highlighting methods will help the reader to understand my story.

My story began in my mid-to-late teens when I was questioning the possible existence of God. I mulled this over for some time before reaching a conclusion that God did not exist, but Jesus did exist in the past. Thus, Jesus could not be the Son of God, but He was still a "good teacher" to follow. Almost immediately, I heard the words *"That's Not Good Enough,"* immediately followed by an ECHO impressed upon my mind. The ECHO was the words "for what I have planned for you."

What I mean by this is that the "words" were as clear in my mind as if I had heard them with my ears, but I knew my ears had not registered any sound. The ECHO is a term that I am going to use to describe the sensation of an indistinct conveyance of a message coming from the spirit world. These words or memories are always indistinct, but I will be putting them into words that may or may not be exactly what I heard or remember.

Needless to say, this first encounter scared me beyond belief. Sadly, I quickly rationalized this encounter away, dismissing it as just my imagination, and I *almost* promptly forgot it. Shortly after this, I started getting IMPRESSIONS of some minutiae, or very small detail, that would happen in my almost immediate future. This IMPRESSION would be properly referred to as a prophecy, but only applicable to my own life in a very small way.

What I can say about them is that 1) They began occurring frequently, usually three or more times per week. I do not remember the exact frequency, but they started off infrequently and become very frequent; 2) I was able to confirm 60 – 75 percent of them as being accurate; and 3) I only remember two of these IMPRESSIONS. These IMPRESSIONS were of a simple nature, like specific questions on an upcoming test in college, or a speed trap just ahead of me. Nothing that was of importance to anyone but me.

The first IMPRESSION that I am going to recount is that of speeding southbound on I-75 toward Tampa, Florida. I was approaching an overpass over Highway 54 and received the IMPRESSION that a cop was approaching northbound on the other side of the overpass. Almost immediately, I dismissed this as my imagination. Sure enough, just as I got to the foot of the overpass, a cop topped the overpass. I got pulled over and was given a speeding ticket.

The only other IMPRESSION that I remember occurred late at night after a date. I was returning from Tampa, driving my girlfriend back to her home, on a backcountry road between Highway 54 and Dade City Florida. As we were running late, I was speeding to make up time. My dad, ex-military / Navy UDT, was a *stickler* for timeliness. So, I did not want to be late and get into trouble. I was also living at home at the time, while going to college (University of South Florida). So, you should have an idea of my motivation to arrive home on time.

I was driving about 80 MPH in a 55 MPH zone. There were no other cars on the road. Suddenly, I saw distant oncoming headlights of a car about two miles away. I immediately got the IMPRESSION that it was a cop. I immediately slowed down to 55 MPH. My date asked me why I slowed down. I responded that "I think that car is a cop." So, I leisurely cruised along at a sedate pace of 55 MPH until we passed the car. As we passed, I saw the door emblem of a county Sheriff's Deputy car. That shook me up too, and I commented on the fact to my date. Did it last? Nope. I immediately sped back up to about 80 MPH to get home on time.

While I only remember these two IMPRESSIONS, I need to stress that I was receiving these IMPRESSIONS on a regular basis. In fact, they were so frequent that they could have been happening multiple times per day, but I do not remember for sure.

After about two and a half years of this, I reached my limit. I wanted further proof. I wanted to see God face-to-face and give Him the "what-for" attitude. If you think this is absurd, I agree. It was. Fortunately, or unfortunately, He granted my request. Again, as I was driving on that lonely backcountry road between Highway 54 and Dade City, I was caught up "IN THE SPIRIT"—all the way to Heaven.

As I was driving, I suddenly "floated" up from my driving position behind the steering wheel to above my car looking down at my car. As I overcame my shock, I realized that I could UNDERSTAND everything I was seeing. I could sense every blade of grass, every insect, tree—well everything. There was nothing that I could see with which I was not *intimately* familiar. I also realized that I could sense a PRESENCE near me, but I could not see anyone. I will refer to this PRESENCE as an ANGEL. Let me be clear on one thing. Many people claiming to have an out-of-body experience claim to have a "string" linking their spirit back to their body. There was no such string in my VISION.

But my VISION was only the beginning. As soon as I UNDERSTOOD everything I viewed, I was taken to the next level up. I could see and UNDERSTAND everything on earth—all its inhabitants, the cities, the animals, everything. But my UNDERSTANDING of the immediate surroundings of my car no longer existed. I could only view and UNDERSTAND the whole of the earth. For each step up that I took, I lost the previous UNDERSTANDING of the lower step. Today, I think that loss was because my mind could not contain all that I UNDERSTOOD for every level. I experienced this change every time I advanced to the next level, so I will not be repeating myself every time I describe going up a level.

The next level up allowed me to UNDERSTAND our solar system. I could view and UNDERSTAND the relationships between the planets and the sun, much like a scientist would understand the relationship between protons, neutrons, and electrons in an atom. In fact, my recollection of that understanding is one like an atom. My ANGEL took me to the next level—I could UNDERSTAND our galaxy. It functioned much like a single cell in the human body. It had its processes and role within the larger perspective—the next level up.

Next, I could UNDERSTAND a whole host of galaxies. They had their functions too, much like a human finger or an organ within the human chest—all working in harmony with each other. Then, my PERCEPTION expanded even further—to the universe. I could UNDERSTAND the entire vast universe and saw it like a living creature. I *think* I also *partially* UNDERSTOOD a larger view—one of multiple universes like people interacting with one another. Suddenly, all this ended. My view switched to one of being in heaven, standing outside the Throne Room of God, Himself.

Once there, my ANGEL left me, saying something along the lines of "wait until He calls you." I looked around me. I saw a vast doorway. The other side of the entrance was at least thirty feet away, but it could have been as much as eighty feet away. I could not perceive the height of the doorway, nor could I perceive the other side of the hallway. The most telling feature of my surroundings was the contrast of the light and darkness.

The hallway that I stood in appeared as near dusk, yet I could see my surroundings clearly. The most notable thing that I saw was a "SUPER BRIGHT, MAGESTIC, PERFECTION LIGHT" that came out of the Throne room into the waiting area. I noticed that it strangely did not have any gray-area, the change between the LIGHT and dark areas, unlike what we see on earth. It was just a razor-sharp line separating the LIGHT from the darkness.

I suddenly realized that I was about to confront *God*. I immediately perceived my fallen nature—a worthless, corrupt person full of junk about to confront complete perfection. I felt more shame and embarrassment than I have ever felt before or since. As soon as that emotion hit me, I FELL from heaven back to behind the steering wheel of my car. While the journey *to heaven* seemed to take several hours, the return journey *from heaven* seemed to take less than a second.

But it did not take long for me to start rationalizing my experience away. "It was just a dream. It *was not* real." But inside—I *knew* it was real. I just did not want to admit it to myself. So, I returned to my sinful lifestyle. I used people and did a lot of other bad things. None of the things that I did would be considered that unusual by today's standards, but inside me, I knew God's standards—and I did not match up *at all*.

Life went on as usual, and the IMPRESSIONS returned after my encounter in Heaven. Shortly thereafter, I got tired of the constant IMPRESSIONS. I confessed to God that I *did* believe that He existed, and that Jesus was His Son. Almost immediately, things changed. I got an ECHO from God, something along the line of "Okay, the IMPRESSIONS will stop, but remember that I'll always be with you even if it doesn't seem like it." And "QUIET" reigned in my life! At the time, it seemed like such a relief.

A little while later, I was returning home from college on a 125 cc Honda motorcycle at night. The high beam was out, so I had angled the low beam to show the road conditions further than is normal for low beam headlights. As usual, I was late and rushing to get home. Because of poor visibility, I barely had time to react to a curve in the road and needed to lean the bike almost over on its side to keep from going off the road and having a wreck.

Almost immediately, I realized that I had overcorrected, and started worrying about wrecking the bike by falling all the way over onto its side. So, I straightened up the bike. Too much. I corrected again by almost leaning it onto its side again, only to realize that I had again overcorrected. This sequence went on several times until I got through the curve. After I got through the curve, I realized that, by all rights, I *should have died* on that curve. Then, I got a faint ECHO from God, saying something like "I told you that I would always be there for you." That day endeared my connection to God for me. Several months passed with complete quiet. Then one day, I got my last ECHO from God.

My dad enjoyed fishing, usually with a partner, but that day he did not have a partner with him. So, he requested that, at sundown, I drive out on my new 1980 450 cc Suzuki motorcycle to help him load his canoe into his truck. I usually rode my bike to and from school / work during daylight hours. So, I had a tinted visor on my helmet to deal with daylight conditions. But it was dusk. I started driving to meet my dad anyway.

About two miles from my home, I pulled up to a stop sign, going from a cross street onto US 301. As usual, I looked both directions for cars—twice. Nothing there, so I started moving forward, leaning my bike into making the left turn. Suddenly, my headlight was reflecting off the chrome of a near and oncoming car bumper. I locked the brakes on the bike, front and rear. However, my bike had traveled the length of the diameter of the front wheel onto US 301—and in front of the oncoming car. Next thing I knew was that I was tumbling in the grass about twenty feet from my, now destroyed, bike. Except for a few scratches and a "burn" on my helmet, I was completely safe.

Imagine my shock! "Why didn't You give me a WARNING of the upcoming accident?" The ECHO that came back was something along the lines of "I *told* you that I would always keep you safe, but that the IMPRESSIONS would stop." He was right. I needed to move from listening for IMPRESSIONS to walking in faith. I had to grow. This came about very slowly in my life.

I first bought the book *Late Great Planet Earth* and learned about God's prophecies. Then, I got a digital copy of the Bible. Then, I read through the entire Bible for the first time in my life. Then I got into debates between

Christians and anti-Christians. This book is about my research that spawned from those debates.

God has always blessed me with the intense and perverse ability and desire to overcome all odds in finding Truth. The harder the challenge, the more enjoyment I get in digging out the empirical facts. Through my journey, I came to realize that I could never trust someone else' conclusions, even my fellow Christians' conclusions. I could only depend upon their summary of empirical facts.

Mulling over my life, I have come to several realizations. I) I am not very good at faith. I need to see the evidence before I can believe it; 2) I am better than most people at digging for facts, in both stubbornness and methodology; 3) I am a very bad person without Jesus actively in my life; 4) I am suited for rooting out falsehoods, digging out obstacles preventing abundant faith, and tearing out the thorny issues plaguing Christianity today.

In short, I am a good "plowman," but I'm not very good at "sowing the seed", nor "watering and nurturing the seedling." But I recognize that God has a place for everyone. And mostly, I am content to be the person God designed me to be—accepting my failures and my "good works" as God's means of tempering my steel plow blade into an effective tool for Christ.

WORKS CITED

Allchin, Frank Raymond. 2023. *Indus civilization.* June 26. Accessed July 13, 2023. https://www.britannica.com/topic/Indus-civilization.

American Heritage® Dictionary of the English Language, Fifth Edition. S.v. n.d. *doctrine.* Accessed July 13, 2023. https://www.thefreedictionary.com/doctrine.

Amino Acids Guide. 2023. *Amino Acids.* May 29. Accessed July 13, 2023. https://aminoacidsguide.com/.

Ashton, David Down and Dr. John. 2010. *A Correct Chronology.* January 21. Accessed July 13, 2023. https://answersingenesis.org/archaeology/ancient-egypt/a-correct-chronology/.

Associates for Biblical Research. 2021. *When Did the Exodus Happen?* September 09. Accessed July 13, 2023. https://www.biblestudytools.com/bible-study/explore-the-bible/recent-research-on-the-date-and-setting-of-the-exodus.html.

Badham, H. Clemney and N. 1982. "Oxygen in the Precambrian atmosphere: An evaluation of the geological evidence." *Geology.* 10 (3), 141.

BAS Staff. 2023. *The Gospel of Thomas's 114 Sayings of Jesus.* March 16. Accessed August 31, 2023. https://www.biblicalarchaeology.org/daily/biblical-topics/bible-versions-and-translations/the-gospel-of-thomas-114-sayings-of-jesus/.

Basyony, Sherine. n.d. *Compilation Of Quran: History, Stages, Purposes, Importance, And More!* Accessed July 13, 2023. https://bayanulquran-academy.com/the-history-of-compilation-of-the-quran/.

Bible Study Tools. n.d. *Apocrypha Books*. Accessed July 13, 2023. https://www.biblestudytools.com/apocrypha/.

Biblica, Inc. n.d. *How were the books of the Bible chosen?* Accessed July 13, 2023. https://www.biblica.com/resources/bible-faqs/how-were-the-books-of-the-bible-chosen/.

Biblical Archaeology Review. 2003. "Summary report of the Examining Committees for the James Ossuary and Yehoash Inscription." *Biblical Archaeology Review 29:5*, September/October.

BiblicalTraining.org. n.d. *Habiru, Hapiru*. Accessed July 13, 2023. https://www.biblicaltraining.org/library/habiru-hapiru.

Biography.com Editors. 2014. *Saul Biography*. September 08. Accessed July 13, 2023. https://www.biography.com/religious-figures/saul.

Biography.com. n.d. *Pontius Pilate*. Accessed July 13, 2023. https://www.biography.com/religious-figures/pontius-pilate.

Black, Riley. n.d. *Who Pays for Dino Research?* Accessed July 13, 2023. https://www.smithsonianmag.com/science-nature/who-pays-for-dino-research-66263095/.

Bolinger, Hope. 2020. *What Is the Codex Vaticanus?* March 18. Accessed July 13, 2023. https://www.christianity.com/wiki/bible/what-is-codex-vaticanus.html.

Bright Hub Engineering. n.d. *What is a Thermodynamic System? Types of Thermodynamic Systems*. Accessed July 13, 2023. https://www.brighthubengineering.com/thermodynamics/3733-what-is-a-thermodynamic-system/.

British Library Board. n.d. *Codex Alexandrinus*. Accessed July 13, 2023. https://www.bl.uk/collection-items/codex-alexandrinus.

Brodribb, Alfred John Church and William Jackson. n.d. *The Annals By Tacitus, Written 109 A.C.E.* Accessed July 13, 2023. http://classics.mit.edu/Tacitus/annals.11.xv.html.

Bush III, L. Russ. 1991. *A Handbook for Christian Philosophy*. Zondervan Academic.

Cambridge Dictionary. n.d. *Indoctrinate.* Accessed July 13, 2023. https://dictionary.cambridge.org/us/dictionary/english/indoctrination.

—. n.d. *Patina.* Accessed July 13, 2023. https://dictionary.cambridge.org/dictionary/english/patina.

Cartwright, Mark. 2014. *Inca Civilization.* September 15. Accessed July 13, 2023. https://www.worldhistory.org/Inca_Civilization/.

—. 2018. *Minoan Civilization.* March 29. Accessed July 13, 2023. https://www.worldhistory.org/Minoan_Civilization.

Cline, Douglas. n.d. *2.14: Newton's Law of Gravitation.* Accessed July 13, 2023. https://phys.libretexts.org/Bookshelves/Classical_Mechanics/Variational_Principles_in_Classical_Mechanics_(Cline)/02%253A_Review_of_Newtonian_Mechanics/2.14%253A_Newton's_Law_of_Gravitation.

Coghlan, Andy. 2014. *Massive 'ocean' discovered towards Earth's core.* June 12. Accessed July 13, 2023. https://www.newscientist.com/article/dn25723-massive-ocean-discovered-towards-earths-core/.

Collins English Dictionary. n.d. *Provenance.* Accessed July 13, 2023. https://www.collinsdictionary.com/us/dictionary/english/provenance.

Conti, S. Tschopp, E., Mateus, O. et al. 2022. *Multibody analysis and soft tissue strength refute supersonic dinosaur tail.* Accessed July 13, 2023. https://doi.org/10.1038/s41598-022-21633-2.

Dawkins, Richard. 1986. *The Blind Watchmaker: Why the Evidence of Evolution Reveals a Universe Without Design.* Penguin Publishing Group.

DeLong, William. 2018. *People Before Columbus Didn't Believe The Earth Was Flat, But Here's Why Some Think So.* February 06. Accessed July 13, 2023. https://allthatsinteresting.com/flat-earth-myth-before-columbus.

Denffer, Ahmad Von. 2022. *What Was the Qur'an Copy of 'Uthman.* October 31. Accessed August 23, 2023. https://aboutislam.net/shariah/quran/introduction-to-the-quran/what-was-the-quran-copy-of-uthman/.

Drake, Gordon W.F. 2003. *Thermodynamics.* June 21. Accessed July 13, 2023. https://www.britannica.com/science/thermodynamics.

Durant, Will. 1953. *The story of philosophy: The lives and opinions of the greater philosophers. [2d ed.].* Simon and Schuster.

Fields, Helen. 2006. *Dinosaur Shocker.* May. Accessed July 13, 2023. https://www.smithsonianmag.com/science-nature/dinosaur-shocker-115306469/.

Genesis Park. n.d. *Ancient Dinosaur Depictions.* Accessed July 13, 2003. https://www.genesispark.com/exhibits/evidence/historical/ancient/dinosaur/.

Geology.com. n.d. *Deepest Part of the Ocean.* Accessed July 13, 2023. https://geology.com/records/deepest-part-of-the-ocean.shtml.

Gleason, Kevin. 2017. *"Sex Limited Inheritance in Drosophila" (1910), by Thomas Hunt Morgan.* May 22. Accessed August 24, 2023. https://embryo.asu.edu/pages/sex-limited-inheritance-drosophila-1910-thomas-hunt-morgan.

Gleason, Kevin M. 2017. *Hermann Joseph Muller's Study of X-rays as a Mutagen, (1926-1927).* March 07. Accessed July 13, 2023. https://embryo.asu.edu/pages/hermann-joseph-mullers-study-x-rays-mutagen-1926-1927.

Gordon, Tim Childers and Jonathan. 2021. *What is a light-year?* December 22. Accessed July 13, 2023. https://www.space.com/light-year.html.

Got Questions Ministries. 2022. *What is partialism in relation to the Trinity?* January 4. Accessed November 17, 2023. https://www.gotquestions.org/Trinity-partialism.html.

Greek New Testament Dot Net. n.d. *Greek New Testament.* Accessed July 13, 2023. https://greeknewtestament.net/.

Hall, Terry. 1990. *How the Bible Became a Book.* Victor Books.

Hawking, Stephen W. 1988. *A Brief History of Time: From the Big Bang to Black Holes.* Cambridge University Press.

Haynie, Donald T. 2001. *Biological Thermodynamics.* Cambridge University Press.

Hendry, Prof Paul Barrett and Lisa. n.d. *Beyond Jurassic World: what we really know about dinosaurs and how.* Accessed July 13, 2023. https://www.nhm.

ac.uk/discover/what-can-scientists-learn-about-dinosaurs-and-how.
html.

History.com Editors. 2023. *Printing Press.* June 29. Accessed August 31, 2023.
https://www.history.com/topics/inventions/printing-press.

—. 2023. *Sumer.* June 06. Accessed July 13, 2023. https://www.history.com/
topics/ancient-middle-east/sumer.

Howe, Norman Geisler and Thomas. 1992. *When Critics Ask: A Popular
Handbook on Bible Difficulties.* Baker Books.

Hunter, Margaret. 2013. *Job is not on the Amazing Bible Timeline with World History.
Why not?* April 29. Accessed July 13, 2023. https://amazingbibletimeline.
com/blog/job-bible-timeline/.

Isaak, Mark. n.d. *Claim CD011.4: A freshly killed seal was carbon-14 dated at 1300
years old.* Accessed July 13, 2023. http://www.talkorigins.org/indexcc/
CD/CD011_4.html.

Johnson, Charles. 2023. *What Is the Heresy of Modalism?* March 17. Accessed
August 28, 2023. https://www.christianity.com/wiki/christian-terms/
what-heresy-modalism.html.

Kenyon, Fredric G. 1941. *Our Bible and the Ancient Manuscripts.* Eyre &
Spottiswoode.

Khattab, Mustafa. n.d. *Al-Ma'idah.* Accessed July 13, 2023. https://quran.
com/5.

Kimberley, Erich Dimroth and Michael M. 1976. "Precambrian atmospheric
oxygen: evidence in the sedimentary distributions of carbon, sulfur,
uranium, and iron." *Canadian Journal of Earth Sciences,* September 01:
1161-1185.

Kirby, Peter. n.d. *Hippolytus of Rome - The Refutation of all Heresies, Book V.*
Accessed July 13, 2023. http://www.earlychristianwritings.com/text/
hippolytus5.html.

—. n.d. *Irenaeus of Lyons: Book V.* Accessed July 13, 2023. http://www.
earlychristianwritings.com/text/irenaeus-book5.html.

KJV. 1611. *King James Version Bible.*

Koppes, Steve. 2022. *The origin of life on Earth, explained.* September 19. Accessed July 13, 2023. https://news.uchicago.edu/explainer/ origin-life-earth-explained.

Kramer, Joel P. 2022. *Evidence for Ancient Israel Discovered in Egypt.* July 22. Accessed July 13, 2023. https://www.youtube.com/watch?v=4z9V-44cLpQ.

Lemaire, André. 2002. "Burial Box of James the Brother of Jesus." *Biblical Archaeology Review 28:6,* November/December.

Lerner, K. Lee. n.d. *Eratosthenes Calculates The Circumference Of The Earth.* Accessed July 13, 2023. https://www.encyclopedia. com/science/encyclopedias-almanacs-transcripts-and-maps/ eratosthenes-calculates-circumference-earth.

LibQuotes. n.d. *Denis Diderot Quote.* Accessed July 13, 2023. https:// libquotes.com/denis-diderot/quote/lbv5d1c.

Lindahl, T. 1993. "Instability and decay of the primary structure of DNA." *Nature 362* 709–715.

Logical Fallacy. 2020. *False Dichotomy.* September 09. Accessed July 13, 2023. https://www.logical-fallacy.com/articles/false-dilemma/.

Loker, Richard Mann and Ryan. 2021. *Flies with Four Wings? Investigating Genes that Pattern Animal Bodies.* August 05. Accessed July 13, 2023. https://zuckermaninstitute.columbia.edu/flies-four-wings- investigating-genes-pattern-animal-bodies.

Lorey, Frank. 1997. *The Flood of Noah and the Flood of Gilgamesh.* March 01. Accessed July 13, 2023. https://www.icr.org/article/noah-flood-gilgamesh/.

Lubenow, Marvin L. 1992. *Bones of Contention: A Creationist Assessment of Human Fossils.* Baker Book House.

Lundström, Peter. n.d. *Manetho.* Accessed July 13, 2023. https://pharaoh. se/manetho-king-list.

Marcombe, Alex. 2023. *How Long Does Embalming Last? (Must Know Guide).* August 12. Accessed August 25, 2023. https://funeralcircle.com/how-long-does-embalming-last.

Marcus, Ivan Oransky and Adam. 2023. *There's far more scientific fraud than anyone wants to admit.* August 09. Accessed August 23, 2023. https://www.theguardian.com/commentisfree/2023/aug/09/scientific-misconduct-retraction-watch.

Mark, Joshua J. 2012. *Ancient China.* December 18. Accessed July 13, 2023. https://www.worldhistory.org/china/.

—. 2009. *Ancient Egypt.* September 02. Accessed July 13, 2023. https://www.worldhistory.org/egypt/.

—. 2013. *Ancient Greece.* November 13. Accessed July 13, 2023. https://www.worldhistory.org/greece/.

—. 2012. *Maya Civilization.* July 06. Accessed July 13, 2023. https://www.worldhistory.org/Maya_Civilization/.

—. 2018. *Roman Empire.* March 22. Accessed July 13, 2023. https://www.worldhistory.org/Roman_Empire/.

—. 2011. *Writing.* April 28. Accessed July 13, 2023. https://www.worldhistory.org/writing/.

McDougall, T.M. Harrison and I. 1981. "Excess 40Ar in Metamorphic Rocks from Broken Hill, New South Wales: Implications for 40Ar/39Ar Age Spectra and the Thermal History of the Region." *Earth and Planetary Science Letters, 55,* 123-149.

McDowell, Josh. 1997. *Josh McDowell's Handbook on Apologetics, electronic ed.* Nashville, TN: Thomas Nelson.

Merriam-Webster.com Dictionary. n.d. Accessed July 13, 2023. https://www.merriam-webster.com/dictionary/esoteric.

Merriam-Webster.com Dictionary. 2023. *Philosophy.* November 11. Accessed November 18, 2023. https://www.merriam-webster.com/dictionary/philosophy.

——. n.d. *ad infinitum.* Accessed July 13, 2023. https://www.merriam-webster. com/dictionary/ad%20infinitum.

——. n.d. *Agnostic.* Accessed July 13, 2023. https://www.merriam-webster. com/dictionary/agnostic.

——. n.d. *antilegomena.* Accessed August 31, 2023. https://www.merriam-webster.com/dictionary/antilegomena.

——. n.d. *Apocrypha.* Accessed July 13, 2023. https://www.merriam-webster. com/dictionary/apocrypha.

——. n.d. *Apologetics.* Accessed July 13, 2023. https://www.merriam-webster. com/dictionary/apologetics.

——. n.d. *Atheist.* Accessed July 13, 2023. https://www.merriam-webster.com/ dictionary/atheist.

——. n.d. *Blasphemy.* Accessed July 13, 2023. https://www.merriam-webster. com/dictionary/blasphemy.

——. n.d. *Centillion.* Accessed July 13, 2023. https://www.merriam-webster. com/dictionary/centillion.

——. n.d. *Cud.* Accessed July 13, 2023. https://www.merriam-webster.com/ dictionary/cud.

——. n.d. *dinosaur.* Accessed July 13, 2023. https://www.merriam-webster. com/dictionary/dinosaur.

——. n.d. *Entropy.* Accessed July 13, 2023. https://www.merriam-webster. com/dictionary/entropy.

——. n.d. *extant.* Accessed July 13, 2023. https://www.merriam-webster.com/ dictionary/extant.

——. n.d. *Globe.* Accessed July 13, 2023. https://www.merriam-webster.com/ dictionary/globe.

——. n.d. *Hypothesis.* Accessed July 13, 2023. https://www.merriam-webster. com/dictionary/hypothesis.

——. n.d. *in vivo.* Accessed July 13, 2023. https://www.merriam-webster.com/dictionary/in%20vivo.

——. n.d. *Ism.* Accessed July 13, 2023. https://www.merriam-webster.com/dictionary/ism.

——. n.d. *-ist.* Accessed July 13, 2023. https://www.merriam-webster.com/dictionary/-ist.

——. n.d. *Mitosis.* Accessed July 13, 2023. https://www.merriam-webster.com/dictionary/mitosis.

——. n.d. *Monotheism.* Accessed July 13, 2023. https://www.merriam-webster.com/dictionary/monotheism.

——. n.d. *Papyrus.* Accessed July 13, 2023. https://www.merriam-webster.com/dictionary/papyrus.

——. n.d. *Polytheism.* Accessed July 13, 2023. https://www.merriam-webster.com/dictionary/polytheism.

——. n.d. *Postulate.* Accessed July 13, 2023. https://www.merriam-webster.com/dictionary/postulate.

——. n.d. *Premise.* Accessed July 13, 2023. https://www.merriam-webster.com/dictionary/premise.

——. n.d. *Programme.* Accessed July 13, 2023. https://www.merriam-webster.com/dictionary/programme.

——. n.d. *quatrain.* Accessed August 31, 2023. https://www.merriam-webster.com/dictionary/quatrain.

——. n.d. *Religion.* Accessed July 13, 2023. https://www.merriam-webster.com/dictionary/religion.

——. n.d. *Space-time.* Accessed July 13, 2023. https://www.merriam-webster.com/dictionary/space-time.

——. n.d. *Sphere.* Accessed July 13, 2023. https://www.merriam-webster.com/dictionary/sphere.

—. n.d. *Tenet.* Accessed July 13, 2023. https://www.merriam-webster.com/dictionary/tenet.

—. n.d. *Theist.* Accessed July 13, 2023. https://www.merriam-webster.com/dictionary/theist.

—. n.d. *Theory.* Accessed July 13, 2023. https://www.merriam-webster.com/dictionary/theory.

—. n.d. *Worldview.* Accessed July 13, 2023. https://www.merriam-webster.com/dictionary/worldview.

Miller, Emma. n.d. *What is the Textus Receptus?* Accessed July 13, 2023. https://gbtimes.com/what-is-the-textus-receptus/.

Miller, F. J. Fitch and J. A. 1970. "Radioisotope Age Determination of Lake Rudolf Artifact Site." *Nature 226*, April 18: 226-228.

Müller-Wille, Staffan. 2023. *Carolus Linnaeus - The Father of Modern Taxonomy.* May 19. Accessed July 13, 2023. https://www.britannica.com/biography/Carolus-Linnaeus.

National Science Foundation. n.d. *The State of U.S. Science and Engineering 2020.* Accessed July 13, 2023. https://ncses.nsf.gov/pubs/nsb20201/.

Newton, Isaac. 1687. *Philosophiae Naturalis Principia Mathematica.*

Nicole, Tiffany. 2023. *Bible Translation Comparison: Top 10 Most Accurate Bible Translations.* Accessed August 31, 2023. https://lavendervines.com/bible-translation-comparison/.

Nida, Johannes P. Louw and Eugene Albert. 1996. *Greek-English Lexicon of the New Testament: Based on Semantic Domains.* New York: United Bible Societies.

Nijssen, Daan. 2018. *Cyrus the Great.* February 18. Accessed July 13, 2023. https://www.worldhistory.org/Cyrus_the_Great/.

Nikolopoulou, Kassiani. 2023. *What Is Straw Man Fallacy?* June 21. Accessed July 13, 2023. https://www.scribbr.com/fallacies/straw-man-fallacy/.

Nix, Norman L. Geisler and William E. 1968. *A General Introduction to the Bible.* Moody Press.

—. 1986. *A General Introduction to the Bible, Rev. and expanded.* Chicago: Moody Press.

NKJV. 1982. *New King James Version Bible.* Thomas Nelson.

NPS.gov. n.d. *Radiometric Age Dating.* Accessed July 13, 2023. https://www.nps.gov/subjects/geology/radiometric-age-dating.htm.

Osanai, Nozomi. 2005. *The Background of the Gilgamesh Epic.* August 03. Accessed July 13, 2023. https://answersingenesis.org/the-flood/flood-legends/the-background-of-the-gilgamesh-epic/.

Pappas, Stephanie. 2013. *Controversial T. Rex Soft Tissue Find Finally Explained.* November 26. Accessed July 13, 2023. https://www.livescience.com/41537-t-rex-soft-tissue.html.

Paul P. Enns, *The Moody Handbook of Theology* (Chicago, IL: Moody Press, 1989), 48.

Patriot, Berean. n.d. *Majority Text vs. Critical Text vs. Textus Receptus – Textual Criticism 101.* Accessed August 24, 2023. https://www.bereanpatriot.com/majority-text-vs-critical-text-vs-textus-receptus-textual-criticism-101/.

Penn State. 2009. *Deep-sea Rocks Point To Early Oxygen On Earth.* March 25. Accessed July 13, 2023. www.sciencedaily.com/releases/2009/03/090324131458.htm.

Rafferty, Karin Akre and John P. 2023. *Miller-Urey experiment.* July 05. Accessed July 16, 2023. https://www.britannica.com/science/Miller-Urey-experiment.

Ramirez, Ainissa. 2020. *The Rise and Fall of Polywater.* February 25. Accessed July 13, 2023. https://sciencehistory.org/stories/magazine/the-rise-and-fall-of-polywater/.

Ray, David Reagan and Andrew. n.d. *The Assyrian Captivity of Israel.* Accessed July 13, 2023. https://www.learnthebible.org/sunday-school-outlines/the-assyrian-captivity-of-israel.html.

Rayne, Elizabeth. 2022. *How do we know the age of the universe?* November 05. Accessed July 13, 2023. https://www.livescience.com/how-know-age-of-universe.

Reichert, Ben. 2023. *What Are the Deuterocanonical Books of the Bible?* April 26. Accessed July 13, 2023. https://www.biblestudytools.com/bible-study/topical-studies/the-deuterocanonical-books.html.

Rhodes, Frank H.T. 1972. *Geology.* Golden Press.

2020. *Science and Engineering Indicators 2020: The State of U.S. Science and Engineering.* Accessed July 13, 2023. https://ncses.nsf.gov/pubs/nsb20201/u-s-r-d-performance-and-funding#performance-and-funding-trends.

Science Learning Hub. 2023. *Radiocarbon calibration curves.* February 02. Accessed August 21, 2023. https://www.sciencelearn.org.nz/resources/3203-radiocarbon-calibration-curves.

Sewell, Curt. 2010. *The Tablet Theory of Genesis Authorship.* October 11. Accessed July 13, 2023. https://biblearchaeology.org/research/contemporary-issues/3072-the-tablet-theory-of-genesis-authorship.

Simeon Burke. n.d. *When was the Gospel of Thomas written?* Accessed July 13, 2023. https://www.bibleodyssey.org/ask-a-scholar/when-was-the-gospel-of-thomas-written/.

Smith, Leonard Lipkin and David. n.d. *Logistic Growth Model - Background: Logistic Modeling.* Accessed July 13, 2023. https://www.maa.org/press/periodicals/loci/joma/logistic-growth-model-background-logistic-modeling.

Snelling, Andrew. 1999. *"Excess Argon": The "Archilles' Heel" of Potassium-Argon and Argon-Argon "Dating" of Volcanic Rocks.* January. Accessed July 13, 2023. https://www.icr.org/article/excess-argon-archilles-heel-potassium-argon-dating/.

Stanford Encyclopedia of Philosophy. 2021. *Imre Lakatos.* April 26. Accessed July 13, 2023. https://plato.stanford.edu/entries/lakatos/.

Strong, James. 1995. *Enhanced Strong's Lexicon.* Woodside Bible Fellowship.

Textus Receptus Bibles. 2022. *Greek Editions of the Textus Receptus.* Accessed August 24, 2023. https://textusreceptusbibles.com/Editions.

The Associated Press. 2005. *Scientists recover T. rex soft tissue.* March 24. Accessed July 13, 2023. https://www.nbcnews.com/id/wbna7285683.

The Editors of Encyclopaedia Britannica. 2023. *Akkadian language.* July 11. Accessed July 13, 2023. https://www.britannica.com/topic/Akkadian-language.

—. 2023. *Codex Sinaiticus.* July 13. Accessed July 13, 2023. https://www.britannica.com/topic/Septuagint.

—. 2023. *Continental drift.* May 31. Accessed July 13, 2023. https://www.britannica.com/science/continental-drift-geology.

—. 2023. *Gospel of Thomas.* August 25. Accessed August 31, 2023. https://www.britannica.com/topic/Gospel-of-Thomas.

—. 2023. *Masoretic text.* March 22. Accessed July 13, 2023. https://www.britannica.com/topic/Masoretic-text.

—. 2023. *Newton's law of gravitation.* August 15. Accessed August 24, 2023. https://www.britannica.com/science/Newtons-law-of-gravitation.

—. 2022. *Steady-state theory.* March 29. Accessed July 13, 2023. https://www.britannica.com/science/steady-state-theory.

TheNIVBible.com. n.d. *15 Surprising Facts About the Dead Sea Scrolls.* Accessed August 21, 2023. https://www.thenivbible.com/blog/15-surprising-facts-about-the-dead-sea-scrolls/.

Tov-Lev, Dr. Rabbi Asher. n.d. *Newly Deciphered Qumran Scroll Revealed to Be Megillat Esther.* Accessed July 13, 2023. https://www.thetorah.com/article/newly-deciphered-qumran-scroll-revealed-to-be-megillat-esther.

Understanding Evolution (UE). n.d. *Defining speciation.* Accessed July 13, 2023. https://evolution.berkeley.edu/evolution-101/speciation/defining-speciation/.

United States Census Bureau. 2022. *Historical Estimates of World Population.* December 05. Accessed July 13, 2023. https://www.census.gov/

data/tables/time-series/demo/international-programs/historical-est-worldpop.html.

University of Bath. 2023. *Newly discovered, primitive cousins of T. rex shed light on the end of the age of dinosaurs in Africa.* August 23. Accessed August 31, 2023. https://phys.org/news/2023-08-newly-primitive-cousins-rex-age.html.

Vulgate.Org. n.d. *VULGATE.* Accessed August 24, 2023. https://vulgate.org/.

Wallace, Daniel B. 2004. *The Majority Text and the Original Text: Are They Identical?* June 03. Accessed August 25, 2023. https://bible.org/article/majority-text-and-original-text-are-they-identical.

Wallace, J. Warner. 2018. *Why Shouldn't We Trust The Non-Canonical Gospels Attributed To Thomas?* April 18. Accessed July 13, 2023. https://coldcasechristianity.com/writings/why-shouldnt-we-trust-the-non-canonical-gospels-attributed-to-thomas/.

Whiston, William. n.d. *Flavius Josephus, Antiquities of the Jews.* Accessed July 13, 2023. http://www.perseus.tufts.edu/hopper/text?doc=urn:cts:greekLit:tlg0526.tlg001.perseus-eng1:18.3.

Wikipedia. n.d. *Anthropic principle.* Accessed July 13, 2023. https://en.wikipedia.org/wiki/Anthropic_principle.

Wikipedia, Royal we (Wikipedia, Accessed November 17, 2023), https://en.wikipedia.org/wiki/Royal_we.

—. 2021. *Argument from ignorance.* May 28. Accessed July 13, 2023. https://simple.wikipedia.org/wiki/Argument_from_ignorance.

—. n.d. *Bhagavad Gita.* Accessed July 13, 2023. https://en.wikipedia.org/wiki/Bhagavad_Gita.

—. n.d. *Carbon-14.* Accessed July 13, 2023. https://en.wikipedia.org/wiki/Carbon-14.

—. 2023. *Cecotrope.* January 23. Accessed July 13, 2023. https://en.wikipedia.org/wiki/Cecotrope.

—. n.d. *Classical element.* Accessed July 13, 2023. https://en.wikipedia.org/wiki/Classical_element.

—. 2022. *Einstein's static universe.* August 22. Accessed July 13, 2023. https://en.wikipedia.org/wiki/Einstein%27s_static_universe.

—. n.d. *GLASS-z12.* Accessed July 13, 2023. https://en.wikipedia.org/wiki/GLASS-z12.

—. n.d. *GN-z11.* Accessed July 13, 2023. https://en.wikipedia.org/wiki/GN-z11.

—. n.d. *HD1 (galaxy).* Accessed July 13, 2023. https://en.wikipedia.org/wiki/HD1_(galaxy).

—. n.d. *Hittites.* Accessed July 13, 2023. https://en.wikipedia.org/wiki/Hittites.

—. n.d. *JADES-GS-z13-0.* Accessed July 13, 2023. https://en.wikipedia.org/wiki/JADES-GS-z13-0.

—. 2023. *List of New Testament papyri.* July 15. Accessed July 13, 2023. https://en.wikipedia.org/wiki/List_of_New_Testament_papyri.

—. 2023. *Mahabharata.* August 17. Accessed August 23, 2023. https://en.wikipedia.org/wiki/Mahabharata.

—. n.d. *Masoretes.* Accessed July 13, 2023. https://en.wikipedia.org/wiki/Masoretes.

—. n.d. *Miller–Urey experiment.* Accessed July 13, 2023. https://en.wikipedia.org/wiki/Miller%E2%80%93Urey_experiment.

—. n.d. *Pathological Science.* Accessed July 13, 2023. https://en.wikipedia.org/wiki/Pathological_science.

—. 2023. *Radiometric dating.* August 17. Accessed August 21, 2023. https://en.wikipedia.org/wiki/Radiometric_dating.

—. 2023. *Ramayana.* August 23. Accessed August 23, 2023. https://en.wikipedia.org/wiki/Ramayana.

—. n.d. *Serpopard*. Accessed July 13, 2023. https://en.wikipedia.org/wiki/Serpopard.

—. 2023. *Solar constant*. April 28. Accessed July 13, 2023. https://en.wikipedia.org/wiki/Solar_constant.

—. 2023. *Steady-state model*. July 09. Accessed July 13, 2023. https://en.wikipedia.org/wiki/Steady-state_model.

—. 2023. *William L. Moran*. August 05. Accessed August 23, 2023. https://en.wikipedia.org/wiki/William_L._Moran.

Wikiwand. n.d. *Classical element*. Accessed July 13, 2023. https://www.wikiwand.com/en/Classical_element.

World History Publishing. 2018. *Africa Timeline*. March 22. Accessed July 13, 2023. https://www.worldhistory.org/timeline/africa/.

Wuethrich, Bernice. 1999. *The Breath of a Dinosaur*. January 22. Accessed July 13, 2023. https://www.science.org/content/article/breath-dinosaur.

Yeager, Ashley. 2015. *Traces of dino blood, soft tissue found even in junk bones*. June 09. Accessed July 13, 2023. https://www.sciencenews.org/article/traces-dino-blood-soft-tissue-found-even-in-junk-bones.

ZA Blog. 2019. *What is Textus Receptus?* July 03. Accessed July 13, 2023. https://zondervanacademic.com/blog/textus-receptus.

ENDNOTES

INTRODUCTION

1   LibQuotes, *Denis Diderot Quote* (LibQuotes, Accessed July 13, 2023), https://libquotes.com/denis-diderot/quote/lbv5d1c.

2   Merriam-Webster.com Dictionary, *Worldview* (Merriam-Webster, Accessed July 13, 2023), https://www.merriam-webster.com/dictionary/worldview.

3   Merriam-Webster.com Dictionary, *Philosophy* (Merriam-Webster, Accessed November 18, 2023), https://www.merriam-webster.com/dictionary/philosophy.

4   L. Russ Bush III, *A Handbook for Christian Philosophy* (Zondervan Academic, July 21, 1991).

CHAPTER 1

1   The Cambridge Dictionary, *Indoctrinate* (Cambridge University Press, Accessed July 13, 2023), https://dictionary.cambridge.org/us/dictionary/english/indoctrination.

CHAPTER 2

1   Merriam-Webster.com Dictionary, *Religion* (Merriam-Webster, Accessed July 13, 2023), https://www.merriam-webster.com/dictionary/religion.

2   Merriam-Webster.com Dictionary, *Ism* (Merriam-Webster, Accessed July 13, 2023), https://www.merriam-webster.com/dictionary/ism.

3   Merriam-Webster.com Dictionary, *-ist* (Merriam-Webster, Accessed July 13, 2023), https://www.merriam-webster.com/dictionary/-ist.

4   American Heritage Dictionary, *Doctrine* (American Heritage® Dictionary of the English Language, Fifth Edition. S.v., Accessed July 13, 2023), https://www.thefreedictionary.com/doctrine.

5   Merriam-Webster.com Dictionary, *Atheist* (Merriam-Webster, Accessed July 13, 2023), https://www.merriam-webster.com/dictionary/atheist.

6   Merriam-Webster.com Dictionary, *Agnostic,* (Merriam-Webster, Accessed July 13, 2023), https://www.merriam-webster.com/dictionary/agnostic.

7   Merriam-Webster.com Dictionary, *Theist* (Merriam-Webster, Accessed July 13, 2023), https://www.merriam-webster.com/dictionary/theist.

8   Merriam-Webster.com Dictionary, *Monotheism* (Merriam-Webster, Accessed July 13, 2023), https://www.merriam-webster.com/dictionary/monotheism.

9   Merriam-Webster.com Dictionary, *Polytheism* (Merriam-Webster, Accessed July 13, 2023), https://www.merriam-webster.com/dictionary/polytheism.

10   Merriam-Webster.com Dictionary, *Hypothesis* (Merriam-Webster, Accessed July 13, 2023), https://www.merriam-webster.com/dictionary/hypothesis.

11   Merriam-Webster.com Dictionary, *Postulate* (Merriam-Webster, Accessed July 13, 2023) https://www.merriam-webster.com/dictionary/postulate.

12   Merriam-Webster.com Dictionary, *Premise* (Merriam-Webster, Accessed July 13, 2023) https://www.merriam-webster.com/dictionary/premise.

13   Merriam-Webster.com Dictionary, *Tenet* (Merriam-Webster, Accessed July 13, 2023), https://www.merriam-webster.com/dictionary/tenet.

14   Douglas Cline. *2.14: Newton's Law of Gravitation* (The LibreTexts Libraries, Accessed July 13, 2023), https://phys.libretexts.org/Bookshelves/Classical_Mechanics/Variational_Principles_in_Classical_Mechanics_(Cline)/02%253A_Review_of_Newtonian_Mechanics/2.14%253A_Newton's_Law_of_Gravitation

15   Merriam-Webster.com Dictionary, *ad infinitum* (Merriam-Webster, Accessed July 13, 2023), https://www.merriam-webster.com/dictionary/ad%20infinitum.

CHAPTER 4

1   Merriam-Webster.com Dictionary, *Programme* (Merriam-Webster, Accessed July 13, 2023), https://www.merriam-webster.com/dictionary/programme.

2   Stanford Encyclopedia of Philosophy, *Imre Lakatos* (The Metaphysics Research Lab, Department of Philosophy, Stanford University, April 26, 2021), https://plato.stanford.edu/entries/lakatos/.

3   Stanford, *Imre Lakatos,* https://plato.stanford.edu/entries/lakatos/.

4   Stanford, *Imre Lakatos,* https://plato.stanford.edu/entries/lakatos/.

5   Roger Stuewer, *Max Planck* (Encyclopedia Britannica, July 7, 2023), https://www.britannica.com/biography/Max-Planck.

6   Stephen W. Hawking, *A Brief History of Time: From the Big Bang to Black Holes,* (Bantam Dell Publishing Group, 1988), 173-174

7   Riley Black, *Who Pays for Dino Research?* (Smithsonian Magazine, March 18, 2010), https://www.smithsonianmag.com/science-nature/who-pays-for-dino-research-66263095/.

8   National Science Foundation, *Science and Engineering Indicators 2020: The State of U.S. Science and Engineering* (National Science Board, 2020), https://ncses.nsf.gov/pubs/nsb20201/.

9   National Science Foundation, *Science and Engineering Indicators 2020: The State of U.S. Science and Engineering* (National Science Board, 2020), https://ncses.nsf.gov/pubs/nsb20201/u-s-r-d-performance-and-funding#performance-and-funding-trends.

10 Ivan Oransky and Adam Marcus, *There's far more scientific fraud than anyone wants to admit* (The Guardian, 2023), https://www.theguardian.com/commentisfree/2023/aug/09/scientific-misconduct-retraction-watch.

11 Oransky, *There's far more scientific fraud than anyone wants to admit*, https://www.theguardian.com/commentisfree/2023/aug/09/scientific-misconduct-retraction-watch.

12 Oransky, *There's far more scientific fraud than anyone wants to admit*, https://www.theguardian.com/commentisfree/2023/aug/09/scientific-misconduct-retraction-watch.

13 Wikipedia, *Pathological science*, (Wikipedia, Accessed July 13, 2023), https://en.wikipedia.org/wiki/Pathological_science.

14 Ainissa Ramirez, *The Rise and Fall of Polywater*, (Science History Institute Museum & Library, 2020), https://sciencehistory.org/stories/magazine/the-rise-and-fall-of-polywater/.

15 Ramirez, *The Rise and Fall of Polywater*, https://sciencehistory.org/stories/magazine/the-rise-and-fall-of-polywater/.

CHAPTER 5

1   Wikipedia, *Einstein's static universe*, (Wikipedia, August 22, 2022) https://en.wikipedia.org/wiki/Einstein%27s_static_universe.

2   The Editors of Encyclopaedia Britannica, *Newton's law of gravitation*, (Encyclopaedia Britannica, August 15, 2023), https://www.britannica.com/science/Newtons-law-of-gravitation.

3   The Editors of Encyclopaedia Britannica, *Steady-state theory*, (Encyclopaedia Britannica) https://www.britannica.com/science/steady-state-theory.

4   Wikipedia, *Steady-state model*, (Wikipedia, July 9, 2023) https://en.wikipedia.org/wiki/Steady-state_model.

5   Stephen W. Hawking, *A Brief History of Time: From the Big Bang to Black Holes*, (Bantam Dell Publishing Group, 1988), 121-122

6   Hawking, *A Brief History of Time*, 132.

7   Hawking, *A Brief History of Time*, 175.

8   Wikipedia, *HD1 (galaxy)*, (Wikipedia, Accessed July 13, 2023), https://en.wikipedia.org/wiki/HD1_(galaxy).

9   Wikipedia, *JADES-GS-z13-0*, (Wikipedia, Accessed July 13, 2023), https://en.wikipedia.org/wiki/JADES-GS-z13-0.

10 Wikipedia, *GLASS-z12*, (Wikipedia, Accessed July 13, 2023), https://en.wikipedia.org/wiki/GLASS-z12.

11 Wikipedia, *GN-z11*, (Wikipedia, Accessed July 13, 2023), https://en.wikipedia.org/wiki/GN-z11.

12   Elizabeth Rayne, *How do we know the age of the universe?*, (Live Science, November 5, 2022) https://www.livescience.com/how-know-age-of-universe.

CHAPTER 6

1   Amino Acids Guide, *Amino Acids*, (Amino Acids Guide, May 29, 2023), https://aminoacidsguide.com/
2   Karin Akre and John P. Rafferty, *Miller-Urey experiment*, (Encyclopaedia Britannica, July 5, 2023), https://www.britannica.com/science/Miller-Urey-experiment.
3   Wikipedia, Miller–Urey experiment (Wikipedia, Accessed July 13, 2023), https://en.wikipedia.org/wiki/Miller%E2%80%93Urey_experiment.
4   Erich Dimroth and Michael M. Kimberley, *Precambrian atmospheric oxygen: evidence in the sedimentary distributions of carbon, sulfur, uranium, and iron*, (Canadian Journal of Earth Sciences, September 01, 1976), Vol.13, 1161-1185.
5   Clemney, H. and N. Badham, 1982. *Oxygen in the Precambrian atmosphere: An evaluation of the geological evidence*, (Geology. 10 (3): 141).
6   Penn State, *Deep-sea Rocks Point To Early Oxygen On Earth*, (ScienceDaily, Accessed July 13, 2023), www.sciencedaily.com/releases/2009/03/090324131458.htm.
7   Steve Koppes, *The origin of life on Earth, explained* (University of Chicago, September 19, 2022), https://news.uchicago.edu/explainer/origin-life-earth-explained.

CHAPTER 7

1   Will Durant, *The story of philosophy the lives and opinions of the greater philosophers [2d ed.]* (Simon and Schuster, 1953 (paperback)), 64.
2   Understanding Evolution (UE), *Defining speciation* (The University of California Museum of Paleontology, Accessed July 13, 2023), https://evolution.berkeley.edu/evolution-101/speciation/defining-speciation/.
3   Kevin M. Gleason, *"Sex Limited Inheritance in Drosophila" (1910)* (The Embryo Project Encyclopedia, May 22, 2017), https://embryo.asu.edu/pages/sex-limited-inheritance-drosophila-1910-thomas-hunt-morgan.
4   Kevin M. Gleason, *Hermann Joseph Muller's Study of X-rays as a Mutagen, (1926-1927)* (The Embryo Project at Arizona State University, March 07, 2017), https://embryo.asu.edu/pages/hermann-joseph-mullers-study-x-rays-mutagen-1926-1927.
5   Richard Mann and Ryan Loker, *Flies with Four Wings? Investigating Genes that Pattern Animal Bodies* (Columbia's Zuckerman Institute, August 5, 2021), https://zuckerminstitute.columbia.edu/flies-four-wings-investigating-genes-pattern-animal-bodies.

CHAPTER 8

1   Richard Dawkins, *The Blind Watchmaker: Why the Evidence of Evolution Reveals a Universe Without Design* (Penguin Publishing Group, 1986), 77-78.

2   Understanding Evolution (UE), *Defining speciation* (The University of California Museum of Paleontology, Accessed July 13, 2023), https://evolution.berkeley.edu/evolution-101/speciation/defining-speciation/.

3   Steve Koppes, *The origin of life on Earth, explained* (University of Chicago, September 19, 2022), https://news.uchicago.edu/explainer/origin-life-earth-explained.

4   Merriam-Webster.com Dictionary, *Centillion* (Merriam-Webster, Accessed July 13, 2023), https://www.merriam-webster.com/dictionary/centillion.

CHAPTER 9

1   T. Lindahl, *Instability and decay of the primary structure of DNA* (Nature 362, 709–715 (1993))

2   Merriam-Webster.com Dictionary, *in vivo* (Merriam-Webster, Accessed July 13, 2023), https://www.merriam-webster.com/dictionary/in%20vivo.

3   Wikipedia, *Temperate climate* (Wikipedia, Accessed July 13, 2023), https://en.wikipedia.org/wiki/Temperate_climate#/media/File:Latitude_zones.png

4   Helen Fields, *Dinosaur Shocker* (Smithsonian Magazine, May 2006), https://www.smithsonianmag.com/science-nature/dinosaur-shocker-115306469/.

5   Helen Fields, *Dinosaur Shocker*, https://www.smithsonianmag.com/science-nature/dinosaur-shocker-115306469/.

6   The Associated Press, *Scientists recover T. rex soft tissue* (The Associated Press, March 24, 2005), https://www.nbcnews.com/id/wbna7285683.

7   Helen Fields, *Dinosaur Shocker*, https://www.smithsonianmag.com/science-nature/dinosaur-shocker-115306469/.

8   Stephanie Pappas, *Controversial T. Rex Soft Tissue Find Finally Explained* (Live Science, November 26, 2013), https://www.livescience.com/41537-t-rex-soft-tissue.html.

9   Pappas, *Controversial T. Rex Soft Tissue Find Finally Explained*, https://www.livescience.com/41537-t-rex-soft-tissue.html.

10 Alex Marcombe, *How Long Does Embalming Last? (Must Know Guide)* (Funeral Circle, August 12, 2023), https://funeralcircle.com/how-long-does-embalming-last.

11 Ashley Yeager, *Traces of dino blood, soft tissue found even in junk bones* (Science News, June 9, 2015), https://www.sciencenews.org/article/traces-dino-blood-soft-tissue-found-even-in-junk-bones.

CHAPTER 10

1   Merriam-Webster.com Dictionary, *Thermodynamics* (Merriam-Webster, Accessed July 13, 2023), https://www.merriam-webster.com/dictionary/thermodynamics.

2   Merriam-Webster.com Dictionary, *Entropy* (Merriam-Webster, Accessed July 13, 2023), https://www.merriam-webster.com/dictionary/entropy.

3   Gordon W.F. Drake, *Thermodynamics* (Encyclopaedia Britannica, June 21, 2003), https://www.britannica.com/science/thermodynamics.

4   Drake, *Thermodynamics*, https://www.britannica.com/science/thermodynamics.

5   Donald T. Haynie, *Biological Thermodynamics*, (Cambridge University Press, 2001), xii.

6   Haynie, *Biological Thermodynamics*, 59.

7   Bright Hub Engineering, *What is a Thermodynamic System? Types of Thermodynamic Systems* (Bright Hub, Inc), https://www.brighthubengineering.com/thermodynamics/3733-what-is-a-thermodynamic-system/.

8   Wikipedia, *Solar constant* (Wikipedia, April 28, 2023), https://en.wikipedia.org/wiki/Solar_constant.

9   Merriam-Webster.com Dictionary, *Mitosis* (Merriam-Webster, Accessed July 13, 2023), https://www.merriam-webster.com/dictionary/mitosis.

CHAPTER 11

1   Wikipedia, *Radiometric dating* (Wikipedia, August 17, 2023), https://en.wikipedia.org/wiki/Radiometric_dating.

2   The LibreTexts libraries, *Stable and Unstable Isotopes* (libretexts.org, Accessed July 13, 2023), https://chem.libretexts.org/Courses/Portland_Community_College/CHI05%3A_Allied_Health_Chemistry_II/07%3A_Nuclear_Chemistry/7.02%3A_Stable_and_Unstable_Isotopes.

3   Wikipedia, *Carbon-14* (Wikipedia, Accessed July 13, 2023), https://en.wikipedia.org/wiki/Carbon-14.

4   Science Learning Hub, *Radiocarbon calibration curves* (The University of Waikato, February 02, 2023), https://www.sciencelearn.org.nz/resources/3203-radiocarbon-calibration-curves.

5   NPS.gov, *Radiometric Age Dating* (US Government, Accessed July 13, 2023), https://www.nps.gov/subjects/geology/radiometric-age-dating.htm.

6   Mark Isaak, *Claim CD011.4: A freshly killed seal was carbon-14 dated at 1300 years old* (The TalkOrigins Archive, 2004), http://www.talkorigins.org/indexcc/CD/CD011_4.html.

7   T.M. Harrison and I. McDougall, *Excess ^{40}Ar in Metamorphic Rocks from Broken Hill, New South Wales: Implications for ^{40}Ar/^{39}Ar Age Spectra and the Thermal History of the Region* (Earth and Planetary Science Letters, 55 (1981)) 23-149.

8   Andrew Snelling, PH.D. *"Excess Argon": The "Archilles' Heel" of Potassium-Argon and Argon-Argon "Dating" of Volcanic Rocks* (Institute of Creation Research, January 1999), https://www.icr.org/article/excess-argon-archilles-heel-potassium-argon-dating/.

9   Frank H.T. Rhodes, *Geology* (Golden Press, 1972), 149.

10 Marvin L. Lubenow, *Bones of Contention: A Creationist Assessment of Human Fossils* (Baker Book House, 1992).

11 F. J. Fitch and J. A. Miller, *Radioisotope Age Determination of Lake Rudolf Artifact Site* (Nature 226 (18 April 1970)) 226-28.

CHAPTER 12

1   Leonard Lipkin and David Smith, *Logistic Growth Model - Background: Logistic Modeling* (Mathematical Association of America, Accessed July 13, 2023), https://www.maa.org/press/periodicals/loci/joma/logistic-growth-model-background-logistic-modeling.

2   United States Census Bureau, *Historical Estimates of World Population* (United States Government, December 5, 2022), https://www.census.gov/data/tables/time-series/demo/international-programs/historical-est-worldpop.html.

CHAPTER 13

1   History.com Editors, *Sumer* (History, A&E Television Networks, LLC, June 6, 2023), https://www.history.com/topics/ancient-middle-east/sumer.

2   Frank Raymond Allchin, *Indus civilization* (Encyclopaedia Britannica, June 26, 2023), https://www.britannica.com/topic/Indus-civilization.

3   Joshua J. Mark, *Ancient China* (World History Publishing, December 18, 2012), https://www.worldhistory.org/china/.

4   Mark Cartwright, *Inca Civilization* (World History Publishing, September 15, 2014), https://www.worldhistory.org/Inca_Civilization/.

5   Joshua J. Mark, *Maya Civilization* (World History Publishing, July 06, 2012), https://www.worldhistory.org/Maya_Civilization/.

6   Joshua J. Mark, *Ancient Egypt* (World History Publishing, September 02, 2009), https://www.worldhistory.org/egypt/.

7   Mark Cartwright, *Minoan Civilization* (World History Publishing, March 29, 2018), https://www.worldhistory.org/Minoan_Civilization/.

8   Joshua J. Mark, *Ancient Greece* (World History Publishing, November 13, 2013), https://www.worldhistory.org/greece/.

9   Joshua J. Mark, *Roman Empire* (World History Publishing, March 22, 2018), https://www.worldhistory.org/Roman_Empire/.

10 World History, *Africa Timeline* (World History Publishing, March 22, 2018), https://www.worldhistory.org/timeline/africa/.

CHAPTER 15

1   Merriam-Webster.com Dictionary, *Apologetics* (Merriam-Webster, Accessed July 13, 2023), https://www.merriam-webster.com/dictionary/apologetics.

2   James Strong, *Enhanced Strong's Lexicon* (Woodside Bible Fellowship, 1995), (Strong's Greek #3056: λόγος /log·os/).

CHAPTER 16

1   Merriam-Webster.com Dictionary, *Papyrus* (Merriam-Webster, Accessed July 13, 2023), https://www.merriam-webster.com/dictionary/papyrus.

2   Merriam-Webster.com Dictionary, *extant* (Merriam-Webster, Accessed July 13, 2023), https://www.merriam-webster.com/dictionary/extant.

3   Merriam-Webster.com Dictionary, *Paleography* (Merriam-Webster, Accessed July 13, 2023), https://www.merriam-webster.com/dictionary/paleography.

4   Vulgate.Org, *VULGATE* (Vulgate.Org, Accessed August 24, 2023), https://vulgate.org/.

5   The Editors of Encyclopaedia Britannica, *Masoretic text* (Encyclopaedia Britannica, Accessed July 13, 2023), https://www.britannica.com/topic/Masoretic-text.

6   TheNIVBible.com, *15 Surprising Facts About the Dead Sea Scrolls* (HarperCollins Publishers, Accessed August 21, 2023), https://www.thenivbible.com/blog/15-surprising-facts-about-the-dead-sea-scrolls/

7   Wikipedia, *List of New Testament papyri*, (Wikipedia, July 15, 2023), https://en.wikipedia.org/wiki/List_of_New_Testament_papyri.

8   Greek New Testament Dot Net, Greek New Testament, (Greek New Testament Dot Net, Accessed July 13, 2023), https://greeknewtestament.net/

9   Hope Bolinger, *What Is the Codex Vaticanus?* (Christianity.com March 18, 2020), https://www.christianity.com/wiki/bible/what-is-codex-vaticanus.html.

10   The Editors of Encyclopaedia Britannica, *Codex Sinaiticus* (Encyclopaedia Britannica, Accessed July 13, 2023), https://www.britannica.com/topic/Septuagint.

11   British Library Board, *Codex Alexandrinus* (British Library Board, Accessed July 13, 2023), https://www.bl.uk/collection-items/codex-alexandrinus.

12   Greek New Testament Dot Net, *Greek New Testament*, https://greeknewtestament.net/.

13   John. E. Kenney, *textual criticism* (Encyclopedia Britannica, March 15, 2021), https://www.britannica.com/topic/textual-criticism.

CHAPTER 17

1   Greek New Testament Dot Net, *Greek New Testament*, (Greek New Testament Dot Net, Accessed July 13, 2023), https://greeknewtestament.net/

2   TheNIVBible.com, *15 Surprising Facts About the Dead Sea Scrolls* (HarperCollins Publishers, Accessed August 21, 2023), https://www.thenivbible.com/blog/15-surprising-facts-about-the-dead-sea-scrolls/

3   Dr. Rabbi Asher Tov-Lev, *Newly Deciphered Qumran Scroll Revealed to Be Megillat Esther* (The Torah.com, Accessed July 13, 2023), https://www.thetorah.com/article/newly-deciphered-qumran-scroll-revealed-to-be-megillat-esther.

4   Wikipedia, *Masoretes* (Wikipedia, Accessed July 13, 2023), https://en.wikipedia.org/wiki/Masoretes

5   Wikipedia, *Masoretes*, https://en.wikipedia.org/wiki/Masoretes

6   Fredric G. Kenyon, *Our Bible and the Ancient Manuscripts* (Eyre & Spottiswoode, 1941), 38.

7   Norman L. Geisler and William E. Nix, *A General Introduction to the Bible* (Moody Press, 1968) 263.

8   Greek New Testament Dot Net, *Greek New Testament*, https://greeknewtestament.net/.

9   Terry Hall, *How the Bible Became a Book* (Victor Books, 1990), 135.

10 Norman L. Geisler and William E. Nix, *A General Introduction to the Bible, Rev. and expanded.* (Chicago: Moody Press, 1986), 194.

11 Josh McDowell, *Josh McDowell's Handbook on Apologetics, electronic ed.* (Nashville, TN: Thomas Nelson, 1997).

12 Tiffany Nicole, *Bible Translation Comparison: Top 10 Most Accurate Bible Translations* (Lavender Vines, 2023), https://lavendervines.com/bible-translation-comparison/.

CHAPTER 18

1   Wikipedia, *Hittites* (Wikipedia, Accessed July 13, 2023), https://en.wikipedia.org/wiki/Hittites.

2   Merriam-Webster.com Dictionary, *esoteric* (Merriam-Webster, Accessed July 13, 2023), https://www.merriam-webster.com/dictionary/esoteric

3   Merriam-Webster.com Dictionary, *Space-time* (Merriam-Webster, Accessed July 13, 2023), https://www.merriam-webster.com/dictionary/space-time.

4   Wikipedia, *Classical element* (Wikipedia, Accessed July 13, 2023), https://en.wikipedia.org/wiki/Classical_element.

5   Wikiwand, *Classical element* (Wikipedia, Accessed July 13, 2023), https://www.wikiwand.com/en/Classical_element.

6   Wikipedia, *Classical element*, https://en.wikipedia.org/wiki/Classical_element.

7   The Editors of Encyclopaedia Britannica, *Continental drift* (Encyclopaedia Britannica, Accessed July 13, 2023), https://www.britannica.com/science/continental-drift-geology.

8   James Strong, *Enhanced Strong's Lexicon* (Woodside Bible Fellowship, 1995), (Strong's Hebrew #776).

9   Strong, *Enhanced Strong's Lexicon*, (Strong's Hebrew #1320).

10 Margaret Hunter, *Job is not on the Amazing Bible Timeline with World History. Why not?* (Amazing Bible Timeline with World History, April 29 2013), https://amazingbibletimeline.com/blog/job-bible-timeline/.

11 Hunter, *Job is not on the Amazing Bible Timeline with World History. Why not?*, https://amazingbibletimeline.com/blog/job-bible-timeline/.

12 Kassiani Nikolopoulou, *What Is Straw Man Fallacy?* (Scribber, Revised on June 21 2023), https://www.scribbr.com/fallacies/straw-man-fallacy/.

13 Merriam-Webster.com Dictionary, *Sphere* (Merriam-Webster, Accessed July 13, 2023), https://www.merriam-webster.com/dictionary/sphere.

14 K. Lee Lerner, *Eratosthenes Calculates The Circumference Of The Earth* (Encyclopedia.com, Accessed July 13, 2023), https://www.encyclopedia.com/science/encyclopedias-almanacs-transcripts-and-maps/eratosthenes-calculates-circumference-earth.

15 Strong, *Enhanced Strong's Lexicon*, (Strong's Hebrew #2328).

16 Strong, *Enhanced Strong's Lexicon*, (Strong's Hebrew #1754).

17 William DeLong, *People Before Columbus Didn't Believe The Earth Was Flat, But Here's Why Some Think So* (All That's Interesting, February 6, 2018), https://allthatsinteresting.com/flat-earth-myth-before-columbus.

18 Merriam-Webster.com Dictionary, *Sphere* (Merriam-Webster, Accessed July 13, 2023), https://www.merriam-webster.com/dictionary/sphere.

19 Merriam-Webster.com Dictionary, *Globe*, (Merriam-Webster, Accessed July 13, 2023), https://www.merriam-webster.com/dictionary/globe.

20 Isaac Newton, *Philosophiae Naturalis Principia Mathematica*, 1687.

CHAPTER 19

1 Wikipedia, *Universal Product Code* (Wikipedia, Accessed July 13, 2023), https://en.wikipedia.org/wiki/Universal_Product_Code.

2 MarcoBarcode, *How to Change UPC E into UPC A in C# IDEs* (MarcoBarcode, 2012), http://www.macrobarcode.com/csharp-barcode/convert_upc_e_to_upc_a.shtml.

3 Peter Kirby, *Irenaeus of Lyons: Book V* (Early Christian Writings, Accessed July 13, 2023), http://www.earlychristianwritings.com/text/irenaeus-book5.html.

4 Merriam-Webster.com Dictionary, *quatrain* (Merriam-Webster, Accessed August 31, 2023), https://www.merriam-webster.com/dictionary/quatrain.

5 Ellie Crystal, *Quatrains of Nostradamus* (Crystalinks, Accessed July 13, 2023), https://www.crystalinks.com/quatrains.html.

CHAPTER 20

1 Stephen W. Hawking, *A Brief History of Time: From the Big Bang to Black Holes*, (Bantam Dell Publishing Group, 1988). 125.

2   Wikipedia, *Anthropic principle* (Wikipedia, Accessed July 13, 2023), https://en.wikipedia.org/wiki/Anthropic_principle

3   The Editors of Encyclopaedia Britannica, *Pascal's wager,* (Encyclopaedia Britannica, Accessed July 13, 2023), https://www.britannica.com/topic/Pascals-wager.

CHAPTER 21

1   Wikipedia, *Argument from ignorance* (Wikipedia, May 28, 2021), https://simple.wikipedia.org/wiki/Argument_from_ignorance.

2   Associates for Biblical Research, *When Did the Exodus Happen?* (BibleArchaeology.org September 09, 2021), https://www.biblestudytools.com/bible-study/explore-the-bible/recent-research-on-the-date-and-setting-of-the-exodus.html

3   Biography.com Editors, *Saul Biography* (A&E; Television Networks, September 8, 2020), https://www.biography.com/religious-figures/saul.

4   ESV.org, *The Divided Kingdom: Kings of Judah (all dates B.C.)* (ESV.org, Accessed July 13, 2023), https://www.esv.org/resources/esv-global-study-bible/chart-11-03a/.

5   David Reagan and Andrew Ray, *The Assyrian Captivity of Israel* (Learn The Bible, Accessed July 13, 2023), https://www.learnthebible.org/sunday-school-outlines/the-assyrian-captivity-of-israel.html.

6   ESV.org, *The Divided Kingdom: Kings of Judah (all dates B.C.)* (ESV.org, Accessed July 13, 2023), https://www.esv.org/resources/esv-global-study-bible/chart-11-03a/.

7   Daan Nijssen, *Cyrus the Great* (World History Publishing, February 21, 2018), https://www.worldhistory.org/Cyrus_the_Great/.

8   Encyclopaedia Britannica, *Akkadian language* (Encyclopaedia Britannica, Accessed July 13, 2023), https://www.britannica.com/topic/Akkadian-language.

9   Encyclopaedia Judaica, *Mari* (Encyclopaedia Judaica, 2008), https://www.jewishvirtuallibrary.org/mari.

10   BiblicalTraining.org, *Habiru, Hapiru* (BiblicalTraining.org, Accessed July 13, 2023), https://www.biblicaltraining.org/library/habiru-hapiru.

11   Encyclopedia.com, *Habiru (Habiri)* (Encyclopedia.com, Accessed July 13, 2023), https://www.encyclopedia.com/religion/encyclopedias-almanacs-transcripts-and-maps/habiru-habiri.

12   BiblicalTraining.org, *Habiru, Hapiru,* https://www.biblicaltraining.org/library/habiru-hapiru.

13   BiblicalTraining.org, *Habiru, Hapiru,* https://www.biblicaltraining.org/library/habiru-hapiru.

14   Joel P. Kramer, *Evidence for Ancient Israel Discovered in Egypt* (Expedition Bible, July 22, 2022), https://www.youtube.com/watch?v=4z9V-44cLpQ.

CHAPTER 22

1   Collins English Dictionary, *Provenance* (HarperCollins Publishers, Accessed July 13, 2023), https://www.collinsdictionary.com/us/dictionary/english/provenance.

2   Norman L. Geisler and William E. Nix, *A General Introduction to the Bible, Rev. and expanded.* (Chicago: Moody Press, 1986), 202.

3   Norman L. Geisler and William E. Nix, *A General Introduction to the Bible, Rev. and expanded,* 211.

4   Norman L. Geisler and William E. Nix, *A General Introduction to the Bible, Rev. and expanded,* 223.

5   Norman L. Geisler and William E. Nix, *A General Introduction to the Bible, Rev. and expanded,* 226.

6   Norman L. Geisler and William E. Nix, *A General Introduction to the Bible, Rev. and expanded,* 226.

7   Norman L. Geisler and William E. Nix, *A General Introduction to the Bible, Rev. and expanded,* 228.

8   Norman L. Geisler and William E. Nix, *A General Introduction to the Bible, Rev. and expanded,* 229.

9   Norman L. Geisler and William E. Nix, *A General Introduction to the Bible, Rev. and expanded,* 428.

10 Biblica, Inc, *How were the books of the Bible chosen?* (Biblica, Inc, Accessed July 13, 2023), https://www.biblica.com/resources/bible-faqs/how-were-the-books-of-the-bible-chosen/.

11 Norman L. Geisler and William E. Nix, *A General Introduction to the Bible, Rev. and expanded,* 295.

12 Merriam-Webster.com Dictionary, *antilegomena* (Merriam-Webster, Accessed August 31, 2023, https://www.merriam-webster.com/dictionary/antilegomena.

13 Merriam-Webster.com Dictionary, *Apocrypha* (Merriam-Webster, Accessed July 13, 2023), https://www.merriam-webster.com/dictionary/apocrypha.

14 Ben Reichert, *What Are the Deuterocanonical Books of the Bible?* (Bible Study Tools, April 26, 2023), https://www.biblestudytools.com/bible-study/topical-studies/the-deuterocanonical-books.html.

15 Bible Study Tools, *Apocrypha Books* (Bible Study Tools, Accessed July 13, 2023), https://www.biblestudytools.com/apocrypha/.

16 The Editors of Encyclopaedia Britannica, *Gospel of Thomas* (Encyclopedia Britannica, August 25, 2023), https://www.britannica.com/topic/Gospel-of-Thomas.

17 BAS Staff, The Gospel of Thomas's 114 Sayings of Jesus (Biblical Archeology Society, March 16, 2023), https://www.biblicalarchaeology.org/daily/biblical-topics/bible-versions-and-translations/the-gospel-of-thomas-114-sayings-of-jesus/.

18 Simeon Burke, *When was the Gospel of Thomas written?* (Society of Biblical Literature, Accessed July 13, 2023), https://www.bibleodyssey.org/ask-a-scholar/when-was-the-gospel-of-thomas-written/.

19 J. Warner Wallace, *Why Shouldn't We Trust The Non-Canonical Gospels Attributed To Thomas?* (Cold-Case Christianity, April 18, 2018), https://coldcasechristianity.com/writings/why-shouldnt-we-trust-the-non-canonical-gospels-attributed-to-thomas/.

20 Peter Kirby, *Hippolytus of Rome - The Refutation of all Heresies, Book V* (Early Christian Writings, Accessed July 13, 2023), http://www.earlychristianwritings.com/text/hippolytus5.html.

21 Curt Sewell, *The Tablet Theory of Genesis Authorship* (Associates for Biblical Research, October 11, 2010), https://biblearchaeology.org/research/contemporary-issues/3072-the-tablet-theory-of-genesis-authorship.

22 James Strong, *Enhanced Strong's Lexicon* (Woodside Bible Fellowship, 1995), (Strong's Hebrew #8435).

23 James Strong, *Enhanced Strong's Lexicon* (Woodside Bible Fellowship, 1995), (Strong's Hebrew #5612).

24 Joshua J. Mark, *Writing* (World History Publishing, April 28, 2011), https://www.worldhistory.org/writing/.

25 Peter Lundström, *Manetho* (Pharoah.SE, Accessed July 13, 2023), https://pharaoh.se/manetho-king-list.

26 James Strong, *Enhanced Strong's Lexicon* (Woodside Bible Fellowship, 1995), (Strong's Hebrew #4714).

27 David Down and Dr. John Ashton. *A Correct Chronology* (Answers in Genesis, January 21, 2010), https://answersingenesis.org/archaeology/ancient-egypt/a-correct-chronology/.

CHAPTER 23

1   Biography.com, *Pontius Pilate* (Hearst Magazine Media, Inc., June 13, 2022), https://www.biography.com/religious-figures/pontius-pilate.

2   Biography.com, *Pontius Pilate*, https://www.biography.com/religious-figures/pontius-pilate.

3   William Whiston, A.M., Ed., *Flavius Josephus, Antiquities of the Jews* (Tufts University, Accessed July 13, 2023), http://www.perseus.tufts.edu/hopper/text?doc=urn:cts:greekLit:tlg0526.tlg001.perseus-eng1:18.3.

4   Translated by Alfred John Church and William Jackson Brodribb, *The Annals By Tacitus, Written 109 A.C.E.* (The Internet Classics Archive, Accessed July 13, 2023), http://classics.mit.edu/Tacitus/annals.11.xv.html.

5   André Lemaire, *Burial Box of James the Brother of Jesus* (Biblical Archaeology Review 28:6, November/December 2002).

6   James Strong, *Enhanced Strong's Lexicon* (Woodside Bible Fellowship, 1995), (Strong's Hebrew #3290).

7   James Strong, *Enhanced Strong's Lexicon*, (Strong's Hebrew #1248).

8   James Strong, *Enhanced Strong's Lexicon*, (Strong's Hebrew #3130).

9   James Strong, *Enhanced Strong's Lexicon*, (Strong's Hebrew #251).

10 James Strong, *Enhanced Strong's Lexicon*, (Strong's Hebrew #3091).

11 The Cambridge Dictionary, patina (Cambridge University Press, Accessed July 13, 2023), https://dictionary.cambridge.org/dictionary/english/patina.

12 Biblical Archaeology Review, *Summary report of the Examining Committees for the James Ossuary and Yehoash Inscription* (Biblical Archaeology Review 29:5, September/October 2003).

13 Biblical Archaeology Review, *Summary report of the Examining Committees for the James Ossuary and Yehoash Inscription*.

14 Biblical Archaeology Review, *Summary report of the Examining Committees for the James Ossuary and Yehoash Inscription*.

15 Biblical Archaeology Review, *Summary report of the Examining Committees for the James Ossuary and Yehoash Inscription*.

CHAPTER 24

1   Logical Fallacy, *False Dichotomy* (Logical Fallacy, September 09, 2020), https://www.logical-fallacy.com/articles/false-dilemma/.

2   James Strong, *Enhanced Strong's Lexicon* (Woodside Bible Fellowship, 1995), (Strong's Greek #4624).

3   James Strong, *Enhanced Strong's Lexicon* (Woodside Bible Fellowship, 1995), (Strong's Hebrew #433).

4   Wikipedia, Royal we (Wikipedia, Accessed November 17, 2023), https://en.wikipedia.org/wiki/Royal_we

5   Paul P. Enns, *The Moody Handbook of Theology* (Chicago, IL: Moody Press, 1989), 48.

6   Merriam-Webster.com Dictionary, *Blasphemy* (Merriam-Webster, Accessed July 13, 2023), https://www.merriam-webster.com/dictionary/blasphemy.

7   Enns, *The Moody Handbook of Theology*, 200.

8   Enns, *The Moody Handbook of Theology*, 200.

9   Enns, *The Moody Handbook of Theology*, 200.

10 Charles Johson, *What Is the Heresy of Modalism?* (Christianity.com, March 17, 2023), https://www.christianity.com/wiki/christian-terms/what-heresy-modalism.html.

11 Got Questions Ministries, *What is partialism in relation to the Trinity?* (Got Questions Ministries, January 4, 2022), https://www.gotquestions.org/Trinity-partialism.html.

12 Merriam-Webster.com Dictionary, *dinosaur* (Merriam-Webster, Accessed July 13, 2023), https://www.merriam-webster.com/dictionary/dinosaur

13 Genesis Park, *Ancient Dinosaur Depictions* (Genesis Park, Accessed July 13, 2023), https://www.genesispark.com/exhibits/evidence/historical/ancient/dinosaur/.

14 Genesis Park, *Ancient Dinosaur Depictions*, https://www.genesispark.com/exhibits/evidence/historical/ancient/dinosaur/.

15 Joshua J. Mark, *Narmer Palette* (World History Publishing, February 04, 2016), https://www.worldhistory.org/Narmer_Palette/

16 Wikipedia, *Serpopard* (Wikipedia, Accessed July 13, 2023), https://en.wikipedia.org/wiki/Serpopard.

17 Andy Coghlan, *Massive 'ocean' discovered towards Earth's core* (New Scientist, June 12, 2014), https://www.newscientist.com/article/dn25723-massive-ocean-discovered-towards-earths-core/.

18 Geology.com, *Deepest Part of the Ocean* (Geology.com, Accessed July 13, 2023), https://geology.com/records/deepest-part-of-the-ocean.shtml.

19 Nozomi Osanai, *The Background of the Gilgamesh Epic* (Answers in Genesis, August 3, 2005), https://answersingenesis.org/the-flood/flood-legends/the-background-of-the-gilgamesh-epic/.

20 Nozomi Osanai, *The Background of the Gilgamesh Epic* (Answers in Genesis, August 3, 2005), https://answersingenesis.org/the-flood/flood-legends/the-background-of-the-gilgamesh-epic/.

21 Modern Warka. William Moran, *The Gilgamesh Epic: A Masterpiece from Ancient Mesopotamia*, CANE, vol. III & IV, p. 2027. Cf. Uruk is recorded as "Erek in Gen. 10:10." Victor P. Hamilton, *Handbook on the Pentateuch*, Baker Book House, Grand Rapids, p. 66, 1982, https://answersingenesis.org/the-flood/flood-legends/the-background-of-the-gilgamesh-epic/.

22 Wikipedia, *William L. Moran* (Wikipedia, August 05, 2023), https://en.wikipedia.org/wiki/William_L._Moran.

23 Frank Lorey, M.A, *The Flood of Noah and the Flood of Gilgamesh* (Institute of Creation Research, March 01, 1997), https://www.icr.org/article/noah-flood-gilgamesh/.

24 Bernice Wuethrich, *The Breath of a Dinosaur* (Science - AAAS, January 22, 1999), https://www.science.org/content/article/breath-dinosaur.

25 Prof Paul Barrett and Lisa Hendry, *Beyond Jurassic World: what we really know about dinosaurs and how* (The Natural History Museum, Accessed July 13, 2023), https://www.nhm.ac.uk/discover/what-can-scientists-learn-about-dinosaurs-and-how.html.

26 S. Conti, E. Tschopp, O. Mateus, et al, *Multibody analysis and soft tissue strength refute supersonic dinosaur tail*, (Sci Rep 12, 19245 (2022)). https://doi.org/10.1038/s41598-022-21633-2.

27 University of Bath, Newly discovered, primitive cousins of T. rex shed light on the end of the age of dinosaurs in Africa (University of Bath, August 23, 2023), https://phys.org/news/2023-08-newly-primitive-cousins-rex-age.html.

28 Merriam-Webster.com Dictionary, *Cud* (Merriam-Webster, Accessed July 13, 2023), https://www.merriam-webster.com/dictionary/cud.

29 Encyclopaedia Britannica, *Carolus Linnaeus - The Father of Modern Taxonomy* (Encyclopaedia Britannica, Accessed July 13, 2023), https://www.britannica.com/biography/Carolus-Linnaeus.

30 Joyce Chepkemoi, *Hyrax Facts: Animals Of Africa* (worldatlas.com, Accessed July 13, 2023), https://www.worldatlas.com/articles/hyrax-facts-animals-of-africa.html.

31 Norman Geisler and Thomas Howe, *When Critics Ask: A Popular Handbook on Bible Difficulties* (Baker Books, 1992).

32 Wikipedia, *Cecotrope* (Wikipedia, January 23, 2023), https://en.wikipedia.org/wiki/Cecotrope.

33 Merriam-Webster.com Dictionary, refection (Merriam-Webster, Accessed July 13, 2023), https://www.merriam-webster.com/dictionary/refection.

CHAPTER 25

1 Berean Patriot, *Majority Text vs. Critical Text vs. Textus Receptus – Textual Criticism 101* (bereanpatriot.com, Accessed August 24, 2023), https://www.bereanpatriot.com/majority-text-vs-critical-text-vs-textus-receptus-textual-criticism-101/.

2 Daniel B. Wallace, *The Majority Text and the Original Text: Are They Identical?* (CARM, June 03, 2004), https://bible.org/article/majority-text-and-original-text-are-they-identical.

3 Textus Receptus Bibles, *Greek Editions of the Textus Receptus* (TextusReceptusBibles.com, 2022), https://textusreceptusbibles.com/Editions.

4 Emma Miller, *What is the Textus Receptus?* (GB Times, Accessed July 13, 2023), https://gbtimes.com/what-is-the-textus-receptus/

5 Textus Receptus Bibles, *Greek Editions of the Textus Receptus*, https://textusreceptusbibles.com/Editions.

6 ZA Blog, *What is Textus Receptus?* (Zondervan Academic, July 03, 2019), https://zondervanacademic.com/blog/textus-receptus.

7 ZA Blog, *What is Textus Receptus?*, https://zondervanacademic.com/blog/textus-receptus.

8 ZA Blog, *What is Textus Receptus?*, https://zondervanacademic.com/blog/textus-receptus.

9 Wikipedia, *Codex Vaticanus* (Wikipedia, Accessed August 24, 2023), https://en.wikipedia.org/wiki/Codex_Vaticanus.

10 Norman L. Geisler and William E. Nix, *A General Introduction to the Bible, Rev. and expanded.* (Chicago: Moody Press, 1986), 346.

11 Luke Wayne, *Differences Between the Majority Text and the Textus Receptus*, https://www.carm.org/king-james-onlyism/differences-between-the-majority-text-and-the-textus-receptus/

12 Berean Patriot, *Majority Text vs. Critical Text vs. Textus Receptus – Textual Criticism 101*, https://www.bereanpatriot.com/majority-text-vs-critical-text-vs-textus-receptus-textual-criticism-101/.

13 Berean Patriot, *Majority Text vs. Critical Text vs. Textus Receptus – Textual Criticism 101*, https://www.bereanpatriot.com/majority-text-vs-critical-text-vs-textus-receptus-textual-criticism-101/.

CHAPTER 26

1   History.com Editors, *Printing Press* (A&E Television Networks, June 29, 2023), https://www.history.com/topics/inventions/printing-press.

2   James Strong, *Enhanced Strong's Lexicon* (Woodside Bible Fellowship, 1995), (Strong's Greek #3340).

3   James Strong, *Enhanced Strong's Lexicon* (Woodside Bible Fellowship, 1995), (Strong's Greek #3340).

4   Wikipedia, *Johannine Comma* (Wikipedia, August 23, 2023), https://en.wikipedia.org/wiki/Johannine_Comma.

OTHER RELIGION

1   Sherine Basyony, *Compilation Of Quran: History, Stages, Purposes, Importance, And More!* (Bayanulquran Academy, Accessed July 13, 2023), https://bayanulquran-academy.com/the-history-of-compilation-of-the-quran/.

2   Sherine Basyony, *Compilation Of Quran: History, Stages, Purposes, Importance, And More!* (Bayanulquran Academy, Accessed July 13, 2023), https://bayanulquran-academy.com/the-history-of-compilation-of-the-quran/.

3   Ahmad Von Denffer, What Was the Qur'an Copy of 'Uthman (Munich, Germany, Islamic Center, October 31, 2022, https://aboutislam.net/shariah/quran/introduction-to-the-quran/what-was-the-quran-copy-of-uthman/.

4   Sherine Basyony, *Compilation Of Quran: History, Stages, Purposes, Importance, And More!* (Bayanulquran Academy, Accessed July 13, 2023), https://bayanulquran-academy.com/the-history-of-compilation-of-the-quran/.

5   Dr. Mustafa Khattab, *Al-Ma'idah* (Quran.com, the Clear Quran, Accessed July 13, 2023), https://quran.com/5.

6   Wikipedia, *Mahabharata* (Wikipedia, August 17, 2023), https://en.wikipedia.org/wiki/Mahabharata.

7   Wikipedia, *Bhagavad Gita* (Wikipedia, Accessed July 13, 2023), https://en.wikipedia.org/wiki/Bhagavad_Gita.

8   Wikipedia, *Ramayana* (Wikipedia, August 23, 2023), https://en.wikipedia.org/wiki/Ramayana.

Printed in the United States
by Baker & Taylor Publisher Services

Printed in the United States
by Baker & Taylor Publisher Services